HOW & WHEN TO
SUE YOUR
LAWYER

WHAT YOU NEED TO KNOW

Robert W. Schachner
John F. Phillips, Esq.

SQUAREONE
PUBLISHERS

D0927288

The information and opinions presented in this book are based upon the training, personal experiences, and research of the authors. The publisher believes that it is the right of citizens of this country to disseminate and obtain such information. Readers should understand that there is no guarantee that any one approach will always produce the desired outcome, for each person and situation is unique. It is therefore urged by the publisher and authors that people always use caution and responsibility in dealing with legal matters, including consultation with qualified professionals. Readers who are in any doubt about their legal situation should seek appropriate professional help. The publisher and authors take no responsibility for any misunderstandings or outcomes resulting from anyone's actions based upon the information and opinions contained in this book.

Cover Designer: Jacqueline Michelus
Editor: Carol A. Rosenberg
Typesetter: Gary A. Rosenberg

Square One Publishers
115 Herricks Road • Garden City Park, NY 11040
(516) 535-2010 • (866) 900-BOOK • www.squareonepublishers.com

Legal documents from West Publications on pages 187, 188, 192, 193, 195–199 have been reprinted with permission from Thomson/West.

Library of Congress Cataloging-in-Publication Data

Schachner, Robert W.
    How and when to sue your lawyer : a client's guide to a lawyer's professional responsibility / Robert W. Schachner ; with John Philips.
        p. cm.
    Includes bibliographical references and index.
    ISBN 0-7570-0043-6
    1. Lawyers—Malpractice—United States. I. Phillips, John Francis, 1956–. II. Title.

KF313.S32   2005
347.73'5041—dc22

                                            2004025253

Printed in the United States of America

10   9   8   7   6   5   4   3   2   1

Contents

Appendices

This book is dedicated to all past, present, and future clients of lawyers in the fervent hope that it will make a difference in their lives.

Acknowledgments

It is with grateful appreciation that I would like to thank the following people:

To Irving Boigen, Esq., one of the most compassionate and intelligent lawyers who ever practiced the art and science of law, for helping to sow the seeds for this book; to the American Bar Association—including Nancy Slonim, Brad Hoffman, George Kuhlman, Chris Tozer, Patrick Sean Ginty, Jane Nosbisch, Neal W. Cox, III, Art Garwin, Denise Eichhorn, and the many other staff members who were kind enough to answer a myriad of questions and provide materials and information; to Professor Russell Engler, Associate Professor of Law and Director of Clinical Programs at New England School of Law, for his input and insight; to Anthony E. Davis, Esq., of Moye, Giles, O'Keefe, Vermeire, & Gorrell, LLP (a legal professionalism and ethics law firm), for his gracious time and discussions; to John Emmett of Emmett, Cobb, Waits, & Kessenich, and to Leo Ross, III of Schreeder, Wheller, & Flint, LLP, for their help; to Martin Zevin and Michael Felton for their counsel; to John Wiley & Sons for their informative publications; to LexisNexis for their excellent Internet legal service; to my brother, Dr. Stephen P. Schachner, for his help and counsel; to the Broward County Law Library in Ft. Lauderdale, Florida, and the Shepard Broad Law Center, Law Library & Technology Center at Nova Southeastern University for the use of their huge collection; and, most of all, to Carol A. Rosenberg, my editor—without her help and diligence, this book would not be what it is—and to my coauthor, John Philips, Esq., who took 9,000 phone calls from me at all hours of the day and night, for his patience and his knowledge of the law. With love and special thanks to Lynn Robitaille and her daughter, Mimi Bilodeua, for their patience with me during the three years I was working on this book.

A Word About Gender

To avoid long and awkward phrasing within sentences, the publisher has chosen to alternate the use of male and female pronouns according to chapter. Therefore, when referring to the third-person attorney or client, odd-numbered chapters use male pronouns, while even-numbered chapters employ female pronouns, to give acknowledgment to attorneys and clients of both genders.

Whatever the motive of the complainant in invoking the grievance procedure, the responsibility of our profession is to provide a fair and full method of ascertaining the validity of the complaint and imposing such sanction on a lawyer's conduct as may be warranted in the public interest. . . . we seek to make sure that all of us who hold ourselves out to the public as counselors and agents in the administration of justice will so conduct ourselves as to merit the trust imposed in us.

—Michigan Supreme Court
in *Lipton v. Boesky,* 110 Mich App 589; 313 NW2d 163 (1981)

Introduction

Why in the world would you ever want to sue your lawyer? Hopefully, the relationship between you and your lawyer (or firm of lawyers) is an amicable one, especially during the course of a lawsuit, business transaction, or personal legal matter. And, hopefully, in representing you, your legal counsel will have acted professionally and responsibly. But what happens if your relationship with your lawyer deteriorates? What if he or she undertakes your case, receives payment, but fails to perform to professional standards? Or what if you discover that had your lawyer researched the legal issue at the heart of your case more thoroughly (or had consulted with an expert), the outcome of your case might have been more in your favor? Or, in the worst-case scenario, what happens if you lose your case, not because the facts were against you, but because your lawyer was inept, negligent, or in breach of his or her legal and ethical responsibilities to you? The failure of your attorney in the proper discharge of his or her duty is called *legal malpractice*.

This book can help you protect yourself from the negative effects of a lawyer's lapses in judgment or, even worse, malpractice. As they say, "To be forewarned is to be forearmed." In the parlance of the legal community, this is called *loss prevention*, and lawyers use it to protect themselves from the very strategy discussed in this book. This book is also designed to arm you with the tools to "get even" or at least get compensated for your lawyer's misdeeds, miscalculations, and mistakes, if necessary.

So, what things can go wrong in the handling of your legal matter? The American Bar Association (ABA) study detailed in Chapter 1 provides some insight into the four most prevalent categories of errors made by the legal community. These are substantive errors, administrative errors, client relations errors, and intentional wrongs (not a pleasant thought).

Chapter 2 outlines the professional rules of conduct for the legal com-

1

munity established by the American Bar Association. These rules have been adopted or substantially adopted by the state bar associations. As you'll learn, the state bar associations in many states are regulated by the state Supreme Court (or intergrated bar), which promulgates—proposes and enforces—rules, regulations, and ethical standards. The state Supreme Court also polices the conduct of the lawyers admitted into the bar for that state. Because lawyers are being asked to review the conduct of their peers, this may not be seen as a favorable situation for the lay community. Unbiased peer review can be clouded by the feelings of kinship among members of a profession. Many committees do have lay members, however. Bar grievance committees review and recommend actions or sanctions against irresponsible attorneys, but they do not afford financial relief.

Chapter 3 describes an attorney's legal responsibilities to his or her clients. This includes official state bar requirements for continuing education. Continuing education is essential because the law is fluid; changes take place on an ongoing basis. The legislature amends existing laws and codifies—places into written law—new laws at each session. Precedents— judicial decisions—are often handed down when an appellate court or Supreme Court makes a ruling that reverses or clarifies a lower court's decision. Even court rules change from time to time, which may have an impact on your case or on the procedures necessary to bring your case to a conclusion. Of course an attorney's responsibilities go well beyond continuing education, and you, as a client, also have certain responsibilities. So read this chapter carefully to know what to expect from your lawyer and what your lawyer expects from you.

Chapter 4 turns to the companion subjects *competence* and *scope of representation*. This chapter will help prepare you to evaluate a lawyer's legal knowledge and skills to determine if he or she is the right lawyer for your case. This chapter also outlines the range in which a lawyer can operate on your behalf and the limits of your business relationship.

Chapter 5 alerts you to the pitfalls of a lawyer's lack of diligence—failure to provide the attention and care legally required—and lack of client communication. You'll learn how to recognize when your lawyer is not giving your case or matter the attention it requires, as well as how important it is to avoid a breakdown of communication.

Conflict of interest can doom attorney-client relationships from the start. Chapter 6 covers the rules and pitfalls of conflicts that can lead to malpractice. This chapter also discusses the all-important subject of fiduciary duty, which includes a lawyer's responsibility to protect any property belonging to a client that may be in his or her possession as well as keeping a client's information confidential.

Chapter 7 deals with the possibility of your representing yourself in a legal matter. This is known as acting *pro se*. Along with this discussion is the companion subject *ex parte*. You'll learn what takes place at an ex parte proceeding—usually a hearing before a judge when one party to a case is absent. This is an important subject, especially if you are a pro se litigant.

Chapters 8, 9, 10, and 11 discuss the four most prevalent areas of abuse by lawyers: substantive acts of malpractice, including failure to know the law, planning errors, and conflict of interest; administrative acts of malpractice, including failure to calendar, procrastination, and clerical errors; acts of malpractice as a result of client relations, including failure to obtain client's consent and failure to follow instructions; and intentional acts of malpractice, including fraud.

Chapter 12 covers a frequent impasse in the attorney-client relationship: legal fees. It discusses the history of legal billing and how the "billable hour" evolved. It also discusses alternative billing systems and fee agreements that may be used.

If you suffer damages due to your attorney's incompetence, ignorance, or negligence despite all your precautions and cooperation, turn to Chapter 13. This chapter will help you determine if you have a cause of action. *Black's Law Dictionary* defines a *cause of action* as "the fact or facts that give a person a right to judicial relief; the legal effect of an occurrence in terms of redress to a party to the occurrence." If you have a valid cause of action (or causes of action), this chapter goes on to describe your remedies, which may include placing your lawyer on notice that you plan to file a bar complaint, demanding a fee reduction, and taking legal action. If you've been damaged, this final chapter will guide you step by step through the process of "getting even." It will help you seek financial compensation for the harm your attorney's negligence caused you.

Some of the chapters close with cases in point—synopses of actual cases that apply to the topic of the particular chapter. You'll learn how the decisions in these cases have become part of our American body of law.

Appendix A contains a glossary of terms used throughout this book, as well as some additional terms you may encounter while researching your case. Appendix B is an informative guide to the common errors that attorneys make in various areas of the law. Being aware of these mistakes may help you and your attorney avoid them. In Appendix C, you'll learn how to use a law library. Knowing how to research the prosecution and defense positions in your case can be your secret weapon when dealing with your lawyer. With the information you find there, you'll be able to determine if your lawyer did, or is doing, a competent job representing you. Appendix D presents the statute of limitations on legal malpractice actions for each state.

Whether you have been badly damaged by your lawyer's actions or inaction, by his or her lack of legal knowledge or diligence, or if you just want to know what to expect from your lawyer to raise your comfort level, *How & When to Sue Your Lawyer* is for you. No longer do injured clients have to suffer in silence. This book will provide the means to replace disappointment, aggravation, and seeming futility with a course of action that may lead to satisfaction.

1

American Bar Association Malpractice Study

In an effort to determine the root cause of legal malpractice claims, the American Bar Association (ABA) established the National Legal Malpractice Data Center, which examined close to 30,000 legal malpractice claims reported between January 1996 and September 1999. The Data Center's findings serve as general indicators of the client-related wrongs that attorneys commit, especially concerning the acts of malpractice that occur most often and for what reasons. The information in this chapter, based on the ABA study, can be your guide to a less troublesome relationship with your lawyer.

MALPRACTICE CLAIM STATISTICS

Almost 80 percent of the claims examined in the ABA study were against firms of five or fewer lawyers. Statistically, this means that the smaller the law firm, the greater the chance that an injured client will find it necessary to file a malpractice claim. About 65 percent of all the claims examined were against lawyers admitted to practice for more than ten years. This may be a sign of complacency on the part of veteran lawyers. Many of the actions lawyers take on behalf of their clients over the years are very similar in nature. Preparing and filing legal documents and even doing legal research may become repetitious and may be performed without much thought or diligence. Such complacency can jeopardize a client's interests.

According to statistics reported at the Lawyers Professional Liability Loss Control Seminar in 1991, a claim for malpractice is made against one out of every fifteen lawyers. As if that were not enough to place the legal community on notice that the profession is facing a crisis of public confidence, appellate decisions dealing with legal malpractice quadrupled during the three-year period of the ABA study. These findings indicate that there is a good chance you may encounter a situation that calls for a claim of malpractice against a lawyer who has performed work for you or your business.

On close examination, the data compiled by the Data Center shows the statistical likelihood that a lawyer's failure in the following nine major areas of legal practice may be the cause of a malpractice claim:

1. Personal Injury (plaintiff)	24.6 percent
2. Real Estate	16.97 percent
3. Collection and Bankruptcy	8 percent
4. Family	10.13 percent
5. Estate	8.7 percent
6. Corporate and Business Organization	8.6 percent
7. Criminal	4 percent
8. Personal Injury (defendant)	4 percent
9. Other	15 percent

See "The Statistical Characteristics of Malpractice" on page 8 for a closer look at malpractice claims relating to firm size, years of legal practice, and malpractice awards.

CATEGORIES OF ERROR

So what can go wrong in the handling of your legal matter? The ABA study provides insight into the categories of errors made by lawyers that can result in their becoming the respondents, or defendants, of legal malpractice claims. The first four categories of error listed below are discussed briefly in this section. More detailed discussions on each of these errors appear in Chapters 8, 9, 10, and 11, respectively. These statistics can be used as a quick guide to the most prevalent types of mistakes that lawyers make. Being aware of this information may help you avert an error on your lawyer's part that could lead to a malpractice claim.

1. Substantive Errors	56.2 percent
2. Administrative Errors	16.4 percent
3. Client Relations Errors	18.7 percent
4. Intentional Wrongs	8.5 percent

Substantive Errors

Substantive errors are mistakes involving the actual practice of law—that is, the way your lawyer handles the practice of law in a case situation or legal matter. When dealing with your lawyer on your case, pay special attention to those areas in your particular legal matter that may be prone to one of the eight substantive errors listed below. For example, a simple real estate closing may not be prone to a conflict of interest but could be susceptible to a math error or title research mistake. Or if you are involved in a complicated trial, a lawyer who doesn't have thorough knowledge of the law could jeopardize your case even if he plans properly. So be sure to observe your attorney's actions on your behalf and be on the alert for possible substantive errors.

1. Failure to Know Law or Properly Apply Law	21.9 percent
2. Inadequate Investigation	6.1 percent
3. Planning Error	3.2 percent
4. Failure to Know Deadlines	15.2 percent
5. Record Search Error	2.65 percent
6. Conflicts of Interest	5.12 percent
7. Tax Consequences	1.57 percent
8. Math Error	0.48 percent

Administrative Errors

The practice of law requires a great deal of discipline. A well-run law office is usually free of administrative error, but unfortunately, not all law offices are well run. The third most prevalent deficiency on the part of a lawyer that results in an act of malpractice is errors in administration. The areas most often at fault in this category are listed below. (Be aware that the law sometimes "forgives" undisciplined lawyers for their errors. This is called *excusable neglect* and is covered more fully in Chapter 9.)

1. Failure to Calendar	7.03 percent
2. Procrastination	4.95 percent
3. Failure to File	1.54 percent
4. Failure to React to Calendar	1.27 percent
5. Clerical Error	1.25 percent
6. Lost File	0.40 percent

Statistical Characteristics of Malpractice

The findings of the ABA study provide some in-depth insight into the statistical likelihood that a lawyer or law firm will commit acts of malpractice based on certain characteristics. According to the study, law firms of two to five attorneys are at greatest risk of error. Let's take a closer look at this finding as well as others relating to the characteristics of the malpractice cases in the ABA study.

Firm Size

In the course of the ABA study, the Data Center found that almost eight out of every ten claims examined stemmed from law firms of five or fewer lawyers. The following are their findings relating to firm size:

Firm Size	Percentage of Claims
Sole practitioners	34.7 percent
Two to five attorneys	38.5 percent
Six to ten attorneys	11.8 percent
Eleven to thirty-nine attorneys	10.9 percent
Forty to ninety-nine attorneys	1.5 percent
More than one hundred attorneys	2.6 percent

One likely reason that the percentages of claims are highest for the category of sole practitioners and small firms is that prevailing in a malpractice claim against a large firm is more difficult and a great deal more costly.

Years Admitted to Practice

The following statistics relating to years admitted to practice seem to suggest that the more experience a lawyer has, the more likely it is that he may let his guard down as the years pass, thereby increasing his chances of committing an act of malpractice. Another possible reason for these statistics is that veteran lawyers are likely to have "deeper pockets" than their fresh-out-of-law-school counterparts, and injured clients know how to recognize a well-heeled lawyer and/or one covered by malpractice insurance when they see one. In other words, it is more likely that a client would pursue a claim for malpractice against a wealthy or insured attorney than one who would not be able to pay up on a judgment.

Years Admitted to Practice	Percentage of Claims*
Fewer than four years	4.5 percent
Four to ten years	29.9 percent
More than ten years	65.6 percent

Based on data from 1983–1985.

Legal Malpractice Awards

Obtaining a malpractice award may be an arduous task, but the following information reveals that it can be accomplished. In the statistics below, the actual dollar amounts awarded to claimants do not reveal the whole story regarding malpractice awards. First, aside from the amount awarded to the plaintiff, a lawyer who is fighting a malpractice claim may have to pay an attorney to defend him. For example, a lawyer cannot bill himself for the hours spent preparing a defense. Moreover, the time spent on a malpractice case takes the attorney away from performing billable work. A second missing component is that many valid malpractice claims never get filed. The legal system is already very intimidating, and becoming involved in litigation against a lawyer is even more so. Therefore, many injured clients just grin and bear it.

The amounts shown below also suggest that the larger the amount of the malpractice claim, the more virile the lawyer's defense will be because there is more at stake. It also suggests that the smaller the claim and the smaller the law firm, the easier it is to prevail.

Amount Paid to Claimant	Percentage of Claims†
Less than $1,000	70.01 percent
$1,001–$5,000	10.72 percent
$5,001–$10,000	5.48 percent
$10,001–$25,000	6.56 percent
$25,001–$50,000	3.61 percent
$50,001–$100,000	2.16 percent
More than $100,000	1.47 percent

† Percentages are rounded up to nearest hundredth decimal place.

Inflation and prevailing jury attitudes may increase the amounts awarded in the future. For example, the current negative public opinion of the legal profession may be a factor in favor of an injured client whose case is tried before a jury.

Client Relations Errors

The relationship between a lawyer and his client should be regarded as sacrosanct, and a climate of mutual respect should prevail. When you hire a lawyer, he is working for you. You are the "boss" to a certain extent, and your lawyer is obligated by law (and professional responsibility) to seek your consent and follow your instructions within bounds. However, some lawyers believe that being knowledgeable of the law and possessing information that a layperson (the client) does not possess renders them superior. Some lawyers think that they can refuse to, or do not need to, explain case strategy to their clients. This leads to the kinds of errors the ABA has called *client relations errors.* Listed below are the most prevalent of these errors.

1. Failure to Obtain Client Consent	11.89 percent
2. Failure to Follow Instructions	3.93 percent
3. Improper Withdrawal	2.93 percent

Intentional Wrongs

The last category is the most unpleasant of all the possible acts of malpractice. These errors, or *intentional wrongs* as they are dubbed in the ABA study, are acts that, in some cases, may be criminal and, if proved, could result in censure or even eventual disbarment—the loss of the right to practice law. Below are the most prevalent intentional wrongs.

1. Malicious Prosecutions	4.2 percent
2. Fraud	4.2 percent
3. Libel	1.5 percent
4. Civil Rights (abuse or violation)	1.7 percent

THE MOST COMMON AREAS OF MALPRACTICE CLAIMS

The ABA study reveals that a little more than 40 percent of all malpractice claims result from personal injury cases and real-estate-related work. Perhaps this is a result of the frequency with which these types of cases occur or the tremendous amount of detail involved in them. In any event, the ABA study shows that lawyers are especially prone to make mistakes in these areas. Therefore, these two areas of law are discussed in more detail in the following sections.

Personal Injury Cases

According to the ABA study, personal injury cases are the most prevalent area of the law in which malpractice occurs. These are cases in which a lawyer is pursuing an award for damages for physical injuries sustained by a client as a result of another's negligence such as slip and fall, product liability, animal bite, dramshop (the serving of alcohol to an intoxicated individual), medical malpractice, or automobile negligence. In malpractice claims related to personal injury cases, 13.9 percent were due to administrative errors, 58.6 percent were due to substantive errors, 11.3 percent were due to client relations errors, and 5.8 percent were due to intentional wrongs. If you are the plaintiff in a personal injury case, be sure that your attorney is qualified in the field and that you are kept informed of the case progress.

Real Estate Law

According to the ABA study, real-estate-related cases are the second most prevalent area of the law in which malpractice occurs. In real-estate-related cases, erroneous public records research represented 31.7 percent of all substantive errors, failure to obtain client's consent represented 57.3 percent of all client relations errors, failure to file documents represented 31.7 percent of all administrative errors, and malicious prosecutions represented 33.5 percent of all intentional wrongs. Real-estate-related work is wrought with the possibility of error. For example, a one-digit mistake in a property description can cause serious problems in any property transaction. Real estate matters are so full of exacting detail, as well as ever-changing property laws, that attorneys who handle these types of transactions must exercise a very high degree of expertise, or they leave themselves open to malpractice claims by clients on either side of the transaction.

CONCLUSION

Now that you know the general areas that can go awry, you can be diligent in your review of what occurs in your case and your lawyer's work on your behalf. Your diligence in this regard is just as important as your lawyer's diligence in protecting and/or accomplishing the task he agreed to undertake.

Before we look closer at the relationship between attorney and client and individual failures of lawyers, let's review the rules of professional conduct that set the stage for the attorney-client relationship.

2

Rules of
Professional Conduct

L awyers are afforded certain privileges by society and are therefore expected to adhere to certain standards of professional behavior. A system of ethical rules, generally known as *rules of professional conduct*, has evolved to govern their conduct. This chapter discusses the evolution and purpose of these rules and will familiarize you with the ethical behavior your attorney is required to uphold during the handling of your legal matter and in her dealings with you.

The portions of the American Bar Association's *Annotated Model Rules of Professional Conduct*, Third Edition, discussed in this chapter are provided as examples of the constraints and responsibilities placed on lawyers. Because each state has a separate and independent bar association or organization, your state's rules may vary somewhat. Reviewing the rules of professional conduct specific to your state will give you a good handle on the responsibility your attorney has in your attorney-client relationship. Meanwhile, use the information in this chapter as a starting point when evaluating a potential case of malpractice and to assess your attorney's degree of compliance with the rules.

THE EVOLUTION OF
THE *MODEL RULES OF PROFESSIONAL CONDUCT*

The American Bar Association has been providing leadership in the field of legal ethics and professional standards for the legal profession for almost 100 years. On August 27, 1908, the ABA adopted the original *Canons of Professional Ethics.* These canons were based on the code of ethics adopted by the Alabama Bar Association in 1887. Alabama, in turn, had borrowed its code largely from the lectures of Judge George Sharswood, whose talks on the subject of ethics were published in *Professional Ethics* in 1854.

In 1964, the ABA created a committee to evaluate the *Canons of Professional Ethics*. This committee came up with the *Model Code of Professional Responsibility*, which was adopted by the ABA's house of delegates in 1969. Through amendments, committee meetings, and conferences, the *Model Rules of Professional Conduct* eventually evolved. Individual states draw upon these "model rules" to craft their own set of regulations for lawyers in their state.

The *Model Rules of Professional Conduct* is constantly being reviewed, revised, and updated to reflect the times in which we live and the prevailing moral convictions of our society. Each year at its convention, the ABA's house of delegates votes on proposals to change, amend, or otherwise alter the rules.

STATE BAR ASSOCIATIONS AND THEIR RULES OF CONDUCT

In order to practice law, a lawyer must be admitted to one or more state bars by passing an exam in the state in which she wants to practice. Each state regulates, controls, and provides a disciplinary system for lawyers duly authorized to practice law in their jurisdiction. The *Model Rules of Professional Conduct* are available to the various state bars as a model for their own set of rules. They have been adopted in whole or in part by the Supreme Courts of forty-four jurisdictions. Other states are considering the adoption of the same or similar rules into their state bar association's rules of conduct.

There are basically two types of state bar associations or organizations. The first is an *integrated* association or organization—that is, it is connected to and governed by the Supreme Court of the particular state. The Florida Bar is an example of an integrated organization. A *non-integrated* bar association or organization is independent, and therefore, its enforcement powers are very limited. The New Jersey State Bar Association is an example of a non-integrated association.

The introduction to Florida's *Rules of Professional Conduct* establishes the Florida Bar as an official arm of the Florida Supreme Court. Consequently, the full weight of the state's highest court is behind the Florida Bar. Therefore, only the state Supreme Court can discipline a lawyer through the bar. And only the state Supreme Court can disbar a lawyer. In states that do not have integrated bars, cases involving the discipline of lawyers are brought to the attention of the Supreme Court by the bar, and then acted upon by the court. It would be useful to become familiar with how your state bar association or organization operates in relation to the discipline and enforcement of its members.

THE PURPOSE OF THE *MODEL RULES*

The original purpose of the *Model Rules* was merely to provide guidelines for the conduct of lawyers. It may seem logical to the layperson that rules established for the ethical and professional conduct of lawyers should form the basis of a lawyer's legal responsibility to her clients and to the system, but that is not what the ABA and the bar associations originally intended. Fortunately, recent court decisions in malpractice litigation have opened the door to the use of a violation of these rules of conduct as evidence of negligence and wrongdoing on the part of an attorney.

If the American Bar Association prevailed in all jurisdictions and in all cases, the following would be the prevailing law:

> Violation of a Rule should not give rise to a cause of action nor should it create any presumption that a legal duty has been breached. The Rules are designed to provide guidance to lawyers and to provide a structure for regulating conduct through disciplinary agencies. They are not designed to be a basis for civil liability.
>
> —Preamble to the *Annotated Model Rules of Professional Conduct*, Third Edition

Some courts have reasoned that if the bar announces and circulates rules of ethical and legal conduct for their members then those same rules should be "evidence per se or at least [be] persuasive authority on the proper standards of lawyer conduct," as stated in *The Lawyer's Desk Guide to Preventing Legal Malpractice* (ABA Chicago, 1992). In other words, the ABA has now accepted the premise that breaking an ABA rule is evidence of a possible act of malpractice. And that, as noted in the *Rules Regulating the Florida Bar* (The Florida Bar, 1996), "Federal, state and local courts in all jurisdictions—even those that have not formally adopted the 'Rules'—look to them [ABA rules] for guidance in resolving lawyer malpractice cases, disciplinary actions, disqualifications issues, sanctions questions and much more." It's no wonder that the courts have begun to hold that the violation of bar rules establishes a precedent for the discipline of an attorney's misbehavior.

The following is a quote from the Florida Bar's Rules of Discipline 3-1.2, which demonstrates the extreme power that a state bar can wield over its members—all lawyers admitted to practice in the state:

> The Supreme Court of Florida has the inherent power and duty to prescribe standards of conduct for lawyers, to determine what constitutes

grounds for discipline of lawyers, to discipline for cause attorneys admitted to practice law in Florida, *and to revoke the license of every lawyer whose unfitness to practice law has been duly established.*

So it seems to this author that if the Supreme Court of a particular state can disbar a lawyer for a breach of the rules, the same breach should be *prima facie* evidence—that is, sufficient evidence to establish a presumption of fact—of an act of malpractice. And, in fact, this is the position many courts are now reaching.

In a pair of cases—*Hansen v. Wightman* and *Gulfwide v. F. E. Wright*—the Washington Court of Appeals established the precedent that the code of professional responsibility is made up of the following:

1. Canons: General concepts of conduct expected of lawyers.

2. Ethical considerations: Behavioral aims lawyers should seek to achieve.

3. Disciplinary rules: Levels of deportment—that is, the manner of personal conduct—that must be met.

The judges of the Washington Court of Appeals said in their decision in the Hansen case, "these rules have the dignity and status of any rule adopted by the Supreme Court. They are the standards of ethics for all members of the Bar. . . . " It is court decisions such as this that contribute to the body of law that a person who is seeking redress in a malpractice claim can turn to for guidance.

THE FORMAT OF THE *ANNOTATED MODEL RULES* OF PROFESSIONAL CONDUCT

The following are the chapter headings and rule numbers and titles of the *Annotated Model Rules of Professional Conduct,* Third Edition. The annotated version of the rules includes case law, discussions about how the rules apply, and some historical background.

The headings and rule numbers are presented here in their entirety to help familiarize you with what your state's rules may contain and to give you an idea of the complexity of the rules. Many of these rules will be discussed in the following chapters.

CLIENT-LAWYER RELATIONSHIPS

COUNSELOR

ADVOCATE

TRANSACTIONS WITH PERSONS OTHER THAN CLIENTS

LAW FIRMS AND ASSOCIATIONS

5.1 Responsibilities of a Partner or Supervisory Lawyer

5.2 Responsibilities of a Subordinate Lawyer

5.3 Responsibilities Regarding Non-lawyer Assistants

5.4 Professional Independence of a Lawyer

5.5 Unauthorized Practice of Law

5.6 Restrictions on Right to Practice

5.7 Responsibilities Regarding Law-related Services

PUBLIC SERVICE

6.1 *Pro Bono Publico* Service

6.2 Accepting Appointments

6.3 Membership in Legal Services Organizations

6.4 Law Reform Activities Affecting Client Interests

INFORMATION ABOUT LEGAL SERVICES

7.1 Communications Concerning a Lawyer's Services

7.2 Advertising

7.3 Direct Contact with Prospective Clients

7.4 Communication of Fields of Practice

7.5 Firm Names and Letterheads

MAINTAINING THE INTEGRITY OF THE PROFESSION

8.1 Bar Admission and Disciplinary Matters

8.2 Judicial and Legal Officials

8.3 Reporting Professional Misconduct

8.4 Misconduct

8.5 Disciplinary Authority; Choice of Law

The Structure of Individual Annotated Model Rules

Take a look at Model Rule 1.1 "Competence" and the following commentary. This should provide you with some insight into the format and construction of the rules as they are presented in the ABA's official publication.

Rule 1.1 Competence

A lawyer shall provide competent representation to a client. Competent representation requires the legal knowledge, skill, thoroughness, and preparation reasonably necessary for the representation.

The *Annotated Model Rules of Professional Conduct* defines each of the principles, tasks, and obligations that Rule 1.1 implies. Headings under this rule include "Legal Knowledge and Skill," "Thoroughness and Preparation," and "Maintaining Competence."

The *Annotated Model Rules* then moves into a detailed breakdown of each area that one might consider an element of competence, with appropriate case-law citations.

The Structure of State Bar Rules

As mentioned earlier, state bar rules may differ from the *Model Rules*. Be sure to review *your* state's bar rules when assessing your attorney's performance. Below are subject headings from the *Rules Regulating the Florida Bar* (Vol. XXVII, September 2002) to acquaint you with what may be found in a state bar set of rules as opposed to the *Model Rules*.

Rules Regulating the Florida Bar

General	Chapter 1
Bylaws of The Florida Bar	Chapter 2
Rules of Discipline	Chapter 3
Rules of Professional Conduct	Chapter 4
Rules Regulating Trust Accounts	Chapter 5
Legal Specialization and Education Programs	Chapter 6
Clients' Security Fund Rules	Chapter 7
Lawyer Referral Rule	Chapter 8
Group and Prepaid Legal Services Rules	Chapter 9
Rules Governing the Investigation and Prosecution of the Unlicensed Practice of Law	Chapter 10
Rules Governing the Law School Practice Program	Chapter 11
Emeritus Attorneys Pro Bono Participation Program	Chapter 12
Authorized Legal Aid Practitioners Rule	Chapter 13
Fee Arbitration Rule	Chapter 14
Review of Lawyer Advertisements and Solicitations	Chapter 15
Foreign Legal Consultancy Rule	Chapter 16
Authorized House Counsel Rule	Chapter 17
Military Legal Assistance Counsel Rule	Chapter 18

ETHICAL VIOLATION VERSUS MALPRACTICE

It is important to make a distinction between an act by a lawyer that is uneth-ical and one that is a violation of law or bar regulations. An ethical violation is not in and of itself an act of malpractice. As a general rule, ethical viola-tions by an attorney, even if she breaches a suggested rule of professional conduct, are not always actionable as a malpractice claim. For example, in the case of *Coleman v. Hick* (433 SE 2nd 621 GA. 1993), it was found that *fee gouging*—uncalled-for billing amounts—does not qualify as grounds for a malpractice action. Despite the fact that the offense is a clear-cut violation of the ethical code as outlined in the *Model Rules,* simply charging too much is not an act of malpractice. However, a breach of fiduciary duty (also an eth-ical violation) may be grounds for a malpractice claim if the breach ulti-mately results in damages to a client. (The fiduciary duty is discussed at length in Chapter 6.)

2.1.   CASE IN POINT
The Thrifty Shoe-Store Owner

Uncle Ed, a shrewd businessman and investor, assembled great wealth and assets during his forty-year career in the shoe business. Over the years, he had placed his hard-earned money in a number of successful and safe investments.

Uncle Ed was proud of his young nephew Len, who, after graduating from law school, became his lawyer. Unfortunately for Uncle Ed, Len's advice was self-serving and erroneous. First of all, Len convinced his uncle to invest in speculative high-tech stock ventures, at a time when the now-retired uncle needed to have safe investments for his golden years. A little at a time, Uncle Ed also loaned Len money for investments, eventually to the tune of $1.5 million. (Ed raised this money by personally mortgaging his properties.)

Although Len personally guaranteed the loans to his uncle, Ed was put-ting himself out on a limb. Remember, a personal guaranty might only be worth the value of the paper it is written on, as was the case with Len's promise to repay.

A year later, Len convinced his uncle to invest another $700,000 in a speculative movie venture. Ed was not aware that Len was personally in-volved in the movie venture nor did he know that Len went bankrupt the year before!

All the ventures were miserable failures. Ed lost more than $4 million as well as his properties to foreclosures because he had pledged them as collateral.

Ed was being sued by a company involved in one of the investments (as was Len), and this gave him the opportunity to sue his nephew for the mess he'd gotten him into. Ed died during the case, and his wife succeeded. A jury awarded Uncle Ed's estate $2.5 million against lawyer Len.

Len filed an appeal, only to be castigated by the appellate court, whose ruling strengthened the protection afforded clients when dealing with attorneys. The appellate court said:

> California law provides that a member of the State Bar shall not enter into a business transaction with a client or knowingly acquire an ownership, promissory, security, or other pecuniary interest adverse to a client unless (1) the transaction and terms in which the member of the State Bar acquires the interest are fair and reasonable to the client and are fully disclosed and transmitted in writing to the client in a manner and terms which should have reasonably been understood by the client, (2) the client is given a reasonable opportunity to seek the advice of independent counsel of the client's choice on the transaction, and (3) the client consents in writing thereto.

Uncle Ed should never have had his nephew represent him. Len should not have involved himself financially with his uncle/client and should have disclosed to him that he had a right to have an independent attorney review the deals to ensure that the terms were fair and reasonable. In all cases, a client must consent in writing to the involvement of a lawyer in an investment in which he has an interest.

The court further affirmed, "that an attorney's duties to his client are governed by the rules of professional conduct. Those rules, together with statutes and general principles relating to other fiduciary relationships, all help define the duty component of the fiduciary duty which an attorney owes to his client."

In a ruling that helps to strengthen the principle that the *Model Rules of Professional Conduct* are being recognized as the standard to which the legal profession is required to adhere, the court said: "An attorney's duties to his client are conclusively established by the rules of professional conduct, which the trial court is required to judicially notice. The attorney's violation of those rules establishes his negligence, even in the absence of expert testimony."

However, the court did say that without a lawyer's having broken a law or statute, "there is no independent cause of action for the breach of a disciplinary rule." (While this may seem contradictory, the particular facts of a case have an influence on how the law is applied.)

The effect of the final ruling in this case is clear. The violation of a bar rule or ethical responsibility on the part of a lawyer is not, in itself, sufficient to bring a cause of action against the errant lawyer. To bring an action, it is necessary to allege a fraud or another tort (crime) or breach of contract in order to have a cause of action and be able to file a complaint in a court of law (although this is gradually changing). However, once the action is filed, the court is obliged to review the lawyer's actions against the fabric of the bar rules.

CONCLUSION

The *Model Rules of Professional Conduct* can guide you in your quest to understand what has gone wrong between you and your attorney or with your legal matter. A review of these rules, as well as the rules specific to your state, will give you insight into the very minimum conduct expected from a member of the legal community. Although it is necessary to check the law in the state in which there is a possible malpractice claim, the *Model Rules* and your state rules can help you determine if your lawyer might have committed an act of malpractice. It is also necessary to check statutes and case law in the jurisdiction where the act of malpractice took place. This information can be found in a law library, which you will learn how to use in Appendix C.

With this said, it is important to understand the responsibilities of each party and interaction between the parties in an attorney-client relationship. The next chapter will set the record straight as to what you should expect from your legal counsel and what your responsibilities are in the very complex attorney-client relationship.

3

Attorney and Client Responsibilities

Despite our conflicting feelings about lawyers and the so-called prestige of the profession, lawyers are just human beings like the rest of us. Some may be a little greedier or more ruthless than others, and some may be more compassionate or craftier, but they are still just flesh and blood. When you retain the services of a lawyer or law firm, you are entering into a contract—an offer and acceptance—for services. If you make a payment to a lawyer or law firm and your money is accepted, a contractual relationship exists between you and the lawyer or law firm that accepted your money. As with any contract, each party has certain responsibilities. But even before the relationship forms, a person who is seeking legal counsel has one very important responsibility: to carefully choose a lawyer. This chapter begins by providing some guidance in this area and then goes on to discuss your responsibilities as a client. Thereafter, the focus is on the many responsibilities a lawyer has to you and to society.

CHOOSING A LAWYER

The old adage "buyer beware" applies to you when you're shopping for a lawyer. If you choose a bad doctor who takes out your spleen instead of your appendix, you won't be able to get your spleen back, but your recourse—a medical malpractice claim—will be on a straight and narrow legal path. If your accountant makes a math error, he can be held responsible. In such situations, if the documented facts are on your side, you will have a good chance of financial recovery. Unfortunately, in the case of attorneys who have committed malpractice, it may be infinitely more difficult to hold them accountable for their mistakes. Theoretically, bar associations should protect the buyers of legal services, but in reality, these associations make winning a malpractice claim more difficult. Coupled with what's been critized by some as the "good old boys club"—favoritism shown to old friends, classmates, and colleagues—the pursuit of compensation from a lawyer can be a considerable challenge. This is partly why the initial selection process of competent legal counsel is so critical.

The process of finding a suitable attorney should be undertaken carefully and should not be rushed. A good way to find appropriate counsel is to develop a list of possible candidates and interview each of them. To begin, decide on the area of the law in which you need special expertise. Hiring an attorney with practical experience in the specialty you need will save time and money, and may give you an advantage over your adversary (who may not have that practical experience). See "Recognized and Approved Specialties of Law" on page 32.

Once you have zeroed in on the specialty, compile a list of attorneys with the experience you need. Seek recommendations from people you trust. Ask family and friends, but make sure they know what they are talking about and that their experiences are similar to yours. If the company you work for has in-house counsel, ask that person for recommendations; if your company uses outside legal help, find out that attorney's name and ask for some suggestions.

Most law libraries, and many public libraries, have a copy of Martindale-Hubbell, a huge tome that lists most lawyers by location and firm, and provides a short biography of each individual, including education and past employment. This book will even give you the names of corporate clients the attorney or firm has represented. You can also access the Martindale-Hubbell database via the Internet. (See the Resources section on page 215.)

Another way to add to your list of possible attorneys is to call the state bar association referral service in the state where you need representation. The bar will gladly give you the names of lawyers who specialize in the area you need. Be aware, however, that this will not be a list of all the lawyers in the area, nor necessarily of the best ones, as the service gives only the names of those lawyers who have registered with it. However, it is probable that if you do call one of these lawyers, he will explore the merits of your case for a nominal fee.

When you have your list of candidates, you must interview your choices (or, at the very least, discuss your case over the phone with them). This will help you narrow your choices to the individual or firm that you judge to be best suited to represent you. Remember, the ultimate decision is yours alone, so evaluate each candidate carefully. The following are some suggested questions to use as you interview each lawyer on your list:

❏ What is your fee arrangement—contingency, hourly, or flat rate (a set fee for the entire job)?

❏ How are expenses handled under a contingency arrangement?

❏ What expenses should I anticipate?

❏ Will you send copies of correspondence and pleadings (court documents that contain the formal statements of the parties in a lawsuit) to me as a matter of course? *With the knowledge of the legal process you gain from this book, you will be able to protect your interests by essentially looking over your attorney's shoulder.*

❏ What is your background? Have you handled other cases like mine? How many?

❏ Will my case require expertise that you (or your firm) do not have? If so, will you agree to consult with someone who has that expertise? Who will pay for this?

❏ If litigation is even a remote possibility, are you an experienced court-room advocate? If not, how will litigation be handled? Who pays, and how much? Who is responsible for trial preparation? *Sometimes a lawyer who does not handle litigation will do the trial preparation and then call in a "star" for the courtroom presentation. This may benefit you, as you will pay less for the lengthier preparation than you would if the star handled the entire process.*

❏ If court action of any type is possible, do you have experience before the judge involved? *A past social, business, or professional relationship with the judge may give you an edge. Ethically speaking, this should not be a factor; realistically, it may be.*

❏ If legal research is needed, do you have your own law library? Who will be responsible for the research, and what will it cost?

If you have the opportunity to visit the lawyers on your list, notice the appearance of each one's office. Check for a neat, organized operation, and for personnel who seem happy as well as professional.

Finally, compare the answers the candidates give you to thin out your list. If you must, depend on your gut feelings and any first impressions the candidates make. Although there is no absolute guarantee that this kind of shopping will ultimately lead to a satisfactory outcome, you will have done your best to provide yourself with adequate representation. You will also have laid the foundation for a strong, safe relationship with your attorney of choice.

How Not to Be the Client Lawyers Turn Down

Loss prevention manuals warn lawyers to watch out for certain behavioral patterns in prospective clients. By understanding the types of behavior that attorney's watch out for, you may be able to modify your own behavior in order to have a wider choice of lawyers who are willing to take your case. So, before you speak to a potential attorney, learn the following client no-noes:

❑ A client should not want to proceed regardless of cost.

❑ A client should not indicate that he is "on a mission."

❑ A client should not change attorneys frequently—especially on the same case.

❑ A client's expectations shouldn't seem unrealistic.

❑ A client should not appear to base his sole financial well-being on the outcome of the case.

❑ A client should not appear to be interviewing many different lawyers in the process of finding one to take his case.

❑ A client should avoid demonstrating knowledge of the law as it applies to his case during the interview. A client who is educated in the law is not necessarily a lawyer's best customer.

❑ A client should not appear to be in a great hurry if time is not of the essence.

Sometimes your search for a lawyer will indicate that a certain individual is particularly suited to your case. His expertise and community stature may be important to you. Therefore, to protect yourself against rejection by the lawyer of your choosing, be sure to follow the above guidelines.

A CLIENT'S RESPONSIBILITIES AFTER CHOOSING A LAWYER

Being the layperson in the relationship, a client has fewer and less-complicated responsibilities than his lawyer. A client's most important responsibility is to be honest and completely forthcoming—to fully disclose all pertinent facts and circumstances involving his case or legal matter. There is no reason for a client not to be completely honest. The attorney-client privilege protects the disclosure of any information a client gives to his attorney. But be careful. If a third party, other than your spouse or another lawyer from the firm you've hired, is present when you disclose this information, the privilege dissolves. Be sure to speak to your lawyer in private on sensitive matters. (See "On the Subject of Privileged Communication" on page 28.)

The ability to pay for an attorney's services is another of the client's responsibilities. A client cannot expect a lawyer or law firm to work for free. A fee must be paid according to the terms of the contract or retainer agreement between the lawyer and client. An exception to this is when a contingency agreement exists between the lawyer and client. When a lawyer agrees to a contingency, he gets paid a percentage from monies recovered by verdict or by settlement. In this case, the agreement must be in writing according to your state bar rules.

A client also has the responsibility to be as helpful as possible in the ongoing matter. The more a client can contribute, the less the case should cost in the long run. After all, who knows better than the client where the evidence lies and what the facts of the case are?

Lastly, the client has the responsibility to respect deadlines and court dates, and to dress appropriately for court appearances and depositions—oral testimonies that are recorded by an officer of the court, or a court reporter. The client should produce required documents in a timely fashion, and, above all, should not display anger at the opposition, especially in courtroom situations. In other words, the client should keep his cool and assist whenever he can in the handling of his legal matter.

A LAWYER'S RESPONSIBILITIES

In our society, a lawyer has a sovereign duty to protect his client to the best of his ability—no matter whether that client is a criminal defendant, an important business tycoon, an injured accident victim, or newlyweds closing on their first house. That duty is reflective of the special place in society a lawyer has as an officer of the court and the moral and ethical cannons of behavior he has sworn to uphold. Understanding a lawyer's responsibility to his clients is the first step in a client's loss-prevention plan.

On the Subject of Privileged Communication

Attorneys and their clients have a very special relationship that reaches back over the many centuries of legal history. This extraordinary privilege mandates that private discussions between attorney and client are completely confidential. The attorney-client privilege allows for complete protection from use as evidence conversations and communications made under circumstances of assured confidentiality. The United States Supreme Court has described the privilege as one of the oldest recognized privileges for confidential communication, and states that it exists even after the death of the client.

Despite this broad mandate from the highest court in the land, the privilege does not hold if a person informs his attorney that he is going to commit a wrongdoing. An attorney is duty bound to divulge potential *criminal* behavior, after warning the client not to carry out the act.

Much of the privilege section of the law is rooted in state laws dealing with evidence. Depending on the particular jurisdiction, the attorney-client privilege may be codified—written down—as a bar rule, ethics rule, regulation, constitutional provision, or legislative enactment (statute). Or it may be drawn from precedent as in case decisions, sometimes referred to as *judge-made law.*

As with so many areas of the law, it is well worth remembering to check *your* state's statutes, bar regulations, precedents, and ethics rules when looking into the subject of attorney-client or any other perceived privilege.

In today's practice of law, the *privilege* of not having to testify as a witness may sometimes protect communications between individuals other than just attorney and client. Much of this is specified in federal rules, which specifically proclaim that it is state law (not federal law) that controls the decision on who is protected by privilege and who may invoke its benefits. Under certain circumstances and based on state law in the particular jurisdiction, there may or may not be a privileged communication between the following individuals:

❑ Insured and insurer

❑ Accountant and client

❑ Corporate client and a corporation's non-management employees

❑ Partners of an unmarried couple who live together

❑ Husband and wife

❑ Client and social worker

❏ Penitent and clergy

❏ Doctor and patient

❏ Personal representative of a deceased client

❏ Psychiatrist and patient

❏ Sexual assault counselor and victim

❏ Domestic violence advocate and victim

❏ Sunshine Law participants

Be aware that if a third party is present during privileged communications, the privilege may be nullified, depending on the third person's function. Also, a wavier of privilege takes place upon voluntary disclosure of privileged information. Be sure to discuss this privilege with your attorney when disclosing confidential information. He should know how to protect your right to privacy.

A Lawyer's Responsibilities to Those Seeking Counsel

A lawyer is a member of a bar association and an officer of the court. Therefore, a lawyer's responsibilities are much more complex than those of a client. Even before a formal agreement to represent a client exists, a lawyer has certain duties and responsibilities. For example, once a conversation begins with a potential client, a lawyer cannot "erase" what he hears. If a possible crime is about to be committed, the lawyer has a legal duty to report that information to law enforcement. Or, if a court deadline is approaching that can adversely affect the potential client, the lawyer must warn the individual of the nature of the imminent danger.

If a lawyer chooses not to represent a person seeking counsel, he will most likely write a letter of non-engagement for self-protection. The lawyer will not leave the subject of representation open at the end of the conversation. He will make his decision emphatically clear to the person seeking counsel.

I've often received lengthy "turn-down" letters explaining why a lawyer I had interviewed would not take my case or legal matter. These lawyers seemed more interested in protecting themselves from the possibility that I misunderstood the outcome of our discussion than providing me with reasons for not taking the case. Such non-engagement letters serve as a lawyer's and/or law firm's protection against any claim that, as a result of an initial meeting, a contract or relationship exists between them and a client whose case they did not take on. More important, such letters tell the clients that they need to find another attorney or to file suit before the statute of limitations expires.

A Lawyer's Responsibility to Advise on the Statute of Limitations

Another important responsibility to a prospective or active client is to inform the client if the statute of limitations is about to run out. Many legal actions are required to be commenced within a specific period of time or according to the particular law or statute. Therefore, a lawyer who declines a case is obligated by law to warn the person or entity that it must seek counsel by a certain date to avoid being precluded by an expired statute of limitations. In a well-known malpractice jury award of over $600,000, a law firm that did not take a medical malpractice case prior to the expiration of the statute of limitations was sued for malpractice themselves when they failed to warn the prospective client that the statute of limitations exists. For more information on this case, see *Togstad v. Vesely, Otto, Miller & Keef*, Minn. 291 N.W. 2d 686 (1980).

A Lawyer's Responsibility to Avoid Conflict of Interest

In general, a lawyer should not represent a client if there is a conflict with the attorney's business interest or law firm or partnership, a third person with whom the attorney is linked, or another client. There are many situations in which an attorney's judgment may be clouded by a conflicting interest. Anytime an attorney is faced with even a potential conflict, the attorney should refrain from representation to avoid even the appearance that his judgment may be compromised and the quality of the work adversely affected. For example, a lawyer may not represent a client if the lawyer's exercise of independent professional judgment is limited by the lawyer's own interests, such as having an ownership in a real estate development that the potential client wants to sue. Whether or not a lawyer believes that an outside interest won't affect his performance, the law does not condone such conduct—as with human nature, it is difficult to serve "two masters." (Conflict of Interest is covered more fully in Chapter 6.)

A Lawyer's Responsibility to Continue Education

Although 21.9 percent of the malpractice cases cited in Chapter 1 are a result of failure to know the law, the bar requirements for continuing education are still a bare minimum. They do exist, however. State bar associations recognize the potential for error and the fluid nature of the law and, therefore, expect their members to continue their education on an ongoing basis. In fact, almost all state bar associations require some form of continuing education for attorneys to remain members of the bar. (Of course, if a lawyer is not in good standing and, therefore, cannot practice in the state, it doesn't matter how much he knows about the law.) From time to time, the ABA and accredited companies and institutions provide continuing education classes for members of the bar. A good attorney will be accepting of the notion that continuing education requirements are beneficial. Clients should beware of those lawyers who try to sneak by without it.

The logic behind a lawyer's responsibility to diligently follow the bars rules for continuing legal education is to insure that he stays abreast of the most recent changes in statutory law and case law. Continued study of the law is to a lawyer what study on the latest treatment protocols is to a physician. It is necessary to perfect and maintain proficiency not only in a specialty area of the law, but in general practice as well.

A Lawyer's Requirements for Practicing a Specialty

The requirements for lawyers who have or wish to have a specialty are more stringent than they are for those lawyers who practice general law. (See "Recognized and Approved Specialties of Law" on page 32.) A lawyer who wishes to be *board certified* in a specialty must show proof of continuing education. He must also submit an application to the bar along with "certification of references" from other lawyers who can attest to his substantial experience in each area of law sought to be designated a specialty. If he cannot provide a "certification of references," he must submit to an examination given by the board. The application for board certification in a specialty must also contain a statement that the would-be specialist will continue legal education in the speciality to enhance his proficiency. This can be accomplished through private study or continuing legal education programs approved by the bar. These requirements are designed to protect clients from lawyers who are not proficient in their designated specialties.

The problem with the above requirements, as well as with the monitoring of a lawyer's responsibilities in general, is that lawyers are policed by their peers. The public cannot always trust a system that allows a lawyer who does not have adequate knowledge of the law to go unchecked due to the "old boys" club. Unfortunately, it is a client who is usually damaged if an unqualified attorney mishandles his case. To make it right, or to "get even," the injured client must find a lawyer who is willing to sue the errant lawyer for malpractice.

A Lawyer's Responsibilities to "Follow the Rules"

Once you have a contractual relationship with an attorney or law firm, a lawyer's responsibilities become even weightier. For the most part, a lawyer's responsibilities to his client are mandated by the state bar organizations. Most of these organizations, in turn, base their rules on the American Bar Association's *Model Rules of Professional Conduct.* At best, the ABA "rule book" is a guidebook for the conduct of lawyers who practice in the United States. Like the law itself, the rules are open to interpretation. A layperson who tries to rely on the *Model Rules,* or on the version of the rules used by a particular state, may find himself in a legal quagmire. With much legal knowledge to rely on, a lawyer may interpret the rules differently.

By far, the largest section of the *Model Rules* is devoted to the attorney-

---

Recognized and Approved Specialties of Law

A lawyer who chooses to specialize in one or more of the recognized specialties listed below must be certified by his peers to represent clients in that specialty. When searching for a lawyer in a specialty, check the lawyer's certification to be sure it's up to date. With the law representing a society that is changing culturally and technologically more quickly than ever before, a lawyer's training can quickly fall behind if he is not diligent with his continuing-education requirements.

Administrative and Governmental Law

Admiralty

Antitrust and Trade Regulation

Appellate Practice

Aviation Law

Bankruptcy

Collections

Corporation and Business Law

Criminal Law

Elder Law

Entertainment, Arts, and Sports Law

Environmental Law

Immigration and Naturalization

International Law

Labor and Employment Law

Medical Malpractice

Patent, Trademark, and Copyright

Personal Injury

Real Property

Securities

Trust and Estates

client relationship. The following is a list of those areas that we will be taking a closer look at in later chapters.

❑ Competence

❑ Diligence

❑ Communication

❑ Fees

❑ Confidentiality of Information

❑ Conflict of Interest: General

❑ Conflict of Interest: Prohibitive Transactions

❑ Conflict of Interest: Former Client

❑ Safekeeping Property

❑ Declining or Terminating Representation

The above list clearly illustrates the complexity of the attorney-client relationship and the weighty obligation lawyers have when it comes to representing their clients.

A Lawyer's Responsibility to Stay Involved

A critical responsibility a lawyer has to his client is to remain on the client's case until the case is settled or concluded—that is, unless a judge grants a lawyer's request to be substituted or excused from the duty to represent the client once that representation commences. In an action brought by the Michigan Bar against one of its attorneys (*State Bar of Michigan v. Daggs*, 384 Mich. 729,187 N.W. 2d 227 [1971]), the appellate judges said: "Once an attorney accepts a retainer to represent a client, he [or she] is obligated to exert his best efforts wholeheartedly to advance his client's legitimate interests with fidelity and diligence until he is relieved of that obligation either by his client or by a court."

A Lawyer's Responsibility to Continue Representation

A lawyer is required, even when a case appears to be over, to continue representation should he receive a document, notice, or indication that something has changed, may change, or is about to change in the case. For instance, if a case appears to be over and the opposition files additional documents that could upset the apparent outcome, the client must have the security to know that his lawyer will protect him from harm.

A Lawyer's Responsibilities to Unrepresented Individuals

The *Model Rules* often refer to individuals who are not represented by counsel as non-lawyers. Be it non-lawyers or unrepresented individuals or lay people, the ethical rules governing lawyers as indicated in Model Rule 4.3 "Dealing with Unrepresented Persons" contain scant guidance for the regulation of contact between lawyers and those not represented by counsel. The rule does say that "a lawyer, shall not state or imply that the lawyer is disinterested." In other words, a lawyer has an ethical duty to act in a professional, non-condescending manner and should not act as if he doesn't have to pay attention to, or can take advantage of, the unrepresented person because he lacks legal knowledge. Also, if a lawyer realizes that an unrepresented party misunderstands the lawyer's role as his adversary in the matter, it is incumbent upon the lawyer "to correct the misunderstanding." Apart from this, it is up to the lawyer's moral compass and sense of ethics to not take advantage of the non-represented party.

In the article "Out of Sight and Out of Line: The Need for Regulation of Lawyers' Negotiations with Unrepresented Poor Persons," which appeared in the *California Law Review* in 1997, Russell Engler, Professor of Law and Director of Clinical Programs at the New England School of Law, states:

> Despite the frequency of . . . encounters between lawyers and lay people, the ethical rules governing lawyers [are] virtually ignored. Neither the Model Rules of Professional Conduct, nor the Model Code of Professional Responsibility, contains a provision specifically regulating negotiations between lawyers and the lay people . . . Only a single subsection of one disciplinary rule of the Model Code focuses exclusively on this section.

As the cost of defending oneself or prosecuting a just claim becomes more expensive in our society (which is known as one of the most litigious in the world), it seems to this author that the ABA and the individual state bar associations should create and enforce additional rules to protect unrepresented individuals from unethical lawyers in situations in which the trained adversary may wish to win at any cost.

Unfortunately, some lawyers may take advantage of a pro se litigant (an individual who is representing himself) or even an individual who is handling a civil non-litigation legal matter and use their position, as well as their superior experience and knowledge, to take the upper hand. This is one of the reasons why pro se litigants must proceed with extreme caution. If one jumps into the legal lions' den, one must be prepared for a fight. It may not always be a clean one. (For guidelines and details concerning pro se advocacy, see Chapter 7.)

3.1. CASE IN POINT
The Shaky Partnership

Leo and Luce formed a partnership to build an office building in Michigan and hired a lawyer to protect their interests. Unfortunately, problems surfaced during construction, and the contractor refused to finish the project without an increase in the price quoted. Negotiations began between the contractor and Leo and Luce, who were represented by their attorney. The parties reached an agreement that included a restructured partnership and more money for the contractor in the form of a promissory note.

Two years after the building was completed, the contractor sued Leo and Luce for the unpaid promissory note, prompting the instant case. (It is not clear in the reported case why they did not pay the monies owed.) At the start of the case, the attorney wished to withdraw as counsel for Leo and Luce and filed a motion to withdraw with the court. The contractor asked the court for a summary judgment—a favorable court decision on the law alone—on the note in its motion to the court. Although the attorney's request to withdraw had not yet been granted by the court, and while he still had a legal and ethical duty to continue to represent and protect Leo and Luce to the best of his ability, he discontinued his representation and allowed his clients to "slowly twist in the wind."

The trial court judge granted the contractor's request for a summary judgment. Then, the judge promptly allowed the attorney to withdraw from the case. He hadn't even tried to defend Leo and Luce against the imposition of a judgment against them by the court. When questioned, the attorney's cop-out was that he was no longer involved in the matter and was, therefore, not connected to the case. In a state of shock, Leo and Luce (represented by a new lawyer) asked the court to reconsider. The court was steadfast in its decision, and so the couple appealed.

The appellate court found the attorney in violation of the code of professional responsibility for allowing a judgment to be assessed against his clients in open court without a trace of a defense. He was still Leo and Luce's lawyer at the time and had a duty to represent them until he had been granted permission to withdraw. The appellate judges stated that it

One Court's Opinion

The following excerpt is from an opinion rendered by the justices of the Court of Appeals of New York in a malpractice case. Their words speak eloquently of the relationship between attorney and client. Few statements by a court have so clearly illustrated the true nature of what is expected of a lawyer in the attorney-client relationship, and what action the client can take when a lawyer lacks reverence and zeal for his case.

From: The Court of Appeals of New York

As we not too long ago observed, [t]he unique relationship between an attorney and client, founded in principle upon the elements of trust and confidence on the part of the client and of undivided loyalty and devotion on the part of the attorney, remains one of the most sensitive and confidential relationships in our society.

Because of the role attorneys play in the vindication of individual rights in our society, they are held to the highest standard of ethical behavior. Yet without this relationship of trust and confidence an attorney is unable to fulfill this obligation to effectively represent clients by acting with competence and exercising proper care in the representation.

Because of the uniqueness of the attorney-client relationship, traditional contract principles are not always applied to govern disputes between attorneys and clients. Thus it is well established that notwithstanding the terms of the agreement between them, a client has an absolute right, at any time, with or without cause, to terminate the attorney-client relationship by discharging the attorney.

Where that discharge is without cause, the attorney is limited to recovering in

had been the attorney's responsibility to file a breach of contract suit against the contractor when the contractor stopped the job midstream and requested more money before continuing the work. The evidence showed that, during that time, the attorney had charged Leo and Luce a large fee to investigate the facts for a possible lawsuit against the contractor. In the appellate procedure, the evidence showed that the lawyer's lack of action against the contractor violated disciplinary rules.

Moreover, the judges found that the atorney had failed to warn his clients of various problems that might occur with the building project. He also misrepresented to Leo and Luce that the execution of an assumption agreement clause in a mortgage they executed would relieve them of any liability for the cost of construction or mortgage financing, further violat-

quantum meruit [payment for work completed under the terms of a breached contract] the reasonable value of the services rendered. Where the discharge is for cause, the attorney has no right to compensation or a retaining lien, notwithstanding a specific retainer agreement.

Th[is] rule is well calculated to promote public confidence in the members of an honorable profession whose relation to their clients is personal and confidential. We view the public policy considerations that underpin this rule as both relevant and sufficiently compelling to warrant denying unearned attorney's fees, or credit for the monetary equivalent, to an attorney who is guilty of legal malpractice that results in the client's loss of recovery upon a valid claim.

The attorney's malpractice constitutes a failure to honor faithfully the fidelity owed to the client and to discharge competently the responsibilities flowing from the engagement. It is especially appropriate to deny credit for a fee where . . . the defendant attorneys performed absolutely no services in connection with the disputed claim [engagement], and thus, even if discharged by plaintiff without cause, would not have been entitled to any *quantum meruit* compensation.

Of course, if plaintiff had learned of defendants' malpractice and discharged them for cause, they could not claim credit for their fee. We see no reason to allow the [lawyer] to benefit by the fact that [the client] belatedly learned of their misconduct and sued for recovery in legal malpractice.

We conclude, therefore, that in these circumstances, the negligent attorney is precluded from claiming credit for an unearned fee.

—From *Kathleen Campagnola, et al., Respondents, v. Mulholland,
Minion & Roe, et al., Appellants 76 N.Y.2d 38,
555 N.E.2d 611, 556 N.Y.S.2d 239 (1990)*

ing disciplinary rules. Then the judges admonished the attorney for breach of the *Canons of Professional Ethics*, the *Model Rules of Professional Conduct*, and the standard of care for lawyers practicing in Michigan who are engaged in such transactions for advising his clients to assign their right, title, and interest in said property to the contractor in support of the promissory note.

Finally, the appellate court found that the "trusted" lawyer had converted to his own use $12,000 worth of valuable oil paintings owned by Luce, which were given to the lawyer under the guise of reducing the amount of the fee payable to him.

The justices' ruling in this case provides insight into what a client should expect from a lawyer:

Once an attorney **accepts** a retainer to represent a client, he [or she] is obligated to exert his **best efforts wholeheartedly** to **advance** his client's **legitimate interests** with **fidelity** and **diligence** until he is relieved of that obligation either by his client or by a court.

In the law, precedents and court rulings as well as law review articles and treatises are called *authorities*. For the folks in Michigan, and for this book, the words of the Court of Appeals of Michigan are an authority in the relationship between a lawyer and client. The bold-faced words, as used in this decision, are indicative of some of the most important responsibilities lawyers have to clients and are therefore discussed below.

Accept—Once an attorney accepts a case, he is expected to pursue the matter with deliberate speed.

Best efforts—*Exerting best efforts* means a lawyer is expected to diligently use the knowledge, tools, and skills to do the job he has accepted. Another component of best efforts is to understand what the client is trying to achieve and to either "go for it" or decline representation.

Wholeheartedly—The word *wholehearted* means "sincerely and earnestly devoted." An attorney is expected to act earnestly in his effort to bring about a speedy resolution to the case at hand.

Advance—An attorney has an obligation to advance a case. In other words, there must be forward movement toward the client's goals as quickly as possible unless it is to the client's advantage to "stonewall" or delay the case (as it may be in defensive matters).

Legitimate interests—Legitimate interests are those endeavors in business and in life that are not against the law. (Attorneys may not help clients carry out underhanded business transactions.)

Fidelity—Fidelity is the quality or state of being faithful or loyal. An attorney has an obligation to be loyal to his client and faithful in his actions concerning his client's interests.

Diligence—A lawyer is obligated to be diligent—that is, to pay attention and provide legal care to all cases accepted. (This area of the attorney-client relationship is certainly one of the most contentious of all.)

Although not specifically used by the Michigan justices in their statement, the words "communication" and "fiduciary relationship" fit well into this discussion.

Communication—Communication is an integral part of the attorney-client relationship. If the lawyer in the above case had made more of an effort to communicate with his clients—especially by obtaining their consent—the malpractice case against him probably wouldn't have been necessary.

Fiduciary relationship—Part of a lawyer's role as fiduciary is to safe keep a client's property. In the above case, the lawyer breached one of the ethical cannons of behavior by converting to his own use his client's property.

CONCLUSION

Now that you have a working knowledge of a lawyer's responsibilities in the attorney-client relationship, you will be in a better position to evaluate whether you have actually been wronged by your lawyer or law firm. Your first job is to identify the specific areas of responsibility that your lawyer has not met or breached. The chapters ahead will help you make this determination.

4

Competence and
Scope of Representation

An attorney's competence—that is, her ability to properly handle your case or matter—should be your first and foremost concern when choosing someone to represent you. Therefore, it's important to understand and to recognize the various elements of competency. Your second concern should be making sure that the scope of representation is clearly defined between you and your lawyer. In other words, at the start of your business relationship with your lawyer, it should be clearly spelled out what your lawyer is expected to do or is legally required to do on your behalf and also what is not expected of her. This chapter discusses these important concepts and alerts you to some of the pitfalls involving the standards of competency and the parameters of the scope of representation as set by the *Model Rules of Professional Conduct*.

ELEMENTS OF COMPETENCY

When you select a lawyer, you expect certain things to be a given. One of the most important of these things is a lawyer's competence. Rule 1.1 of the *Model Rules of Professional Conduct* states: "A lawyer shall provide competent representation to a client. Competent representation requires the legal knowledge, skill, thoroughness and preparation reasonably necessary for the representation."

But how do you determine if the lawyer you choose to handle your matter or case is competent? Do you judge competence by the law school an attorney attended? For instance, perhaps a diploma from Harvard Law School is hanging on the wall of your attorney's office. To the average person, such a sight might indicate that this lawyer is well educated and should have a high degree of competency. On the other hand, a diploma from an unknown university might give rise to concerns about whether this attorney can competently handle your case. You already know that appearances may be deceiving, so don't rely on a diploma alone to ascertain an attorney's competence. Also, the size of a law firm is not indicative of the quality of legal care you and your matter will receive. Instead of relying solely on appearances, become familiar with the elements of competency—legal knowledge, thoroughness and preparation, knowledge of legal principles, skills, and successful experience with similiar cases. Knowing this information will place you in a better position to determine if your lawyer, or a lawyer you are interviewing, can competently handle your case.

Legal Knowledge

Your lawyer is expected to have knowledge of the field of law in which she is representing you; otherwise, she should not take your case. Alternatively, she can consult with a specialist or a lawyer who has the knowledge required. Under the bar rules, as another possible alternative, your lawyer is permitted to analyze precedent, evaluate evidence, learn the specifics of a particular area of law, and then proceed to represent you in that area.

A lawyer should not represent you in a matter if she doesn't have the required knowledge, doesn't consult with a specialist, and doesn't pursue study in the specific field. Ask a potential attorney if she has resources (experts) available to her. In complex legal matters, her answer might sway your decision to hire her.

Thoroughness and Preparation

To quote the *Annotated Model Rules of Professional Conduct*, "The required attention and preparation are determined in part by what is at stake; major litigation and complex transactions ordinarily require more elaborate treatment than matters of lesser consequence." But who is to judge what matters are of lesser consequence? For instance, a $95,000 home that is in foreclosure is a major matter to the homeowner. However, to an attorney who deals in millions of dollars worth of real estate transactions each year, this matter may seem inconsequential. Therefore, the standard of care becomes *forbidding neglect*—not to let something go wrong that could have been prevented with normal care—and requiring *adequate preparation* for all matters represented by a lawyer. Under established rules, your lawyer must be diligent and act competently on your behalf. Preparation and thoroughness are functions of not being neglectful as is the prompt handling of all matters—especially legal deadlines—related to your case. Preparation includes investigation, research, and verification of client's information. Without these three elements of a lawyer's duty to be thorough, no amount of preparation is complete.

Knowledge of Legal Principles

Basic research, knowledge of procedure, and *knowledge of court rules* are subcategories of knowledge of legal principles. In other words, a lawyer is expected to be familiar with all applicable principles and the practice of law that may impact on a client's needs in the jurisdiction in which the case is proceeding. It is incumbent upon your lawyer to do basic research and keep abreast of new additional rules of law that may affect your case. This includes court rules that, if not followed precisely, could have an adverse effect on your case regardless of how right you are in your position. In Re Belser, 277 S.C. 250, 287 S.E.2d 139 (1982) was a case in which a lawyer filed improper exceptions to a hearing and then failed to serve them on the opposing counsel, claiming ignorance of the rule requiring the need to provide service. In that case, the court held that Attorney Bresler had violated rule DR 6-101 (A)(2)(3) by handling a legal matter without sufficient knowledge of the practice and by neglecting to inquire concerning a legal matter entrusted to him. The court said, "We also take a dim view of the [attorney's] lack of knowledge and familiarity with basic rules of practice in the South Carolina courts. Under these circumstances a public censure is warranted. Attorney Henry Belser Jr. stands publicly reprimanded by this court . . . ."

Skills

Your lawyer is required to have certain basic skills necessary to practice her craft and properly represent you. One of those skills is being able to draft legal pleadings and other documents. Pleadings that are sloppy, incoherent, incomplete, and misleading on their face are possible grounds for malpractice. In Re Hogan, 440 N.E.2d 1280 (ILL 1986), nineteen pleadings or briefs in which arguments or writings were incomprehensible were grounds for a finding of "incompetent practice." However, in this case, the court held that since no corrupt motive or moral turpitude was shown, "suspension, not disbarment is an appropriate sanction." The court further held, "an examination of the brief and pleadings drafted by (the lawyer) makes it clear that he is presently incapable of adequately serving the public." Then the court ordered the lawyer to remedy his disability.

Another responsibility of an attorney under the heading of *skills* is the proper management of her office. Secretarial problems are no excuse for the neglect of client matters and/or the failure to respond to client inquiries. This was covered in *Sanchez v. State Bar*, 555 P.2d 889 (CAL 1976), which is a good starting point for legal research if you have a problem along these lines. Of particular importance in the proper operation of a law office is a calendaring system. This is necessary to prevent missing important legal dates and deadlines, which can easily happen in a busy office if a good system is not in place.

To recap, under the heading of skills, an attorney is responsible for the following:

❑ Drafting pleadings, including checking grammar, spelling, and even typing.

❑ Being familiar with local, state, and federal court rules, especially concerning the forms of pleadings.

❑ Office management: preventing secretarial problems, supervision of non-lawyer personnel, internal calendaring systems, adequate record keeping, and case management, among others.

Some of the above may seem obvious and even mundane, but when a client's way of life and property are at stake, they take on a much greater importance.

In the case of *Gulfwide v. F. E. Wright* (554 SO. 2d 1347) (A. App. 1C1R. 1989), the Court of Appeals of Louisiana's First Circuit made a strong statement regarding the rules of professional conduct and their effect as evidence of a lawyer's behavior and practice. The court held, "There is little doubt that if a case of malpractice is going to be made, the rules of professional conduct if broken or violated, become strong evidence against the malpracticing attorney." Attorneys who do not prepare, who are not knowledgeable of the law, and who do not use basic legal skills in representing their clients run the risk of rebuke by the court system. Not only can they be sanctioned by the bar association or organization in their state, but the courts are increasing their attention to the breaking of bar rules as evidence that a lawyer may have committed malpractice.

Federal Rules of Civil Procedure Rule 11— Protection From an Opposing Side's Attorney's Abuse

When a lack of lawyering skills results in an inadequate pleading, the federal court has provided some protection for those who may have suffered the results of incompetence. Sanctions—fines or other punishments—may be levied and/or disciplinary action may be taken for violation of federal pleading rules. Disciplinary action can take the form of a reprimand, suspension from practice, or even disbarment.

Under Federal Rules of Civil Procedure Rule 11, sanctions against an attorney or law firm are possible under certain conditions. Rule 11 is based on the assumption that if a lawyer signs a court document, the contents thereof are known to be true and accurate by the signer. This rule is also supposed to protect against a lawyer's knowingly filing sham pleadings or other documents or malicious prosecution of a case. Rule 11 has a number of differing sanctions if a violation takes place as determined by the court. The following is F.R.C.P. Rule 11 in its entirety.

Federal Rules of Civil Procedure (F.R.C.P.) Rule 11

Rule 11—Signing of Pleadings, Motions, and Other Papers; Representations to Court; Sanctions

(a) Signature. Every pleading, written motion, and other paper shall be signed by at least one attorney of record in the attorney's individual name, or, if the party is not represented by an attorney, shall be signed by the party. Each paper shall state the signer's address and telephone number, if any. Except when otherwise specifically provided by rule or statute, pleadings need not be verified or accompanied by affidavit. An unsigned paper shall be stricken unless omission of the signature is corrected promptly after being called to the attention of the attorney or party.

(b) Representations to Court. By presenting to the court (whether by signing, filing, submitting, or later advocating) a pleading, written motion, or other paper, an attorney or unrepresented party is certifying that to the best of the person's knowledge, information, and belief, formed after an inquiry reasonable under the circumstances,—

(1) it is not being presented for any improper purpose, such as to harass or to cause unnecessary delay or needless increase in the cost of litigation;

(2) the claims, defenses, and other legal contentions therein are warranted by existing law or by a nonfrivolous argument for the extension, modification, or reversal of existing law or the establishment of new law;

(3) the allegations and other factual contentions have evidentiary support or, if specifically so identified, are likely to have evidentiary support after a reasonable opportunity for further investigation or discovery; and

(4) the denials of factual contentions are warranted on the evidence or, if specifically so identified, are reasonably based on a lack of information or belief. (c) Sanctions. If, after notice and a reasonable opportunity to respond, the court determines that subdivision (b) has been violated, the court may, subject to the conditions stated below, impose an appropriate sanction upon the attorneys, law firms, or parties that have violated subdivision (b) or are responsible for the violation.

(1) How Initiated.

(A) By Motion. A motion for sanctions under this rule shall be made separately from other motions or requests and shall describe the specific conduct alleged to violate subdivision (b). It shall be served as provided in Rule 5, but shall not be filed with or presented to the court unless, within 21 days after service of the motion (or such other period as the court may prescribe), the challenged paper, claim, defense, contention, allegation, or denial is not withdrawn or appropriately corrected. If warranted, the court may award to the party prevailing on the motion the reasonable expenses and attorney's fees incurred in presenting or opposing the motion.

Absent exceptional circumstances, a law firm shall be held jointly responsible for violations committed by its partners, associates, and employees.

(B) On Court's Initiative. On its own initiative, the court may enter an order describing the specific conduct that appears to violate subdivision (b) and directing an attorney, law firm, or party to show cause why it has not violated subdivision (b) with respect thereto.

(2) Nature of Sanction; Limitations. A sanction imposed for violation of this rule shall be limited to what is sufficient to deter repetition of such conduct or comparable conduct by others similarly situated.

Subject to the limitations in subparagraphs (A) and (B), the sanction may consist of, or include, directives of a nonmonetary nature, an order to pay a penalty into court, or, if imposed on motion and warranted for effective deterrence, an order directing payment to the movant of some or all of the reasonable attorneys' fees and other expenses incurred as a direct result of the violation.

(A) Monetary sanctions may not be awarded against a represented party for a violation of subdivision (b)(2).

(B) Monetary sanctions may not be awarded on the court's initiative unless the court issues its order to show cause before a voluntary dismissal or settlement of the claims made by or against the party which is, or whose attorneys are, to be sanctioned.

(3) Order. When imposing sanctions, the court shall describe the conduct determined to constitute a violation of this rule and explain the basis for the sanction imposed.

(d) Inapplicability to Discovery. Subdivisions (a) through (c) of this rule do not apply to disclosures and discovery requests, responses, objections, and motions that are subject to the provisions of Rules 26 through 37.

(As amended Apr. 28, 1983, eff. Aug. 1, 1983; Mar. 2, 1987, eff. Aug. 1, 1987; Apr. 22, 1993, eff. Dec. 1, 1993.)

SCOPE OF REPRESENTATION

Under the terms of Model Rule 1.2 "Scope of Representation and Allocation of Authority Between Client and Lawyer," a lawyer is obligated to, "abide by a client's decision concerning the objective of representation . . . to accept an offer of settlement of a matter [and] in a criminal case the lawyer shall abide by the client's decision as to a plea to be entered." Also in a criminal matter, an attorney must abide by her client's decisions on whether to waive jury trial and whether the client will testify on her own behalf.

There are three conditions to the above rule, as follows:

1. A lawyer's representation of a client does not constitute an endorsement of the client' s political, economic, social, or moral views or activities.

2. A lawyer shall not counsel a client to conduct criminal or fraudulent behavior. However, a lawyer may discuss the validity, scope, meaning, or application of the law.

3. If a lawyer determines that a client expects assistance not permitted (legally or ethically or under the rules of professional conduct), the lawyer shall consult with the client regarding an attorney's limitations.

Basically, the meaning and implications of this rule are simple. Under the legal principle of *agency* (which falls under the scope of representation), a lawyer once retained acts as your agent and cannot make any binding decisions affecting your legal matters in the absence of express, implied, or inherent authority. For some insightful information, refer to *Kaiser Fund v. Doe*, 903, P2 2d 375 (OR. CT. App. 1995).

The following paragraph from page 15 of the *Annotated Model Rules of*

Professional Conduct, **Third Edition,** clearly describes the attorney-client relationship insofar as the principle of agency is concerned.

> Although agency principles provide the most familiar framework with which to describe the attorney-client relationship, the allocation of authority and control between lawyers and clients differs significantly from that in a standard agency-principal situation. In a traditional agency relationship the principal has total right of control over the agent, so much so that liability for misdeeds of the agent can be imputed to the principle. Between lawyers and their clients, the division is somewhat different. It is generally agreed that a lawyer has a right to control the tactics or procedural elements of a case, by virtue of his or her superior knowledge of the law and status as a member of the bar.

Retainer agreements usually spell out a lawyer's degree, or scope, of authority. In the absence of a written agreement, be sure to clearly inform your lawyer why you are hiring her and what you expect her to accomplish on your behalf. For your lawyer to make decisions for you without your knowledge and consent beyond that which is agreed upon is to expand, or go beyond, the scope of representation, which may result in damages to you. From personal experience, however, the area to be most concerned with in scope of representation is the diligent transmittal to clients of offers made by the other side. An attorney has the duty to pass on all offers made to the client for consideration. It may not always be in the attorney's best self-interest to settle under the terms being proposed by the other side, but it is a decision that the client must make (with input from the attorney and, possibly, other experts). An attorney who tries to control a settlement by not passing along an offer is committing an act of malpractice.

As stated in the above extract, one area that definitely belongs to a lawyer is tactics. After discussion with a client, it is the special domain of the attorney to make all technical and procedural decisions in a case. For further information, refer to *Darden v. Wainwright,* 477 US 168 (1986).

4.1.   CASE IN POINT
Honesty Is the Best Policy

Gene had worked as a commissioned salesperson for Leonard who, according to Gene, owed him commissions and refused to account for and pay the money owed. He filed a suit against Leonard in federal court. Leonard responded by claiming that Gene owed *him* money, "several hundred thousand dollars" to quote from the affidavit that Leonard filed in the case. The defendants wanted a set-off, or credit, against the claimed commissions, the subject of the original lawsuit. Meanwhile, the law firm working for the defendant was dissolved and replaced by a new attorney.

Almost two years after the start of the case, Gene's attorney filed a motion for sanctions against opposing counsel under Rule 11, alleging that the statements included in Leonard's affidavits were false. In response to that charge, the defendant's lawyer filed a request for summary judgment and attached an affidavit, used earlier in the case, to the summary judgment pleading. After the initial review by the magistrate judge, the judge ordered sanctions against the defendant's attorney for the false statements contained in the affidavits submitted by his client.

After reviewing the evidence, the court ruled that Leonard had made false statements in his affidavits and other filings and that Gene was entitled to $2,000 as sanctions against the defendant's attorney. Of course, the attorney countered that there should be no sanctions at all and so the case went to appeal.

On appeal, the attorney contended that he came in after the start of the case and that he should not be held responsible for his client's false statements and that he "made a reasonable investigation of the statements contained in the documents [affidavits] which were filed." The court disagreed, noting that, as stated in Rule 11, "the signer of a document acknowledges that the information contained in it is well-grounded in fact to the best of his knowledge after reasonable inquiry."

The attorney tried to assert to the appeals court, as reported in the case that, "he performed a reasonable investigation and thus should not be sanctioned for any inaccurate information. The district court had already rejected that argument and [claimed] that Blain [had] relied on the investigation by the previous attorneys and his client's sworn affidavits. The court also found the lawyer had ample time to conduct his own investigation into the [factual] basis for the numbers provided by [his] client Leonard." In response to the attorney's appeal, the appellate court made an important statement: "Although Rule 11 does not require exhaustive inquiry, attorneys must make an objective reasonable inquiry into the facts of a case . . . The level of an investigation required depends on the facts of each case."

The appellate court also said, "The purpose of the rule is to deter baseless filings."

The lesson here is clear: Any information that you give to your attorney must be accurate; it is also incumbent upon your attorney to investigate any facts you provide if she has even a hint of a doubt. If your attorney relies on your information and it is not truthful and then tries to use this baseless information to outmaneuver your opponent, you and your attorney are heading down the path of sanctions and possibly dismissal of your actions. Frivolous suits do not belong in court.

4.2. CASE IN POINT
The Missed Opportunity

The prospect to settle a case for a reasonable amount without a trial is a valuable right that could be lost due to an attorney's negligence. The negligence may be rooted in lack of skill, lack of communication, or both. Whatever the reason, not passing along an offer of settlement may be grounds for a legal malpractice action depending the outcome of the case. A good example of this principle comes from a Massachusett's case.

The Superior Court of Massachusetts heard this case about a Massachusetts city council that was sued by several of its citizens. The council wanted to offer $375,000 to $400,000 to settle the case; however, the offer was not communicated to the plaintiffs by their attorney.

In its memorandum of decision, the court's words remind us of the criteria that are necessary to prevail on a legal malpractice claim when a lawyer fails to communicate to a client the terms of a proposed settlement offer. The court said:

> The opportunity to settle a case for a reasonable amount without a trial is itself a valuable right, which may be lost because of an attorney's negligence. In such a situation, the client could seek to recover in a legal malpractice suit the difference between the lowest amount at which his case probably would have settled on the advice of competent counsel and the amount of the settlement or the amount of the verdict. Under this approach there is no need for a trial within a trial.

A malpractice claim arising out of a lost settlement even when the client received nothing at trial may be maintained. In other words, the loss at trial by the client does not preclude a claim for malpractice. A plaintiff might contend that the defendant in the previous action made a settlement offer, that the plaintiff's lawyer negligently failed to inform plaintiff of the offer, and that, if informed, the plaintiff would have accepted the offer. If the plaintiff can prove this, she can recover the difference between what the plaintiff would have received under the settlement offer and the amount, if any, the plaintiff received through later settlement or judgment.

In this case, the city council made an offer that was not transmitted to the plaintiffs. Depending on the outcome of a trial, the plaintiffs could recover, through a legal malpractice action, the difference between what the offer was intended to be and what they would have actually received with a favorable verdict.

CONCLUSION

An attorney's neglect of a client's case will sometimes do damage to the client. Nothing can be more important in a legal matter than a competent, skilled, and diligent attorney sent on a well-defined mission. Use what you have learned in this chapter when you select your next lawyer and be sure to clearly define her mission, committing the scope of representation to writing. In the event of a legal catastrophe, this chapter may help you determine what went wrong and allow you to take appropriate action.

Next, we'll move on to a lawyer's obligation to be diligent and to communicate clearly and when necessary with a client.

5

Diligence and Communication

When you hire a lawyer, you expect him to act with reasonable diligence—that is, to give your case the attention and care it requires. You also expect your lawyer to communicate with you from time to time to inform you of the status of your matter and to explain, when necessary, what you need to know in order to make decisions that affect your case. If you find yourself in a position where you must chase after your lawyer for information and must prod him to make the next move, this may be a sign of trouble to come. For this reason, this chapter takes an in-depth look at *diligence* and its partner *communication*. These twin subjects, which can affect every attorney-client relationship, are also rule headings in the *Model Rules of Professional Conduct*. This chapter will help you recognize a lawyer's lack of diligence and his failure to communicate with a client. Be sure to apply what you learn to your own legal situation.

REASONABLE DILIGENCE

There's a good chance you've had or have heard the following complaint: "I gave my lawyer the fee he asked for and so far nothing's happened. He doesn't even return my phone calls. I don't know what to do!" This lack of responsiveness to clients and even occasionally to the courts on the part of many attorneys is certainly one cause for the bad rap attached to the legal profession. Whether due to the attorney's busy schedule, inadvertence, or worse, purposeful avoidance to cover up a mistake, it cannot be tolerated.

Reasonable diligence keeps a case moving forward in a timely fashion to avoid exposing a client to unnecessary risk.

It's important to know what the ABA and most state bars have to say about an attorney's diligence. Rule 1.3 of the *Model Rules of Professional Con-*

duct states: "A lawyer shall act with reasonable diligence and promptness in representing a client."

Most bar rules interpret the duty to be diligent also as a duty to carry through to conclusion all matters related to the representation of a client on a particular matter unless the lawyer files a motion to withdraw from the case and it is granted by the court. Moreover, the ABA's Standing Committee on Ethics and Professional Responsibility (informal opinion 86-1520 [1986]) states that, "while the lawyer client relationship exists, the duty of diligence governs regardless of the client's non-payment of fees." This rule is one of the reasons why many lawyers are reluctant to take on a case without having first received a sufficient retainer or deposit—or, in the case of a contingency arrangement, without believing the case will pay off down the road. Once a lawyer signs on to a case, he becomes obligated to continue to work on the case even in the absence of payment of fees. (Of course, clients have an obligation to pay their attorneys as agreed and on time.) Still, an attorney cannot simply choose to stop working for the client without taking appropriate action; only a court can allow an attorney to withdraw from a case. This protects not only you as a client, but also anyone involved in the case.

In practical terms, there is anecdotal evidence that if a lawyer wants out of a case—like a marriage partner who claims " irreconcilable differences"— most judges will allow the lawyer to withdraw representation, especially in a civil matter. Occasionally, if a trial is pending or if life or property is at stake, the court may, and has the discretion to, force the lawyer to continue representation.

Violations of Diligence

The following are some of the classic signs of a violation of the duty to be diligent:

1. **Failing to file a complaint or other documents or pleadings on time.** If a lawyer does not file a complaint or an answer pleading on time, how could one expect any of the other legal steps and responsibilities to be provided in a timely fashion? If your attorney fails to file documents in a timely manner, this is an indication that you may have to replace your lawyer.

2. **Taking on a new matter and, after some initial activity, neglecting the work.** Some lawyers use what is called the "new matter strategy." They take retainers for as many cases as possible and work on the backlog as

time allows. If you are in the backlog, get out and get new counsel! By the way, payment in advance can potentially lead to a lawyer's lack of diligence since it may remove the incentive to work diligently. Especially in small firms and in one-person or two-person operations, many attorneys look at new matters as their cash cow—a steady source of income. They know that taking on a new matter will surely lead to the immediate payment of a fee. An appointment with a new client may take precedence over everything else, including yesterday's new matters. Contingency fees and periodic payments offer a greater incentive to get the job done. (See Chapter 12 for some enlightening information on billing practices.)

3. **Failing to communicate with a client.** A lack of communication can occur for several reasons. For instance, failure to communicate may be due to a lawyer's procrastination—he may have put things off for so long that communication with the client has become embarrassing for him; or perhaps his schedule is so overwhelming that he's too busy to get to his client's work and fails to return his client's calls or contact his client when the need arises. Whatever the reason, there is no excuse for not keeping in touch with a client. Failure to communicate with a client for whatever reason demonstrates a lawyer's lack of respect for that client. Keeping a client "in the dark" about his case is no way to maintain an attorney-client relationship. (Communication is discussed more fully later in this chapter.)

4. **Constantly failing to work for the client on a timely manner.** As soon as a lawyer agrees to take on a client's matter, it is implied that the attorney will provide his services in a timely fashion. Whether it is fact finding, preparing or submitting documents, showing up at a meeting, or any other legally related task, a lawyer has agreed to provide his client with a level of service that meets his profession's standards. If a lawyer puts off what he is supposed to do or is required to do within a certain time frame, this behavior can result in a detrimental outcome of the legal matter.

5. **An unreasonable delay in informing a client of important developments.** Although a lawyer may communicate with his client, this communication may not include an update on important actions that take place in the case. This lack of information can be damaging to the client, especially in an ongoing case. Such behavior clearly demonstrates a lack of diligence on the part of a lawyer.

6. **Misleading a client as to the status of the work.** Being told by your lawyer that he is working on your matter when he is clearly not or being told that an action has been carried out when it has not is tantamount to fraud. If your trusted counsel should ever deliberately mislead you, quickly find a new lawyer.

If you recognize any of these signs of a lack of diligence in your attorney's behavior, it might be helpful to call your lawyer and quote the diligence rule before your situation becomes a clear-cut malpractice claim. If you cannot get your lawyer on the phone, send a letter by certified mail, return receipt requested. In the letter, remind your attorney of the following bar rules, appearing on page 25 of the *Annotated Model Rules of Professional Conduct*, Third Edition.

A lawyer should pursue on behalf of a client despite opposition, obstruction, or personal inconvenience to the lawyer . . . a client's case or endeavor.

A client's interest often can be adversely affected by the passage of time or the change of conditions; in extreme instances, as when a lawyer overlooks a statute of limitations, the client's legal position may be destroyed. Even when the client's interests are not affected in substance, however, unreasonable delay can cause a client needless anxiety and undermine confidence in their lawyer's trustworthiness.

Unless the relationship is terminated as provided in [the rules] a lawyer should carry through to conclusion all matters undertaken for a client. If a lawyer's employment is limited to a specific matter, the relationship terminates when the matter has been resolved.

COMMUNICATION

The subject of communication between a lawyer and his client is so important that the model rule for communication contains two parts. Rule 1.4 "Communication" of the *Model Rules of Professional Conduct* states:

(a) A lawyer shall keep a client reasonably informed about the status of a matter and promptly comply with reasonable requests for information.
(b) A lawyer shall explain a matter to the extent reasonably necessary to permit the client to make informed decisions regarding the representation.

Under this rule, a lawyer is obligated to provide all pertinent information to his client except in the following situations: 1) a court has provided information to a lawyer under a court order governing its disclosure, or 2) a lawyer may receive, for instance, psychological evaluation reports and deem that they may damage a client's state of mind.

The duty to communicate stems in part from a lawyer's fiduciary responsibility (discussed in Chapter 6) to a client consisting of, at most, good faith. As part of the fiduciary relationship between attorney and client, a lawyer is obligated to look out for his client's best interest; therefore, communication must be maintained between both parties. In Re Marriage of Petula, 491 N.E. 2d 90 (ILL. App. Ct. 1986), the court said, "Time-honored ideals of the legal profession and the continuing need for public confidence in the profession require the conclusion that a client always has the right to know what the attorney did or does, and how much time it took to do it." Good communication also serves to keep the lawyer informed regarding possible changes in the client's status and the status of the client's case.

The specifics of the duty to communicate include, but are not limited to, the following:

❏ Duty to advise a client in a meaningful way about possible options in pursuing or defending a case. (Obviously, a lawyer must be educated sufficiently in a subject to provide meaningful advice.)

❏ Duty to relay settlement offers.

❏ Duty to brief clients in negotiations.

❏ Duty to explain what the possible *net recovery* will be—that is, what the client can expect to go home with at the end of the day.

Failure to Communicate

Obviously, the failure to keep a client abreast of developments in a case is potentially harmful to a client and, in addition, may cause great inconvenience and unwarranted expense to a client. One of the most contentious areas of communication is a lawyer's responsibility and duty to respond to a client's request for information. Some lawyers have a reputation for not returning phone calls or for not returning them within a reasonable amount of time. It seems that if lawyers as a whole respected the rule concerning communication, they would not have such a reputation.

5.1. CASE IN POINT
The Noncommunicative Attorney

Some courts have held that lawyers are not responsible for answering clients' inquires in writing. Therefore, if a client has a routine question regarding the status of his matter, an answer in writing may be considered a courtesy—not an obligation—as the following case demonstrates.

The parents of Michael C. hired a lawyer to represent their son, who—a month shy of his twenty-first birthday—had been seriously injured when a drunk driver traveling the wrong way on Route 66 collided with his car. The lawyer took all of the appropriate action: Claims were filed against the health insurer and the insurer of the drunk driver's car. In addition, the attorney filed a suit against the tavern that served liquor to the drunk driver. (This type of suit is called a *dramshop action*.) It appeared that the attorney was literally and figuratively "on the case."

The attorney obtained $17,000 on behalf of his client from the two insurance companies. Since not all issues in the case were settled, the lawyer deposited the funds in his attorney's trust account. With the dramshop claim pending, both insurance carriers, hoping to recover the money they had paid out, filed liens totaling $17,000 against the money that Michael's parents were hoping to collect from the tavern.

On numerous occasions, Michael and his parents sent letters to their attorney, pleading to know the status of the case. None were ever answered in writing, although the lawyer claimed that he gave them answers over the phone.

Having heard nothing about the status of Michael's case, they filed a disciplinary complaint. After reviewing the evidence against the lawyer, the disciplinary board said, "[he has] an ungracious resistance to his client's demands that the status of his claim be repeatedly explained to him." But the commission also said of Disciplinary Rule 6-101, "[it] does not require that letters from clients be responded to in writing." The noncommunicative lawyer was off the hook and with a profit to show for it—keeping the funds in his account, all $31,000, for his billable hours. Michael was the loser all around.

5.2. CASE IN POINT
Too Little, Too Late

Bob wanted to change his will to include his nephews and nieces as beneficiaries under his Florida estate. (They had not been named under a prior will.) In March, he hired his attorney to prepare a new will to accomplish this. When he met with the attorney to discuss the changes, he paid him a retainer for the work. Thereafter, the attorney prepared a draft of the will and sent it to his client along with a cover letter, seeking Bob's approval.

The attorney knew that Bob's health was failing and that time was of the essence. However, unfortunately for the would-be-beneficiaries, the lawyer did not get around to preparing the key document until May—two months after Bob originally retained his services. By that time, Bob's health had deteriorated so much that he could not sign the revised will. He died a short while later, and his wishes to include his nieces and nephews in his will were never carried out.

Understandably upset, Bob's nieces and nephews filed suit against the lawyer. However, the trial court ruled that they lacked standing as "third party beneficiaries" since they were not named in any prior will or document. Therefore, they were not able to bring an action against the attorney. In other words, unless the intended beneficiaries can prove that a lawyer committed a mistake in drafting a will that included them incorrectly (and the will was subsequently signed), they cannot bring suit against a lawyer for a mistake in an unsigned will, even if it would have been signed if the lawyer had acted promptly.

In this case, the nieces and nephews were left out in the cold, so to speak. Although the lawyer was morally responsible for his mistake, he was able to avoid legal repercussions.

CONCLUSION

Although diligence and communication may seem like simple concepts, they are all too often ignored by lawyers or just not made part of a lawyer's practice. Your case or legal matter cannot move forward if your attorney doesn't diligently pursue a resolution or a conclusion to your legal matter. Likewise, if your lawyer fails to communicate with you on important issues that can potentially affect the outcome of your matter, you may suffer damages. Hopefully, this chapter has given you some insight into these two important areas of the practice of law. Knowing these two basic model rules will help you determine if your lawyer is acting, or acted, diligently on your behalf, and whether or not he communicated with you on all important matters concerning your case or legal matter.

6

Conflict of Interest and Fiduciary Duty

At a meeting between an attorney and her client, the client handed her counsel a crisp one-hundred-dollar bill as a deposit for her services. After the client left, the partner in the two-person firm leaned back in her comfortable leather chair to contemplate the arrival of her next client. As she did so, the attorney happened to twist the bill between her well-manicured fingers. Suddenly, the bill separated into *two* one-hundred-dollar bills! The crisp greenbacks had been stuck together. The lawyer thought to herself, *Hmmm, it seems I have a conflict of interest here, and I just don't know what to do. I have but two choices: the first, keep the extra hundred for myself; the second, share it with my partner.*

In this chapter, you'll learn what a *real* conflict of interest is. You'll also learn about a lawyer's responsibility to protect and safeguard a client's property as well as her confidences.

CONFLICT OF INTEREST

The subject of conflict of interest is an all-important one for both attorney and client. The word *loyalty*—that is, a lawyer's diligent efforts to ensure that she is being loyal to her clients—is a good starting point for understanding conflict of interest. As stated in the *Annotated Model Rules of Professional Conduct*, "Loyalty is an essential element in a lawyer's relationship to a client." The word *loyalty* as used in this quote should be construed in the broadest possible sense.

Making sure that a conflict does not exist is one of a lawyer's most important responsibilities to a client. There are a few reasons why it should not be, and cannot be, the client's responsibility to make this determination. First, a layperson may not understand the very concept of conflict of interest as it applies to a lawyer or law firm. For example, a person who is not

61

educated in legal matters may have difficulty understanding how a lawyer's relationship with one client may affect her other clients. Second, it would be difficult, if not impossible, for most clients to learn enough about a lawyer or a law firm's client roster to determine if a conflict of interest exists. Third, most clients would not know about the details of a lawyer's personal business interests. And last, the conflict of interest rules are complex and spelled out in great detail as guidelines for the legal community to follow. A layperson is not expected to know the ins and outs of the labyrinth of conflict of interest rules and regulations.

For all of these reasons, lawyers are supposed to take the conflict rule very seriously, as well they should. It is an attorney's responsibility to thoroughly review with a potential client any conflicts that may arise out of a possible representation of that client's interest and/or case. Most firms perform a "conflict check" before they even consider taking on a new case. Perhaps the field looks clean. Then upon further review of the potential client's case, it is discovered that one of the client's key witnesses had been a client of the firm. If it were to become public at trial, for instance, that a key witness had been a client of the firm now representing the plaintiff, that witness's testimony may very well be questioned to the detriment of the client. Even if it were not actually tainted, the appearance of a conflict will diminish the weight of the witness's testimony in the eyes of the judge and/or jury. If so, the client's own lawyer has done the client a disservice by not discussing the potential.

Should a lawyer fail to run a conflict check to advise a client of the possibility of an adverse effect due to a potential conflict of interest, the lawyer may be subject to a malpractice claim if the client is ultimately harmed.

Several of the rules that fall under the main heading of the client-lawyer relationship cover conflict of interest. These rules are too lengthy to include here in their entirety. Therefore, following are some of the pertinent parts of the conflict of interest rules (with important exceptions noted) as stated in the *Model Rules of Professional Conduct:*

❑ A lawyer shall not represent a client if the representation of that client would be directly adverse, or harmful, to another client.

❑ A lawyer shall not represent a client if the representation of that client may be materially limited by the lawyer's responsibilities to another client or to a third person, or by the lawyer's own interest.

Exception: If the client is informed of a conflict and consents to that conflict or potential conflict after consultation, the lawyer may proceed with representation provided that she reasonably believes the representation will not adversely affect the relationship with the other client. If a lawyer's representation of a client is materially—substantially—limited by the lawyer's responsibilities to another client or to a third person or even to the lawyer's own interest, and the client is informed of the conflict, and the lawyer believes that the representation will not adversely affect the client, then this also may be considered an exception. The key words here are "informed consent" and, of course, if you are the client, it should be in writing.

❏ A lawyer shall not enter into a business transaction with a client or knowingly acquire an ownership, possessory, security, or other pecuniary—financial—interest adverse to a client.

Exception: A lawyer can enter into a business transaction with a client if the terms on which the lawyer acquires the interest are fair and reasonable to the client and are fully disclosed, and having been transmitted in writing to the client in a manner that can be reasonably understood by the client. Another exception to the prohibition of doing business within the context of a attorney-client relationship is that it may be okay if the client is given a reasonable opportunity to seek the advice of independent counsel.

❏ A lawyer shall not use information relating to representation of a client to the disadvantage of the client.

Exception: A lawyer may reveal information in her possession to third parties if the lawyer believes that revealing such information will prevent the client from committing a criminal act that might result in imminent death or substantial bodily harm. The lawyer may also reveal information if it is to establish a claim or defense on behalf of the lawyer in a controversy between the lawyer and client or to establish a defense to a criminal charge or civil claim against the lawyer based upon conduct in which the client was involved. A lawyer may also reveal information in her possession in any proceeding concerning the lawyer's representation of the client.

❏ A lawyer shall not prepare an instrument giving a lawyer or a person related to the lawyer as parent, child, sibling, or spouse any substantial gift from a client including a testamentary gift.

Exception: If the client is related to the donee, the lawyer is exempt from this conflict rule.

❏ Prior to the conclusion of representation of the client, a lawyer shall not make or negotiate an agreement giving the lawyer literary or media rights to a portrayal or account based in substantial part based on information relating to the representation.

❏ A lawyer shall not provide financial assistance to a client in connection with pending or contemplated litigation.

Exception: A lawyer may advance costs and expenses of litigation, and a repayment of those costs and expenses can be contingent on the outcome of the matter. The lawyer who takes a case on a contingency is, in effect, advancing the cost of her work based on the outcome of the case.

❏ A lawyer shall not accept compensation for representing a client from anyone other than the client.

Exception: A lawyer may accept compensation from a third party, if the client consents after consultation, or if there is no interference with the lawyer's independence of professional judgment or with the attorney-client relationship, or if information relating to the representation of the client is protected as required by the rules.

❏ A lawyer who represents two or more clients shall not participate in making an aggregate settlement of the claims of or against the client—or in a criminal case, an aggregated agreement as to guilty or *nolo contendere* pleas (meaning "no contest").

Exception: If each client consents after consultation, the lawyer may make an aggregate settlement.

❏ A lawyer shall not make an agreement in advance limiting the lawyer's liability to a client for malpractice unless permitted by law and the client is independently represented in making the agreement. The lawyer may not settle a claim for such liability with an unrepresented client or former client without first advising that person in writing that independent representation is appropriate in connection therewith.

❏ A lawyer related to another lawyer as parent, child, sibling, or spouse shall not represent a client in a representation directly adverse to a person who the lawyer knows is represented by the other lawyer.

Exception: The lawyer receives the client's consent after consultation regarding the relationship.

❏ A lawyer shall not acquire a proprietary interest in the cause of action or subject matter of litigation the lawyer is conducting for a client.

Exception: The lawyer is working on a contingency arrangement.

The following sections provide further insight into some of the situations covered by the conflict of interest rules discussed above. While it is your attorney's responsibility to ensure that no conflict exists, becoming as familiar as you can with these rules will help you determine if your attorney has acted responsibly and with loyalty in your attorney-client relationship.

Improper to Represent Client If Attorney Has Financial Interest

Other than a desire to be paid a fee for services rendered, a lawyer cannot take on a case in which the lawyer stands to profit. For example, in the case of *DuPont v. Brady,* 646 F. Supp. 1067 S.D. NY (1986), an attorney advised a client to invest in a tax shelter, but failed to advise the client of the potential negative tax risks or that the attorney would receive a substantial commission from the deal. The court found that this was a clear breach of the attorney's duty of undivided loyalty to the client. Additionally, in the case of *Gomez v. Hawkins Concrete Construction Company,* 623 F.S. 194 N.D. FL. (1985), the court found that if an attorney has an ownership interest in a lender and was hired to represent the borrower in a loan from that lender, the attorney had a duty to decline representation. This case also presents a situation in which an attorney was representing two parties with adverse interest, which is also improper.

Improper to Represent Separate Clients With Conflicting Interests

This prohibition extends to representing two parties at the same time that have actual adverse interests in the subject matter that the lawyer would be asked to resolve or counsel, as well as two parties with interests that are not necessarily adverse at the time but are potentially adverse.

Representation of ex-spouses would not present a conflict if the legal matters involved were totally unrelated, would not adversely affect one party over the other, would not affect the lawyer's independent judgment, and would not present a conflict in the future. For example, let's say that an ex-husband wants to set up an offshore account for creditor protection and seeks the advice of his attorney to accomplish this; the ex-wife wants the same lawyer to represent her at a real estate closing. The divorced couple has minor children together. The ex-husband might be setting up this offshore account to make it difficult for creditors, including his ex-wife (for child support and alimony), to collect. In this case, even if there is no present dispute, a potential conflict exists for the lawyer.

Furthermore, an attorney shall not represent a client if the representation of the client will harm the interests of another client, unless 1) the lawyer reasonably believes the representation will not adversely affect the lawyer's responsibilities to and relationship with the other client, or 2) each client consents after consultation (Florida Bar Rule 4-1.7, as adapted from the *Annotated Model Rules of Professional Conduct*, Third Edition). This rule stems from the principle that a lawyer shall not represent any client if the lawyer's exercise of independent professional judgment in the representation of the client may be materially or substantially limited by the lawyer's responsibilities to another client or to a third person or by the lawyer's own interests.

If a lawyer were to represent two unrelated clients (and the clients had related interests, such as business interests), the lawyer might have information about each client that could be used to the disadvantage of one client to the benefit the other. A lawyer's disclosure of such potential conflict and subsequent consent by both clients are important steps to take *before* either client discloses information to the lawyer. For example, in *Simpson v. James*, 903 F. 2d 372, 5th Cir. (1990), an attorney represented both the seller and the buyer of a business that was in desperate financial condition. The attorney did not inform the buyer of the financial condition of the business, nor did he protect the buyer in several ways that would have served the buyer's best interest. In another case, *LZ Properties v. Tampa Obstetrics, P.A.*, 753 So. 2d 721 Fla. 2nd DCA (2000), an attorney represented a party in a lawsuit against a partner in business despite the fact the attorney had an ongoing attorney-client relationship with the partner who was being sued. The attorney believed his judgment was unimpaired, but the court found that he should be disqualified from representing one partner against the other.

Improper to Enter Into Business Deals With Client

It may not be strictly forbidden for an attorney to do business with a client. However, the old saying that the best way to lose a friend is to lend her money rings true here. The courts look very closely at such transactions, as the interests of the attorney are not to conflict with the best interests of the client. In the event that an attorney and client do decide to transact business, the attorney should, at the very least, insist that the client seek independent legal counsel.

Improper to Have Family Relationship With Opponent's Attorney

Television would make it seem that lawyers beat up on one another in court only to go home to the same house. However, in Florida, for example, it is specifically forbidden to represent a client when it is known that the adverse party is represented by a parent, child, brother, sister, or spouse of the attorney.

Improper to Not Promptly Report Receipt and Disburse Money or Property of Client

It is the solemn duty of an attorney to promptly notify a client of her receipt of money or property due the client and to pay the client that due within a reasonable time. The American Bar Association, as well as individual state associations and organizations, has very specific rules governing an attorney's handling of client's money. No other transgression gets more attorneys in trouble with the bar and clients than this area, as there is a virtual no-tolerance standard.

THE FIDUCIARY DUTY

The word *fiduciary* stems from a Latin term meaning "trust." As a noun, it means "a character analogous to that of a trustee." As an adjective, it refers to the nature of a trust or confidence. A fiduciary relationship is a relationship based on the trust and confidence of one person in the fidelity—faithfulness—and interests of another. The attorney-client relationship is only one example of a fiduciary relationship. It also is recognized to exist between principal and agent, guardian and ward, executor and heir, and even between landlord and tenant. A fiduciary or confidential relationship is one in which one person places confidence in another person, thereby placing the other person in a position of superior power and influence. (Such a relationship can occur not only in a formal/legal sense, but also in moral, social, familial, and other personal circumstances.) Some of the characteristics of this special legal and moral relationship are as follows:

❏ Neither party may exert influence or pressure upon the other.

❏ Neither party may take selfish advantage of the other's trust.

❏ Neither party may use the trust in such a way to benefit herself.

❏ Neither party may prejudice the other except in the exercise of good faith and with the consent of the other.

❏ Neither party may take advantage of the other's forgetfulness or negligence.

❏ Neither party may use business shrewdness, hard bargaining, or special knowledge to take advantage of the other.

As you can see from the foregoing, a fiduciary is bound by a very high moral, ethical, and—since the law recognizes this special relationship— legal responsibility. In *Williams v. Griffin* (35 Mich. App. 179, 192 N.W. 2d 283, 285), the court said:

> A fiduciary relationship exists when there is a reposing of faith, confidence, and trust and the placing of reliance by one upon the judgment and advice of another. . . . the substantial reliance [of one party on another] justified the trial court's decision to impose upon Griffin, as Donnelly's fiduciary the burden of presenting credible evidence as to the fairness of his business dealings with Donnelly.

An understanding of a fiduciary relationship and its attendant obligation between client and lawyer, between lawyer and lawyer, between two individuals in business, between officers of a corporation, and even between workers for and with a company will be useful to you in many situations in your business and personal life. Insofar as lawyers are concerned, in addition to the obligations discussed above, the primary fiduciary duties to a client as stated by a California court in *Worth v. State Bar*, 551 P. 2d 16 (CAL 1976) are:

❏ Segregation

❏ Notification

❏ Record Keeping

❏ Delivery

❏ Accounting

Let's look at each of these obligations to understand what a lawyer's main fiduciary responsibilities are to her clients. Although not specifically in the California court's list, *safekeeping property* and *confidentiality* are two important elements of the fiduciary duty and are, therefore, also addressed below.

Segregation

A lawyer must separate a client's funds from her own or from those of her firm. Segregation accomplishes several important goals. By not commingling the client's funds with the lawyer's or those of her firm's funds, a client is protected from a lawyer's creditors. Segregation of funds also simplifies record-keeping and accounting responsibilities. Some state governments—or departments maintained by the Supreme Court, as is the case in New Jersey—actually check lawyers' trust accounts in an effort to protect clients from a lawyer's mishandling of their money. The inadvertent misuse of segregated funds is less likely to occur than with commingled funds. So, for these and other similar reasons, lawyers set up trust accounts to facilitate the segregation of funds. Be aware, however, that misappropriation can occur regardless of segregation. In other words, if a lawyer wants to steel or surreptitiously "borrow" her client's money, it matters not which "pocket" the funds are in.

Notification

A lawyer has an obligation to promptly notify a client, or designated third party, of the receipt of funds or property, such as stock certificates, bonds, and deeds. In Re James, 548 A.2d 1125 NJ (1988) a lawyer used his client's funds to cover his own day-to-day expenses (without the consent of the client) and failed to disburse settlement monies on a timely basis. The lawyer was disciplined by the New Jersey Supreme Court.

When funds or property are expected to be delivered on your behalf as a client to your lawyer or law firm, it's good practice to put them on notice in writing that you wish to be contacted immediately when the funds or property are received so that the disposition of the item can be arranged.

Record Keeping

Although a lawyer may delegate this responsibility, she is ultimately responsible for keeping detailed records of a client's funds and/or property as well as the accuracy of those records. In Re Monpetit, 528 N.W. 2d 243 Minn (1995), the lawyer defended himself by blaming his secretary for sloppy bookkeeping. The defense did not fly. The lawyer was found guilty of negligence, as in "the buck stops" with the lawyer. The record-keeping requirement is so stringent that it can be considered violated even if funds have been segregated. For more information, refer to In Re Gilchrist, 488 A. 2d 1354 D.C. (1985).

Delivery

Notification to the client of receipt of funds or property is not sufficient. A lawyer is obligated to promptly deliver a client's funds or property to the client if directed to do so. This may even include the client's file. In Re

Hartke, 529 N.W. 2d 678 Minn. (1995), a lawyer retained a client's file, claiming that expenses had to be paid before the file was released. The lawyer claimed as one of the expenses the cost of copying the file for his own use. A lawyer may be entitled to charge for the service and file a retaining lien, allowing the lawyer to retain a client's file under certain circumstances, as long as the client's case is not placed in harm's way.

Accounting

A lawyer must maintain accurate books and records in order to substantiate the whereabouts of clients' money. It is irrelevant that a client may not suffer a loss if funds are not *delivered* and not *accounted* for. The obligation as a fiduciary requires accurate accounting of all transactions that take place.

Safekeeping Property

While Model Rule 1.15 "Safekeeping Property" does not address or actually use the word *fiduciary,* the act of safekeeping property by a lawyer is a component of her *fiduciary relationship* or *fiduciary duty* to a client.

A lawyer has a special responsibility to protect a client's property. The same responsibility goes for the property of third parties who have entrusted a lawyer with items for safekeeping even if they are not using the legal services of that attorney. This is covered in the *Model Rules of Professional Conduct* under Rule 1.15, which states in part:

a) A lawyer shall hold property . . . in his possession in connection with a representation separate from the lawyer's own property.

b) Upon receiving funds or other property in which a client or third person has an interest, a lawyer shall promptly notify the client or third person.

c) When in the course of representation a lawyer is in the possession of property in which both the lawyer and another person claim interests, the property shall be kept separate by the lawyer until there is an accounting or severance of the interests.

In simpler terms, property of others or property in dispute should not and cannot be commingled with a lawyer's own property. This may include cash from a closing, estate proceeds or assets, tangible property, and the like. It is important to note that a lawyer should not attempt to unilaterally arbitrate a dispute between a client and a third party—each state may have different laws regarding third party claims for property in the control and safekeeping of a lawyer. The lawyer is thus barred from getting in the middle of the dispute. If an attorney has funds that two parties claim, she can deposit the funds into a court's registry and ask the court to decide. This type of action is called *interpleader*.

A Breach of Fiduciary Duty

The term *fiduciary duty* often arises in dispute situations, in which a person in whom confidence and trust were placed takes advantage of the situation to the detriment of the individual or entity she was supposed to protect.

A breach of the fiduciary duty is not the same as negligence or legal malpractice, per se. Although a breach of fiduciary duty may be its own cause of action in a malpractice claim, the term, when used in the legal malpractice context, describes an attorney's *standard of care* toward the client. And the standard of care may have a number of components such as skill, diligence, and competence. These must be separated out of any cause of action for breach of fiduciary duty. However, it should be remembered that while breach of the *standard of care* is a different concept, involving negligence, lack of skill, and lack of diligence in the particular legal service being provided, breach of the standard of care and breach of the fiduciary duty both may be elements of a malpractice action. For example, an attorney can totally mess up a case, breaching her duties to perform in accordance with the proper standard of care, but still not have violated or breached her fiduciary duties of loyalty and confidence. In other words, you can have an incompetent attorney, who is very loyal to you, keeps your best interests at heart, and preserves your confidences, but simply blows your case.

A cause of action in a legal malpractice case against an attorney for breach of the fiduciary duty of loyalty and confidentiality is different from a claim for legal malpractice for not performing according to the standard of care required for the particular case. The focus of a claim of breach of fiduciary duty is whether an attorney obtained an improper benefit from representing a client, while the focus of a legal malpractice claim is whether an attorney adequately represented a client. Breach of fiduciary duty often involves the attorney's failure to disclose conflicts of interest, failure to deliver funds belonging to the client, improper use of client confidences, or benefiting at the detriment of the client. When the breach of fiduciary duty is a separate cause of action against an attorney, a finding of malpractice based on the preceding factors will almost always require a showing of self-dealing on the part of the attorney to be successful.

Confidentiality

A lawyer's obligation to her clients, as well as to prospective clients, regarding confidentiality stems from both the attorney-client privilege (see page 30) and the model rule covering confidentiality. Secrets, work product (documents used in preparation of the case and legal research), and property are all to be kept safe. There are two fiduciary obligations or duties of an attorney to the client: 1) undivided loyalty, and 2) confidentiality. These obligations must be satisfied diligently, competently, and completely.

The attorney-client privilege is designed to protect the client from her lawyer being called as a witness in matters concerning the client. The other side of the confidentiality coin is a client's right to speak freely to an attorney and to disclose, without undue concern, the nature of the case and all pertinent details. To quote Model Rule 1.6 "Confidentiality of Information":

> . . . clients come to lawyers in order to determine what their rights are and what is, in the maze of laws and regulations, deemed to be legal and correct. The common law recognizes that the client's confidences must be protected from disclosure. Based upon experience, lawyers know that almost all clients follow the advice given, and the law is upheld.

The attorney-client privilege is rooted in the law of evidence and law of agency as handed down and codified throughout the ages. It is important to remember that these two principles merge in confidentiality. However, the attorney-client privilege has now become a matter of law, and its exact application may vary from jurisdiction to jurisdiction. (If the attorney-client privilege becomes an issue, check your state's Code of Evidence.)

There are certain exceptions to the rule of confidentiality. Some of these exceptions, which permit a lawyer to disclose information obtained from a client, include the following:

1. Disclosures that the client has given informed consent to.

2. Disclosures about a client when carrying out a lawyer's duty to represent a client.

3. Disclosures when seeking diagnostic opinion about a disabled client.

4. Disclosures concerning mentally impaired clients.

5. Disclosures to prevent serious bodily harm or imminent death to a client or others.

6. Disclosures in self-defense—that is, fee collection and/or malpractice

defense, such as "When the lawyer reasonably believes disclosure is necessary to support a claim against a client or to defend against the charge of misconduct," as stated on page 80 of the *Annotated Model Rules of Professional Conduct,* Third Edition.

7. Client perjury. (Knowledge that the client is lying.)

8. Disclosure of client crime or fraud.

9. Disclosure when imposed by statute or court order, which supersedes all other privileges and ethical considerations.

A lawyer's responsibility and obligation as a fiduciary and confidante under the attorney/client privilege continues even after the lawyer's attorney-client relationship has been concluded.

CONCLUSION

Although it is difficult to rate one abuse of a client or breach of the ethical standards over another, a breach of confidentiality and trust is high on the list of abuses. Stealing is bad enough, but when one's trusted counselor is the culprit, it is indefensible. You must document the circumstances of any breach of the rules a lawyer has sworn to abide by. This is absolutely essential to recovery.

The next chapter takes up the subject of going it alone in a legal matter, known as *acting pro se,* and the related subject *ex parte.*

7

Ex Parte Proceedings and Pro Se Advocacy

Maybe it's true that in some third-world countries legal proceedings might take place in the absence of the subject of a proceeding and/or his legal representative. That's not the practice in this country—or is it? Under certain circumstance, justice *is* carried out in the United States without the presence of one or more of the parties in a legal matter—and sometimes even without notice to the other party or parties. In a civil matter, this is called an *ex parte* proceeding. (*Ex parte* is a Latin term meaning "from one side.") This chapter begins with a discussion of how and why an ex parte proceeding may take place and how this can affect you and your legal position.

This chapter also discusses pro se advocacy and litigation. *Pro se* is a Latin term meaning "on one's own behalf." If you are acting pro se, you are acting on your own behalf in a legal matter without the aid of an attorney. If you wish to act pro se, reading this chapter is a good starting point. If you decide this course of action is for you, *How and When to Be Your Own Lawyer* (Avery Publishing, 1992) can guide you through the process.

EX PARTE PROCEEDINGS

In an ex parte proceeding, a party—individually or by counsel—appears before a judge in a matter without his adversary present. Although the concept of an ex parte hearing contradicts all notions of fairness in our legal system, such hearings may sometimes take place.

An ex parte proceeding may occur if, for example, one side does not attend a previously notified and scheduled hearing and the judge decides to proceed anyway, if a judge initiates a discussion with one side without both sides present, or if a request for a legal action is made where it is known by the respondents that there may be an attempt to thwart the action. (In the latter example, the court will agree to this in only the most serious cases.) Since our legal system, as well as our government, is based on openness, it is a rare and unusual occurrence for a court to consider a dispute without both sides being present.

An ex parte proceeding places an extra responsibility on a lawyer and the court. As in all matters, but especially in ex parte proceedings, a lawyer should be truthful, fair, and balanced in his presentation of the facts to the court. And, according to the *Annotated Model Rules of Professional Conduct* with regard to Rule 3.3 "Candor Toward the Tribunal," the judge has "an affirmative responsibility to provide the absent party just consideration." A *just* outcome may depend on a lawyer's disclosing facts and potential claims that could be adverse to his own client. (This is not something that a lawyer is anxious to do.) An attorney must disclose all material facts, whether or not the facts are adverse. This is where a lawyer's moral character and ethical standing are especially challenged—to present a balanced case while trying to win as a client's advocate.

A lawyer's legal responsibility to the absent party and the legal system as an officer of the court is covered under Model Rule 3.3 "Candor Toward the Tribunal." Although only part (d) of this rule discusses ex parte specifically, this responsibility—that is, being truthful to the court—is so important for the protection of the absent party that Rule 3.3 is provided in its entirety below for your review.

Rule 3.3. Candor Toward the Tribunal
(a) A lawyer shall not knowingly:
    (1) make a false statement of material fact or law to a tribunal;
    (2) fail to disclose a material fact to a tribunal when disclosure is necessary to avoid assisting a criminal or fraudulent act by the client;
    (3) fail to disclose to the tribunal legal authority in the controlling jurisdiction known to the lawyer to be directly adverse to the position of the client and not disclosed by opposing counsel; or
    (4) offer evidence that the lawyer knows to be false. If a lawyer has offered material evidence and comes to know of its falsity the lawyer shall take reasonable remedial measures.
(b) The duties stated in paragraph (a) continue to the conclusion of the proceeding, and apply even if compliance requires disclosure of information otherwise protected by Rule 1.6.
(c) A lawyer may refuse to offer evidence that the lawyer reasonably believes is false.
(d) In an ex parte proceeding, a lawyer shall inform the tribunal of all material facts known to the lawyer which will enable the tribunal to make an informed decision, whether or not the facts are adverse.

Although ex parte hearings occur much less frequently than other legal proceedings, these hearings are important—especially to the party who is not present. In this author's experience, ex parte proceedings must always be viewed as suspect and must be scrutinized carefully by the absent party if it is learned that such a proceeding has taken place. If an ex parte proceeding has occurred, take the following steps to determine if there was legal justification to attempt the action taken at the ex parte hearing.

1. Check any order that the judge may have signed ordering the hearing or as a result of the hearing.

2. Check with the judge's judicial assistant to learn what transpired in the case.

3. Confer with opposing counsel about what took place.

4. Contact the court to arrange to review a transcript of the ex parte hearing if one was made.

If it is discovered that it was improper or illegal, ask the court for sanctions against the party that was present at the ex parte hearing through a motion for sanctions. Because of the very nature of an ex parte proceeding, it may be difficult to sustain a claim of malpractice against an attorney who initiated or participated in such a hearing or communication since the attorney represents your opponent, not you. A legal malpractice action lies against your own attorney, with whom you have privity. The remedy would be to file a motion to set aside or a motion for rehearing.

PRO SE ADVOCACY

In most states, you can sue your attorney for malpractice *pro se*—on your own without an attorney—by using your local court system. However, there are many pitfalls for a layperson who uses the court system. It is possible to get caught up in a procedural nightmare of rules and regulations, deadlines, and requirements that might prevent you from prevailing even if the facts are on your side. One missed step and a knowledgeable attorney will ask for a dismissal, and the court may grant it.

Even if you master the procedural details of filing a pro se action against your lawyer, you will still have to deal with the "old boys club"—the relationships between attorneys and judges that may date back to their days in law school. Such relationships may give your opponent an unfair advantage in the case.

Some courts have special rules for individuals who are not represented by an attorney. These courts even go so far as to provide special forms and instructions for an individual who is attempting to steer through the legal system without the aid of a lawyer. Therefore, if you are acting pro se, check with your local court for any information they might have for the pro se litigant.

A comparison can be drawn between the need for fairness in an ex parte proceeding and the same need for fairness when a lawyer is in an adversarial position against an individual acting *pro se*. Unfortunately—and perhaps somewhat self-serving—the legal profession has not seen fit to establish ethical standards or model rules for the conduct of the lawyer in dealings with an unrepresented person or a pro se advocate, except in the area of truthfulness and loyalty. Model Rule 4.3 "Dealing with Unrepresented Persons" states:

In dealing on behalf of a client with a person who is not represented by counsel, a lawyer shall not state or imply that the lawyer is disinterested. When the lawyer knows or reasonably should know that the unrepresented person misunderstands a lawyer's role in the matter, the lawyer shall make reasonable efforts to correct the misunderstanding.

Most ethical lawyers will advise a non-represented party to get a lawyer. This may not be possible or desirable due to the high cost of legal representation, however. If this is the situation, then the non-represented individual or pro se individual must be on guard. Don't depend on Rule 4.3 to protect you. Learn what you need to know to be on an equal footing or hire an attorney to represent you.

Setting aside a lawyer's ethical responsibility, the pro se litigant must know from the outset that he is not on a level playing field when opposing a skilled attorney. Therefore, an individual who chooses to represent himself must be on guard at all times. A friendly lawyer with a charming disposition is still a skilled professional in the field of law. It is important to proceed carefully and not to be hoodwinked, disarmed, or entranced by one's opponent.

The decision to oppose an attorney should not be taken lightly. In rare circumstances, you may find yourself with an advantage when opposing a lawyer pro se, but opposing a lawyer in the theater of law is almost always an uphill battle. If you decide to represent yourself in such a matter, you should consider the following guidelines of critical concern when opposing a well-trained and well-practiced lawyer who wants to win—perhaps at any cost:

❑ Be careful of what you say to a lawyer who is representing your adversary. A person who is trained in the law can take advantage of unguarded utterances.

❑ Try to get legal advice from another lawyer on any agreement you make with opposing counsel. You could be walking into a trap.

❑ Lawyers know legal procedure inside and out. You do not. Therefore, use rule books to check court rules and procedure.

❑ Be sure to confirm every agreement in writing, especially changes in hearing dates and times.

❑ Learn proper courtroom etiquette and procedure. Watch out for attorneys who may try to take advantage of your perceived lack of knowledge.

❑ With respect to discovery, especially depositions—oral testimonies— learn what types of questions are out of bounds prior to conducting or attending a deposition.

❑ When you are acting pro se, try not to let ex parte proceedings take place. Review the first half of this chapter once again to familiarize yourself with important information concerning ex parte proceedings.

❑ Engage the services of a court reporter. The availability of a transcript will help level the playing field. If those present at the hearing know that an officer of the court is making an official record of the proceeding, they will more carefully choose their words. Having an official record of the proceeding should prevent a lawyer from trying to get the upper hand by using statements out of context.

❑ Usually at the end of a court hearing, the judge's decision is recorded in an order. If you are acting pro se, it is advisable to ask the court to prepare the order. This should result in the most accurate reflection of the judge's ruling. However, if the court does not agree to write the order, ask the lawyer opposing you to write the order with the stipulation that you will be able to review the document before it is submitted to the judge for signature. Unless it is a very simple matter, try to get some legal advice to be sure the order accurately embodies the ruling of the court.

Russell Engler, Associate Professor of Law and Director of Clinical Programs at the New England School of Law, offers the following additional commentary on pro se litigation:

❑ Not all opposing lawyers are unethical, and many may be helpful and friendly. However, even the most ethical lawyer is there to help his client, not to help you. Develop a mechanism to check information from the opposing lawyer before you act on it. Opposing counsel's comments to you may be informative and accurate, but may also be misleading and manipulative. Consider placing yourself in a position to verify the accuracy of statements by opposing counsel by repeating them, before you act on them, to a judge or other designated member of the court; to a lawyer for the day or other designated advisor, if the court provides one; and/or to your own legal advisor if you have one. (Keep in mind that you cannot speak to a judge without the presence of opposing counsel or opposing party.)

❑ Both the opposing lawyer and the court personnel, including the judge, will expect and hope that you will settle your case. You should expect pressure to settle from all sides. You should understand that the words and actions of the people you encounter, including the opposing lawyer, are designed to induce you to settle your case. Most cases are, in fact, settled, and settlement may well be in your best interest. Remember the old adage, "a bird in the hand is worth three or four in the bush." (We have allowed for inflation and high legal costs.) Whether settlement is a good idea depends on how the terms of the settlement compare to the likely outcome of the case if you do not settle.

Resisting pressure to settle is difficult. To protect yourself, plan your court preparation, think about what you would consider to be an acceptable settlement, and discuss your thoughts with a knowledgeable advisor, if possible. Also, try to learn about realistic and typical outcomes in cases similar to yours where the parties did not settle. Litigants often turn down advantageous settlements and accept poor ones based on unrealistic assessments of what will happen if they do not settle. But be aware of the hazards of rejecting a formal offer when an offer of judgment (in federal litigation, under F.R.C.P. Rule 68) or proposals for settlement (in some state courts—for example, under FL Rule 1.442) is made. If the offer of judgment is rejected and the plaintiff receives less than the offer at the conclusion of the case, then the plaintiff must pay all the defendant's legal costs under Federal Rule 68. Make sure you understand the financial implications of turning down an offer.

Remember that all court appearances, and even all encounters with the opposing side, are potential settlement conferences. Never appear in court, and try to avoid speaking to the other side, without having considered what you would settle for and why, and how you might achieve the settlement.

It is hoped that the legal profession will someday look at the issue of lawyers dealing with pro se individuals, and then develop and enforce rules that protect the layperson, not the legal profession. Until those rules are in place and vigorously enforced, however, every non-represented person must be extremely careful when dealing with lawyers.

7.1. CASE IN POINT
The Marital Home

In a Georgia divorce action filed by a wife against her husband, an ex parte hearing almost cost the husband his fair share of the marital home. The wife filed the divorce petition, which the husband ignored by not filing an answer or other response. In Georgia, a party who fails to file any papers or responses after having been served in a divorce action waives notice of the final hearing on the final divorce decree and, therefore, is barred from appearing in any further proceedings. It is a case of "speak up now or forever hold your peace."

In this case, the husband's failure to respond to the divorce petition gave the wife the opportunity to have an ex parte hearing, during which she asked the judge for ownership of the marital house—despite the fact that she had not asked for it in the original pleadings to the court. In paragraph five of the wife's divorce complaint, she stated that she and her husband were entitled to possession and title to the house owned by the parties. However, during her testimony at the ex parte hearing, at which the husband was absent, she requested that the trial court award this house to her. The trial court complied.

The husband hadn't been put on notice by the wife's divorce petition that he would have to defend himself against the wife's claim to the marital home. Later, when he learned that he had lost his home, he filed an appeal. His appeal was based on the argument that he was denied due process of the law by not being notified of the hearing in which the trial court was making a determination on property division, which was not included in the wife's original complaint.

Fortunately for the husband, the appellate court agreed with him. It ruled that even though a party fails to file defensive pleadings in a divorce action and, therefore, waives notice of the hearing on the final divorce decree, that party is still entitled to receive notice of issues not raised in the complaint. Additionally, a statute provides that a judgment by default shall not be different in kind from, or exceed in amount, that pleaded for in the demand for judgment.

This case illustrates the importance of answering legal proceedings brought against you. By not responding, you're essentially allowing your opponent to waltz into court without any opposition and setting yourself up for loss by default. Ex parte rulings can be devastating, so be sure to protect yourself against this occurrence by filing timely responses.

CONCLUSION

In this chapter, you learned that under certain circumstance, justice may be carried out in our country without the presence of one or more of the parties in a legal matter. You've also learned how to determine if such a proceeding was carried out properly and legally. This is important information, especially if you are acting pro se. This chapter has also addressed the process and pitfalls of acting pro se. You can now make a more informed decision on whether or not this is a good course of action for you. If you do find yourself going down the slippery, winding road of self-representation, hopefully this chapter has helped.

The next chapter takes up the subject of the first of the four most prevalent areas of abuse by lawyers—substantive acts of malpractice.

8

Substantive Acts of Malpractice

Substantive errors are mistakes involving the actual practice of law. According to the malpractice study discussed in Chapter 1, there is a litany of substantive errors. Many of them seem so basic that it's almost inconceivable that such mistakes are actually made by those schooled in the practice of law. However, failure to know the law, inadequate investigation, planning errors, failure to know deadlines, record search errors, conflicts of interest, and even math errors do occur—unfortunately, quite often. Read this chapter to be aware of what can go wrong in this area of the practice of law. This may place you in a position to catch your lawyer's mistakes before they are damaging to your case or legal matter. If it's too late, however, then at least you will be able to evaluate the lawyer's substantive errors in the context of legal malpractice.

FAILURE TO KNOW THE LAW

Statistically, failure to know the law is the most common pitfall for a lawyer. With law libraries and Internet services chockfull of case law, annotated statutes, and other materials on every aspect and speciality of the law, there is no excuse for a lawyer not to know the intricacies of a general or even a specialized area of law. In addition, lawyers who have a specific specialty will generally help their brethren in the profession with advice on their area of expertise as a matter of courtesy.

The following are some possible reasons why failure to know the law is one of the most common errors on the part of a lawyer.

1. **Time is money.** Some lawyers want to do as little as possible for the fee quoted. If you are paying an hourly fee, however, your lawyer may study the law or research the issue at your expense. It is one thing for a lawyer to study case law on your behalf (and bill you for the research), but it is

quite another for a lawyer to learn the law (statutes and procedure) and charge you for it. In this author's opinion, the latter is out of bounds in any situation other than in very complex matters.

2. **Laziness.** Sometimes lawyers who do not have a research staff and/or a complete law library or subscriptions to costly Internet services may tend to "wing it" in the hopes that they can get by with whatever limited knowledge they may possess of the specific case at hand.

3. **Ego.** Some lawyers may not want to admit to a client, or even to themselves, that there is an area of law that they do not know.

4. **Incompetence.** Some lawyers may be lacking quality lawyering skills and legal know-how simply as a result of limited intellectual abilities or failure to receive quality training.

5. **Time constraints.** Some lawyers may take on more work than they can handle and do not have the time to properly research case issues.

INADEQUATE INVESTIGATION

Much can be learned thorough investigation of public records. (The Internet is making that job easier each passing day.) It is incumbent upon a lawyer to do investigative work if a case depends on it. It may be necessary to search public records, research statutes and/or case law, and review the matter in the light of all possible and available knowledge. Failure to adequately investigate a case or legal matter shortchanges the client and is potentially damaging. In fact, I once lost a case before the planning commission in a small New Jersey community because my lawyer did not investigate public records properly—if he investigated at all. My experience is described in "The Case of the Missing Document" on page 85.

PLANNING ERROR

No matter whether it's a busy law firm or single-practitioner law office, scheduling is fundamental when, for instance, legal matters are time sensitive, judges have set deadlines, and statutes require action within certain time frames. Careful planning to avoid scheduling conflicts is essential to meeting these deadlines. For instance, if a court hearing is set for 2:00 P.M., and your attorney arrives at 2:15 because she had been at a business lunch on the other side of town, you are put in a bad light in the judge's eyes. If your attorney had planned properly, perhaps she would have scheduled the business lunch for another day or closer to the court to ensure her timely arrival. Enough blunders by your lawyer and your case may be unfairly prejudiced. Even worse, if your attorney misses a legal deadline, you may miss out on your day in court and on the possibility of a successful outcome.

The Case of the Missing Document

My ex-wife and I were living in suburban New Jersey. We were breeding dogs and needed to expand the kennel area. Unfortunately, not many people like to live near a dog kennel. We were often besieged with various complaints from our neighbors, but our kennel was licensed and in good standing with the local governing body.

The property, which we had purchased as a non-conforming use dog kennel—a grand-fathered exception to current zoning laws—had on it a building separate from the house that we believed would make an ideal additional kennel. A contractor was hired. Our neighbors began complaining when the workmen started pouring the concrete slab in which to embed fence posts to hold a chain-link fence. The city quickly "red tagged" our construction site and construction was halted. In an effort to resume construction, I retained a so-called prominent lawyer in Basking Ridge, New Jersey.

The lawyer examined the case and indicated that we had to apply for a zoning variance for the expansion. We did. With dozens of opposing neighbors voicing their opposition at the zoning meeting, the city commissioners did not have the courage to grant the variance. We appealed and lost. End of story. No expanded kennel.

One day while I was at the county courthouse on another matter, I decided to look up what information was available on the kennel property. To my utter dismay, I found tax records that indicated the very building that I was not allowed to use as a kennel was, in fact, listed in the tax records as a *kennel building*.

The lawyer had never checked the county records before recommending that we go though the failed re-zoning process—which wasn't necessary in the first place. But now, with an adverse decision of the planning board and the court on record, it would have meant starting a new case. We neither had the time nor the money to take on that task.

This story represents one of the most common forms of malpractice. Perhaps if I had known then what I know now about lawyers and the law, my matter might have had a different outcome. We may have been able to avoid the heartbreaking disapproval of our dog-boarding business expansion.

The lesson here is obvious and is one of the reasons that I have written this book and its companion, *How and When to Be Your Own Lawyer*. I am not suggesting that you represent yourself (in most cases), but knowledge of the law can serve you well in our complicated society.

FAILURE TO KNOW DEADLINES

Elementary, my dear lawyer, elementary! The legal system runs on the calendar and, sometimes, by the clock. Your lawyer must know and respect deadlines or your case or situation may be jeopardized. Here is just a small handful of examples of the various deadlines your attorney must be aware of: objections to the findings of a magistrate judge's report in federal district court must be filed within ten days; a request for a rehearing in an appellate court ruling must be filed within fourteen days from entry of judgment; and the deadline for an answer in a civil matter depends on the jurisdiction in which the case is filed. The list goes on and on. These deadlines are absolute. Failure to meet them may result in a loss of an individual's or entity's rights to pursue a legal matter.

RECORD SEARCH ERROR

Because of the openness of our legal system, almost all legal activities are a matter of public record and are open to public scrutiny. This includes the sale of property, the issuances of licenses and certificates, court-case files, property tax records, and so on. Record searches are routinely performed to determine such things as the ownership of real property, the amount and creditor of any encumbrance on the property, the date of birth of an individual, outstanding judgments against an individual or entity, and the like. If an error occurs in a search, such as not discovering a lien on a property, and that property is purchased with the lien still in place or without escrow funds to protect the buyer, the buyer may suffer a catastrophic loss.

CONFLICTS OF INTEREST

Conflict of interest, which was discussed in Chapter 6, accounted for 3.4 percent of substantive errors in the malpractice study cited at the beginning of this book. If your attorney does not run a conflict check, how can she know that her interests or the interests of other clients will not conflict with yours and thereby negatively affect your case or legal matter or vice versa? Many attorneys, unfortunately, fail to run conflict checks. For instance, what would happen if you retained a lawyer to review loan documents from a bank and then found out later that your lawyer's partner represents the loan official's boss on personal matters? Or, how can you trust a lawyer to preside over your divorce if she has slept with your spouse in the past?

Be sure to discuss potential conflicts with your attorney and be aware of possible issues between you and your legal counsel that could rise to the level of conflict of interest. If you suspect that your former attorney should be held accountable for a conflict of interest that harmed your legal matter or case, Chapter 6 should help you make this determination.

TAX CONSEQUENCES

Many transactions in our complex and convoluted legal system have tax consequences. For example, under certain circumstance, you may be taxed on the appreciation (profits) of your house when you sell it, on money you have inherited, or on monetary gifts you have received. When an attorney represents you in a legal matter that involves a transaction, involving but not limited to the exchange, transfer, or acquisition of money and/or property, she should advise you to seek the advice of a tax expert or accountant. Failure to advise on tax consequences is a substantive error and is, therefore, grounds for malpractice if you have been harmed as a result. Be sure to ask your lawyer if your legal case or matter has, or will have, tax consequences. Then double-check with your accountant or a tax expert just to be on the safe side.

MATH ERROR

Legal transactions involving the exchange of money and property often require basic calculations, which we all learned in elementary school. Checking the math with the use of calculators, adding machines, and computer programs should eliminate any possibility of a math error. Unfortunately, math errors still occur, and the only reason they do is simple carelessness. If you suffer the consequences of a lawyer's math error, that lawyer is guilty of an act of malpractice.

8.1.   CASE IN POINT
A Lawyer's Lack of Knowledge

According to California law, a lawyer who fails to perform adequate research for a client on the effects of that state's community property law on retirement benefits is guilty of legal malpractice and can be held financially responsible for her client's loss based on the faulty advice and services. The following case in which the court ruled against the attorney set the standard by which the performance of attorneys is often judged.

Rosemary was married to Clarence for twenty-one years. Clarence was a general in the National Guard, and as Rosemary testified in her divorce case, her husband "was paid by the state . . . it was a job just like anyone else goes to."

For the first sixteen years of the couple's marriage, the general belonged to the State Employees' Retirement System, a contributory plan. Then, for the five years prior to his retirement, he belonged to the National Guard retirement program, a non-contributory plan. In addition, by attending National Guard reserve drills, he qualified for separate retirement benefits from the federal government, also through a non-contributory plan. The state and federal retirement programs each provided lifetime monthly benefits that terminated upon the death of the retiree. The programs made no allowance for the retiree's widow.

Prior to his retirement, the state began to pay the general gross retirement benefits of $796.26 per month. Payments under the federal program, however, did not begin until seventeen years after his actual retirement, when he reached age sixty. All of the retirement benefits that he was entitled to receive were earned during the time he was married to Rosemary.

Rosemary wanted a divorce and retained an attorney to represent her in a divorce action against her husband. According to Rosemary's testimony, the attorney advised her that her husband's retirement benefits were not community property. Three days later, he filed Rosemary's complaint for divorce. The general's retirement benefits were not pled as items of community property and, therefore, were not considered in the litigation or apportioned by the trial court.

The divorce was uncontested and the court's divorce decree divided the minimal community property and awarded Rosemary $400 per month in alimony and child support.

Six months later, Rosemary learned from a friend that her lawyer may have been mistaken concerning her ex-husband's retirement benefits. She asked her lawyer to file a motion on her behalf to amend the divorce decree, alleging under oath that because of the lawyer's mistake (carelessness and excusable neglect), the general's retirement benefits had been omitted from the list of community assets owned by the parties and that such benefits were in fact community property. The court denied the motion on the grounds of being untimely.

Rosemary was upset and went to another lawyer to recover her share of the retirement benefits that the general was receiving by filing a malpractice action against her former counsel and now the defendant in the malpractice case filed by her new attorney.

In court, the attorney admitted in his testimony that he assumed the general's retirement benefits were separate property when he assessed Rosemary's community property rights. It was his position that, as a matter of law, an attorney is not liable for mistaken advice when well-informed lawyers in the community that he spoke with also entertained reasonable doubts as to the proper resolution of the particular legal question involved. His argument did not carry the day; Rosemary won.

The attorney appealed to the state Supreme Court. He asserted that the law defining the character of retirement benefits was uncertain at the time of his legal services to the plaintiff. He contended that the trial court committed an error in refusing to grant his motions for nonsuit—that is, to strike out the suit—and judgment, which amounted to dismissal of Rosemary's complaint against him. He claimed that the trial court also erred by submitting the issue of negligence to the jury under inappropriate instructions. The appellate court did not agree with the lawyer; Rosemary won again.

Regarding instructions to the jury at the trial level on the subject of performing legal services, the appellate justices said:

> It is his further duty to use the care and skill ordinarily exercised in like cases by reputable members of his profession practicing in the same or a similar locality under similar circumstances, and to use reasonable diligence and his best judgment in the exercise of his skill and the accomplishment of his learning, in an effort to accomplish the best possible result for his client. . . . A failure to perform any such duty is negligence.

The appellate judges then placed a note of caution in their decision:

> An attorney is not liable for every mistake he may make in his practice; he is not, in the absence of an express agreement, an insurer of the soundness of his opinions.

In its decision regarding the attorney's actions in the original divorce case between the general and his wife, the court set the standard for a lawyer's failure to know the law:

> We cannot, however, evaluate the quality of defendant's professional services on the basis of the law as it appears today. In determining whether defendant exhibited the requisite degree of competence in his handling of plaintiff's divorce action, the crucial inquiry is *whether his advice was so legally deficient when it was given that he may be found to have failed to use "such*

skill, prudence, and diligence as lawyers of ordinary skill and capacity common-
ly possess and exercise in the performance of the tasks which they undertake."

The appellate judges then went on to cite examples of law available to the attorney that would have given him the knowledge he did not possess when he advised Rosemary on her claim for community property. For instance, "In evaluating the competence of an attorney's services, we may justifiably consider his failure to consult familiar encyclopedias of the law." Then the appellate court said of the attorney's work:

Regardless of his failure to undertake adequate research, defendant through personal experience in the domestic relations field had been exposed to community property aspects of pensions. Representing the wife of a reserve officer in the National Guard in 1965, defendant alleged as one of the items of community property "the retirement benefits from the Armed Forces and/or the California National Guard." On behalf of the husband in a 1967 divorce action, defendant filed an answer admitting retirement benefits were community property, merely contesting the amount thereof. In 1965 a wife whom he was representing was so insistent on asserting a community interest in a pension, over defendant's contrary views, that she communicated with the state retirement system and brought to defendant correspondence from the state agency describing her interest in pension benefits. And representing an army colonel, defendant filed a cross-complaint for divorce specifically setting up as an item of community property "retirement benefits in the name of the defendant with the United States Government.

It is difficult to understand why the attorney deemed the community property claim of three of his former clients deserving of presentation to the trial court but not the similar claim of this plaintiff. In any event, as indicated above, had the defendant conducted minimal research into either law book or case law, he would have discovered with modest effort that the general's state retirement benefits were likely to be treated as community property and that his federal benefits, at least arguably, belonged to the community—that is, the general and his wife.

The trial court had given Rosemary an award of $100,000 against her attorney. Valuation is a question of fact for the jury, and its award of $100,000 in this case was well within the range of damages suggested by substantial evidence.

8.2. CASE IN POINT
Getting Beat Twice

A half-million dollar verdict was rendered by a jury against a law firm that had mishandled the case of a client who was brutally attacked at a gas station. Fortunately for the client, the appellate court to which the law firm appealed upheld the verdict of the jury that awarded the damages.

Early in 1992, a customer was brutally attacked and robbed at a gas station, where numerous and predictable attacks regularly occurred. (The gas station had a duty to protect its customers from such attacks.) The customer's injuries were so severe that three head operations were required. The large personal injury firm hired by the customer (the plaintiff) investigated the case and brought suit against the small company that leased the gas station along with the multinational oil corporation that franchised its name to the small local company.

The lawyers informed their client that, under the law, the multinational company had no liability and that they had better accept a consent settlement from the local company for $1 million—even though the company had no insurance or assets! Moreover, the customer's damages were worth much more than that. The lawyers told their unfortunate client that there was no other person or party that they could find who would be financially responsible for this terrible and predictable assault on him. The personal injury firm said nothing more could be done—case over.

Unfortunately, the law firm's assertion that there were no other responsible parties was wrong. The lawyer the client hired to collect the $1 million judgment discovered that, at the time of the assault, the gas station was not leased to the small local company, but rather to two individuals, who the personal injury firm did not name in the lawsuit. Later investigation revealed that the names of these individuals were actually included in the personal injury firm's original files, but were still not named in the suit!

The client—now eight years later with no money collected—sued the personal injury firm, only to have the trial court let the firm off the hook. The client appealed, and the appellate court overruled the trial court, stating that a law firm is liable if they fail to sue all potentially responsible parties and to fully advise their clients. When the case was heard before a jury, it found in favor of the client. The personal injury firm appealed the decision to the same appellate court, but the appellate court upheld the jury verdict. Thirteen years later, the client received the half million dollars awarded to him—too little and way too late.

CONCLUSION

Hopefully, this chapter has given you some understanding of substantive acts of malpractice and how the work of your trusted counsel carries with it the enormous responsibility to know the law. The fluid nature of the law is not an excuse to not know the law. A busy schedule does not justify missing a deadline or a court date. An inadequate public records search is no excuse for allowing a client to be damaged in a real estate transaction. And so on. In other words, there is no room for error, substantive or otherwise, by a trained member of the bar.

The next chapter discusses the problems that can occur in the administration of a law office.

9

Administrative Acts
of Malpractice

A wise person once said, "It's the little things that count." One would think that lawyers would keep that especially important phrase in mind when holding their clients' lives or property in their hands. Unfortunately, lawyers do not always realize the degree of responsibility they have to their clients. This chapter describes some of the "little" pitfalls that can turn an otherwise okay legal situation into a disaster. Some of these pitfalls are as simple as a failure to record the date and time of a legal obligation, to procrastinate and not pursue a matter at an opportune time, and a failure to file documents at the appropriate time. Other administrative acts of malpractice include a failure to react to a calendered date and clerical error. This chapter begins with one of the most basic tasks: keeping appointments and meeting deadlines.

FAILURE TO CALENDAR

A legal malpractice claim for failure to calendar can result from a case that is lost or defaulted due to a lawyer's missing a deadline or court date. Important legal deadlines are often set by statute, by judges, by rules, and by agreement. Attorneys are responsible for keeping track of procedural and statutory deadlines. Most attorneys have a system to calendar the due date. In addition to the lawyer's own calendar, a well-run law office usually keeps a backup calendar commonly known as a *tickler system*.

Simply keeping track of due dates may seem basic, but in a busy law firm, time has a way of slipping by and things may not get calendared. This may leave an attorney in the embarrassing position of having to ask opposing counsel for a favor to save his "professional neck" or having to claim *excusable neglect*. (This excuse is discussed further in the inset "Excusable Neglect" on page 94.)

Excusable Neglect

Only in a world of lawyers policed by their peers could neglect be excusable. But the doctrine of excusable neglect exists nevertheless. Many of this doctrine's ramifications could be important to the progress, or lack of progress, of a case when a lawyer or a pro se individual claims excusable neglect before a judge.

The doctrine is rooted in the concept within the Constitution of the United States that provides for the court system to be the final decision maker within the justice system. The constitution leaves to judges the task of preventing any harsh application (or a too literal application) of a law, statute, or rule that may deprive a party or entity of a fair and equitable hearing before the court. This doctrine is an attempt to prevent court procedure and rules from taking precedence over the facts of the case.

The Supreme Court flexibly interpreted the excusable neglect standard in a bankruptcy case know as *Pioneer Inv. Services v. Brunswick Associates,* 507 U.S. 380, 399, 113 S. Ct. 1489 (1993). In this case, the Supreme Court concluded that excusable neglect is a somewhat elastic concept. While recognizing that excusable neglect may extend to inadvertent delays, the court stated that inadvertence, ignorance of the rules, or mistakes concerning the rules do not usually constitute excusable neglect. Basically, the determination of whether neglect should be considered excusable neglect is an equitable one, taking account of all relevant circumstances surrounding the party's omission. Factors relevant to this inquiry include the length of the delay and its potential impact on judicial proceedings, the reason for the delay, including whether it was within the reasonable control of the [party or lawyer], and whether the [party or lawyer] acted in good faith.

A lawyer may make an excuse in court for missing a deadline or other error, claiming that circumstances were out of his control or that an office worker did not do his job. If the court grants a lawyer's plea for excusable neglect, both the lawyer and the client are off the hook and the case continues as if nothing happened. However, if the court refuses to grant such a plea and the client is harmed as a result, he will have a very good case of legal malpractice (with court documentation) against his attorney.

There is one catch to the use of the doctrine. When it comes to asking a judge to vacate—remove from the record—a default due to excusable neglect, for say, a lawyer's failure to file an answer, most judges will want to know that a meritorious, or worthwhile, defense exists for that unfiled answer. Alternatively, the lawyer may have to proffer the facts of the case for the judge so that the court's time is not wasted by allowing an answer to be filed late in a case that will later be lost on its merits when the facts are revealed. If a meritorious defense does exist, and excusable neglect is therefore granted, no one will be harmed.

PROCRASTINATION

There is anecdotal evidence that procrastination by lawyers is one of the most complained about deficiencies in the process of legal representation. Nothing is as vexing to a client as procrastination. The study detailed in Chapter 1 indicates that the failure of attorneys to act diligently is the second most common cause of malpractice suits in the administrative category.

When a person makes a decision to practice law, he is aware that it is a time-sensitive job. Any delay in the handling of a matter that an attorney has agreed to take care of could be devastating to your life—financially, socially, or in a myriad of other ways. And there should be no excuse for it!

If your lawyer doesn't do the small things he said he would do, don't expect a better performance when major tasks come around. Find a new lawyer quickly, before you are hurt and his procrastination jeopardizes your legal matter!

Regardless of the reason a lawyer procrastinates—marital problems, financial problems, substance abuse, or mental health problems—clients are put at an unnecessary risk. During representation, a lawyer must put his clients' interest above his own.

FAILURE TO FILE

Not filing documents on time is a serious matter. If a lawyer fails to respond to a pleading, fails to file a response if one is required, fails to record a deed at the proper time, or fails to file any number of other important documents, the results could be catastrophic for the client. For instance, the failure to file a pleading or an answer to a lawsuit may cause the loss of a case by default, when the case would have continued otherwise. Often, the filing of the correct document "tolls the clock"—that is, stops legal deadlines—providing time for further action. In the case of a deed, not filing could cause the loss of property under certain circumstance.

FAILURE TO REACT TO CALENDAR

As mentioned earlier, the court system runs on a calendar. Court deadlines must be respected, or a case, motion, or other action could be lost by default. The only thing worse than not calendaring is not paying attention to what has already been calendered. Although only court deadlines have been mentioned with regard to calendaring, be aware that settlements, contracts, purchase agreements, and even the payment of some debts rely on the calendar. Failing to react to calendar can be damaging to a client's case or legal matter. Therefore, it's a good idea to ask your attorney to inform you of deadlines and to keep track of them yourself as a backup.

CLERICAL ERROR

Clerical errors can be made by an attorney or by someone who works for an attorney. No matter who makes the mistake, it can have equally devastating effects on the client's case or legal matter. Clerical errors may include the transposition of numbers, failure to properly type up a legal description, or a proofreading oversight. Since it is an attorney's responsibility to review the work of his employees, clerical errors in a law office reflect on the lawyer, not on the hired help.

LOST FILE

It is the sacred responsibility of every lawyer to safeguard that which is in his position. And that goes for a client's file, which may contain evidence or documents involved in a case or legal matter. Even after a case or matter has been concluded, a client's files must be stored and be readily retrievable to both protect the client and the lawyer if the matter is revisited in the future. It is unthinkable that a lawyer would lose a file, but it does happen.

9.1. CASE IN POINT
Excuse Me Please, I Forgot Something

Whether or not a court will set aside a default resulting from an attorney's failure to appear on behalf of his client based on the doctrine of excusable neglect depends on a few factors: 1) the facts of the case, 2) the court, and 3) whether the defaulted party can demonstrate to the court that it has a meritorious defense. For example, in the case of *White v. Tranthan* (513 SO. 2d 641) Ala. Civ. App. 1987, an appellate court eventually ruled in favor of a party against whom a default was entered.

In this case, White brought an action against the commissioner of the Alabama Department of Revenue in an attempt to obtain information pursuant to the state's unclaimed property act. On the day the case was scheduled for trial, the defendant's lawyer did not appear. The judge ordered a default judgment to be entered against the defendant. The defendant then filed a motion to vacate the judgment (and the resultant order) on the basis that the failure to appear was "due to a mistake of counsel in calendaring the trial date."

The defendant asserted that a meritorious defense existed, as set forth in his answer to the complaint, which was attached to the motion to vacate the default. When the trial judge denied the motion to vacate the default, the defendant appealed to the appellate court, which reversed the judge's order. The justices held that counsel for the commissioner (defendant) demonstrated "excusable neglect" for his absence at the original hearing. However, in a similar case, *Richel v. Brookdale Hospital Medical Center* (448 N.Y. S 2d. 771) App. Div. 2d 1982, the appellate court ultimately denied the doctrine of excusable neglect because it found that the plaintiff had failed to demonstrate a meritorious defense.

The lesson here is that if a lawyer claims excusable neglect for failure to calendar, resulting in a default, it is necessary for that lawyer who is asking to be excused from negligence to quickly demonstrate that the case has merit on its face.

9.2. CASE IN POINT
Forty Phone Calls and Counting

The following case demonstrates the patience a bar association has with its own when a member is accused of hurting a client through procrastination. Despite forty phone calls from his client asking for service, the lawyer in this case did not exercise his responsibility to his client.

A lawyer represented a client in a licensing proceeding before the National Transportation Safety Board (NTSB). The client retained the attorney to represent him in an administrative hearing challenging the NTSB's denial to allow him to upgrade his pilot's license. The attorney's representation in that matter was satisfactory, but the administrative law judge ruled against his client anyway.

The client then retained the same attorney to handle an appeal of the administrative law decision. The attorney obtained three extensions of time for the filing of his brief for the appeal. But, unfortunately for the client, the lawyer never filed the brief, despite the extensions. Not having heard from the lawyer, the NTSB dismissed the appeal. Counsel for the Federal Aviation Administration, the adversary in the proceeding, assured the attorney she would not object to reopening the appeal, but no petition for reopening was ever filed on the client's behalf.

From the commencement of the appeal until the client fired the attorney some two years later, the client made about forty telephone calls to his attorney to determine whether the brief had been filed and to urge him to do so. Although the client did reach the attorney on several occasions, most of the calls reached an answering machine or the lawyer's secretary. On each occasion, the client requested that the attorney return his call. Not one call was returned.

The client was aware of the need to create a record so he kept notes of the date and content of each of the telephone conversations when he did reach the lawyer. The pattern of each conversation was similar: The lawyer claimed to be working on the brief and said that it would be filed soon and that he would send the client a copy. On one occasion, the lawyer even told the client that he had finished the brief and had filed it. In his only written reply to the client, the lawyer wrote, "I will complete our appeal by the end of this week and send it to Washington with a copy to you which you should receive by Monday." Nothing arrived.

A year later, the client hired a second lawyer. This lawyer pressed the first lawyer to petition the board to reopen the appeal and to file the brief. The attorney assured the second lawyer that he would do so immediately. But, in reality, nothing was done for the frustrated client.

The grounded pilot had had enough. He complained to the bar association and the matter went before the State Bar. The attorney told an investigating member of the committee that he would promptly file a motion to reinstate the appeal and the brief.

Three months later, the client sent a registered letter to the attorney, officially terminating the relationship and requesting the return of his file. The letter was returned unclaimed. The unhappy and damaged client sent it once more. This time, the attorney's secretary acknowledged receipt. However, the request to return the file was not complied with.

The local bar ethics committee found:

> We . . . find that the accused's conduct constituted misrepresentation in violation of [DR 1-102(A)(4) . . . [his conduct was] intended to mislead the client and the representatives of the Bar so they would not take action which would be appropriate if they knew that the accused was not working on the brief and would not file it and the petition in the near future. We also find that the accused violated DR 7-101(A)(2) by intentionally failing to carry out a contract of employment entered into with a client for professional services. . . . The accused disputes only whether his failure to carry out the contract was intentional. He testified that at all times he intended to serve the client, but was unable to bring himself to actually do the work.

As intolerable as the accused's conduct was, the purpose of this proceeding is not to punish him but to restrict his license to practice law to the extent necessary for the protection of the public from future unethical conduct. We conclude that the conduct of the accused was an isolated event caused by emotional difficulties with which he is now dealing effectively. Disbarment is not required for the protection of the public. On the other hand, his conduct is serious enough to warrant suspension.

Although true, this case is almost unbelievable. Why would an intelligent, trained, and skilled lawyer accept responsibility for a client's matter and then do nothing on the client's behalf? To attempt to answer this question, we would need a psychological profile of the lawyer, which of course is not available to us.

We may never know why the attorney refused to act. What we do know is that this type of behavior on the part of a lawyer can endanger the outcome of a legal matter and should not be tolerated if recognized by a client, the court, or the bar association.

9.3. CASE IN POINT
The Half-Million Dollar Clerical Error

Chris and Rosemary were the owners of a holding company that owned a wholesale gasoline business and a convenience store. For almost twenty years, the couple was represented in their legal matters by a large law firm. Chris and Rosemary trusted their lawyers with their most intimate business and personal dealings. In the fall of 1988, represented by their lawyers, they began negotiations with a company that wished to purchase their business. This began an unhappy saga in their relationship with their trusted lawyers.

By spring, the purchaser acquired the gasoline business and the convenience store. Although it should have been an occasion to celebrate, it was not too long after the closing that the purchasers discovered that they either did a poor job on their due diligence—that is, the examination of the deal and documents—or that the couple had duped them into paying for something that was represented to be worth a great deal more than they had paid. And they were angry. The purchasers began to review the closing documents, financial documents, and corporate papers and found that the seller's law firm had failed to include a key financial statement in the package of closing documents.

Chris and Rosemary were upset with their law firm. However, the attorneys assured their clients that the omission did not expose them to liability and then attempted to resolve the matter with the purchasers. But to no avail. The purchasers were just not satisfied that they had paid considerably more for the business than it was worth. So, in the summer, they filed suit against the Chris and Rosemary in the United States District Court. They were seeking damages for securities fraud, breach of contract, and misappropriation of funds. The purchasers even alleged "inappropriate acts" by the sellers during the negotiations.

Since Chris and Rosemary's lawyers might be called as witnesses, they informed Chris that "the firm would not be able to represent him in the lawsuit. . . . the rule is that you cannot be both the witness and the lawyer in the same lawsuit." They recommended a new law firm and Chris took that advice, as he had taken the firm's advice for almost twenty years.

The firm vehemently maintained to the their clients, right up to the period before the trial, that ". . . throughout the litigation, the firm's . . . actions surrounding the negotiations and closing transactions [did not expose them] to legal liability from the suit brought by [the purchasers]." The lawyer who handled the transaction for Chris and Rosemary was forced to testify at the trial that "a clerical error" resulted in omission of a financial statement that would have accurately disclosed the value of the couple's business.

Unfortunately, that "clerical error" cost Chris and Rosemary an adverse jury verdict for securities fraud and breach of contract. The dollar award against them was $585,000.

CONCLUSION

As you've learned in this chapter, many things can go wrong in the course of legal representation in the form of administrative errors. You've also learned that to prevail in a legal malpractice case, sometimes referred to as a *case within a case,* the underlying action—the case in which the lawyer botched up—must have had a reasonable chance of going in your favor. In other words, if you didn't have a chance of winning your original case, you will not prevail in a malpractice action, despite your attorney's mistakes in the original case.

The next chapter discusses acts of malpractice due to client relations.

10

Acts of Malpractice Due to Client Relations

It is imperative that a lawyer and client have a working relationship based on mutual trust. However, it's important to remember that a lawyer is working for her client, that the client is paying the bill, and that the client is supposed to be in control—not the other way around. Before decisions are made, a lawyer and client should discuss all available options; then, the client should instruct the lawyer to take the course of action from the available options she has chosen. If a lawyer fails to obtain the consent of her client, or fails to follow instructions, she is acting as if she has authority when, in fact, she does not. There may even be grounds for malpractice if a lawyer takes control of a client's affairs without the client's consent. Another contentious area of client relations is the withdrawal process, which must be handled in an orderly and proper manner to avoid harming the client's interest.

This chapter takes up the subject of client relations errors, including the failure to obtain a client's consent, failure to follow instructions, and improper withdrawal. Being aware of what can go wrong in the area of client relations can help you avoid such problems with your attorney or recognize problems—or acts of malpractice—that may have occurred in the attorney-client relationship between you and your former counsel.

FAILURE TO OBTAIN CLIENT CONSENT

As discussed in Chapter 5, a lawyer is duty bound to obtain her client's consent for most major actions taken in the client's legal matter or case. This duty stems from the agency relationship between a lawyer (the agent) and her client (the principal). The distribution of authority in the agency relationship between attorney and client differs from traditional agency relationships. In traditional settings between agent and principal—real estate agent and homebuyer, for instance—the principal has total control over her affairs. However, between a lawyer and client, according to the *Annotated Model Rules of Professional Conduct,* Third Edition, "a lawyer has the right to control tactics or procedural elements of a case, by virtue of his or her superior knowledge of the law." But—again according to the *Model Rules*—a lawyer is bound by her client's instructions. Therefore, failure to obtain the client's consent is a breach of a lawyer's duty under the *Model Rules* and the ethical practice of law.

It is important not to get confused between the *agency relationship* and the *fiduciary relationship.* In a fiduciary relationship, we are talking about trust, loyalty, and the safeguarding of property (tangible and intangible); in the agency relationship, it is a matter of the interaction between the two parties (the conducting of the business of prosecuting or defending a case) in which the attorney is acting only under the client's authority.

When hiring an attorney, be sure to clearly spell out what you expect her to accomplish on your behalf. Also, while this should be a given, inform your attorney that you expect to be consulted on all decisions every step of the way. If you discover that your attorney made decisions on your behalf that negatively affected the outcome of your legal matter or case, it may be the basis for a malpractice claim or, at the very least, cause for termination or a bar complaint.

FAILURE TO FOLLOW INSTRUCTIONS

A lawyer must obtain a client's consent and communicate with the client regarding any decision or circumstance that requires the client's informed consent. For instance, if a lawyer is negotiating a business deal for a client, she must keep the client informed of the details of the negotiations and the various options open to her. As discussed in Chapter 5, a lawyer is bound by Model Rule 1.2 (and appropriate case law) to follow her client's lawful instructions, even if the lawyer recognizes that it's not the best business stance to take and despite her contrary advice to the client. If what a client proposes is illegal, an attorney is not bound to carry it out and, in many cases, will prompt the attorney to withdraw.

This duty to take instructions from a client and to obtain a client's consent continues throughout representation until the matter is resolved. An attorney's failure to carry out her client's instructions is a clear breach of the lawyer's duty to the client. Depending on the severity of this breach, the lawyer's defiance could lead to a bar complaint or a malpractice action.

Be sure that your attorney discusses all available options with you regarding your legal matter or case. If you don't understand something, ask her to explain it more clearly. Thereafter, using this information, decide upon a course of action and discuss it with your attorney. Put your decision in writing to make sure your attorney understands your desires and is in agreement with your goals. Keep a file containing hard copies of your communications.

IMPROPER WITHDRAWAL

Withdrawal of representation is an important area of client relations and a contentious area of malpractice. Whatever the reason—disagreements, fee disputes, lack of payment, or other issues—an attorney must file a motion to withdraw from a case or legal matter before the proper court with proper notice and must continue to represent the client until the court grants the withdrawal. This is usually accomplished by certified mail. (Legal work for a client other than litigation or another matter being heard before a court does not require the court's permission to withdraw.) The court will not permit an attorney to withdraw if it will negatively impact the client's case. For example, if a lawyer were to withdraw just before the summation to a jury was due, her withdrawal could have a material effect—that is, a major or damaging effect—on the outcome of the case and possibly damage the client. Courts will usually allow a client time to find another attorney.

Model Rule 1.16 "Declining or Terminating Representation" discusses a myriad of reasons a lawyer may withdraw representation. However, it is important to note that according to this rule, "When ordered to do so by a tribunal, a lawyer shall continue representation notwithstanding good cause for terminating the representation." In other words, if a judge orders an attorney to remain on the case, she must continue to represent the client regardless of her reasons (valid or invalid). Withdrawing from a case without the client's consent, without the judge's consent, or for reasons that are not related to the case (such as a planned vacation) may be considered improper withdrawal. In certain circumstance, even if a client were to give consent, the court may not allow the attorney to withdraw. For instance, if a case is in the final stages of a jury trial and the client agrees to let the lawyer out of the case, the court may not want to waste the jury's time and begin the case again with new counsel.

A client may discharge a lawyer at will with or without cause. And, under Model Rule 1.16, the lawyer is still obligated—even if discharged unfairly in the lawyer's opinion—to "take all reasonable steps to mitigate the consequences to the client." Under this rule, a lawyer must also "carry through to conclusion all matters undertaken for a client." This would include providing new counsel with all files and pertinent documents, providing notice to all parties involved (in the event litigation is involved), and taking whatever other steps are necessary to protect the client from the exposure of the lawyer's withdrawal.

If a lawyer has had a longstanding relationship with a client—perhaps she has represented the client on a number of different matters—the client may believe the lawyer is still serving in her representative capacity. However, any doubt as to whether the attorney-client relationship still exists should be clarified in writing as soon a possible.

10.1.   CASE IN POINT
The Missing Yacht

I was the principal shareholder in a corporation that had been sued and had a judgment entered against it. Unable to collect, the creditor's attorney brought a supplemental action against a second company I was involved in, attempting to collect the judgment against the first company by enforcing it against the assets of the second company. This can be accomplished under certain circumstances using the theory of *alter ego*, in which one company can be liable for the debts of another company if both companies are so interrelated as to ownership, control, and interrelated finances that the shareholders disregard the formal integrity of each (such as using the funds of one company to pay all the unrelated bills of the other). I knew that the creditor's attorney would be aggressively pursuing this tact, so I retained a large law firm to protect my second company's interests. I gave them specific warnings, asked them to be prepared to protect my interests, and demanded that they keep me informed. When I received the expected summons and complaint for collection on the second company, I visited my attorneys to discuss the next move.

After service of a summons and complaint, a response is usually due to be filed within twenty days. I asked my law firm to send me proof that they had filed the response by sending me a copy. I asked three times for a copy, only to be told by the firm that it was in the mail.

Then, while out of town on business, I found out that the main asset of the second company—a yacht—was seized by the sheriff because my attorneys did not file an answer. My negligent and misrepresenting attorneys tried, in vain, to set aside the default judgment by claiming excusable neglect.

The aggressive plaintiff's attorney won by default, without a fight! By simply waiting twenty days and applying for a default, the creditor's attorney seized the yacht, a valuable asset that he otherwise never would have been able to collect. The yacht was put up for public auction. At the time of the seizure, my law firm paid the outstanding judgment to prevent the auctioning off of the asset, and later paid an additional amount to resolve the legal malpractice case filed against them. All of the worry, stress, and potential financial disaster could have been avoided if my attorneys had simply followed my instructions. Luckily for me, they had the financial resources to cover their mistake. But many lawyers would not have been able to do so.

10.2. CASE IN POINT
Toys' Story

The Toys were shareholders in a company that had a retail and wholesale division. They decided to sell the retail division after having owned it for over twenty years. A business broker introduced the Toys to the buyers, who then introduced the Toys to their attorney. (Previously, the Toys had never met this attorney.) The buyers identified this attorney as one they had recently used. What happened next illustrates the danger of an attorney's representing both sides of a transaction and not being honest with a client.

The attorney met with both sides to the transaction and stated that he could only represent one side; he chose the Toys, the sellers of the retail division. The Toys insisted that the sale pertain only to the retail division and also that it include language about inventory valuation. It was important for the Toys, the sellers, to get the highest valued price for their inventory being sold, while it was obviously important for the buyers to get the inventory at the lowest possible cost. Unknown to the Toys, the double-dealing attorney was in contact with the buyers, and according to the suit for malpractice eventually filed against the attorney by the Toys, the attorney was still acting on the buyers' behalf on issues related to the transaction.

The attorney prepared the final contract for sale, based on provisions provided by the buyers, without the Toys' knowledge. Rather than inventory being valued at wholesale price plus 10 percent, the contract provided that the Toys would be paid based on the manufacturer's invoice plus 10 percent, a significant financial hit for the Toys.

At closing, the Toys signed the agreements, after exacting from their attorney assurance that the lawyer protected their interests, that the contract contained all that they wanted, and that it reflected all the prior draft changes. The contract for sale did not protect the Toys; rather, it hurt them. It even made them personally responsible for damages, rather than keeping the protection of the corporation format. Again, they relied on their attorney. (Important: a client must read and reread every document, even the fine print of the backside of an invoice. She should not simply rely on her lawyer's assurances that it is okay to sign.)

Naturally, a lawsuit developed between the Toys and the buyers. The Toys were out of the retail business, lost control of the day-to-day operations, and suffered financial losses, legal fees for the litigation, and personal liability.

They eventually sued the double-dealing attorney for breach of contract and professional negligence. A trial court dismissed the action against the attorney initially, though fortunately the appellate court reversed it, remanding to the trial court to allow the suit to proceed to trial. This case illustrates a major failure in client relations, as the attorney did not follow the Toys' specific instructions—he failed to obtain his clients' consent. Moreover, it illustrates the danger of an attorney's trying to represent two sides to a transaction—a classic example of conflict of interest.

CONCLUSION

Litigation is costly and time consuming. It also detracts from life's more productive endeavors. In an effort to prevent the breakdown of the attorney-client relationship, be sure to closely supervise your lawyer's work. Demand communication and insist that your lawyer keep you informed of the status of your matter by letter, by E-mail, or by sending you copies of all or selected documentation. Doing so will help assure you that your attorney is following your directions and obtaining your consent. Should you be damaged as a result of improper actions by your attorney, a legal malpractice case may ensue. If your attorney no longer wants to represent you due to the breakdown in communication and mutual trust, she can withdraw from your matter. This will require that you find another attorney and start all over again. If your attorney does something as your agent without your approval and consent, and such action eventually causes you financial damage, you may pursue a legal malpractice action against her.

The next chapter discusses the most distressing of an attorney's "errors"—intentional acts of malpractice.

11

Intentional Acts
of Malpractice

This chapter helps clarify the differences between a situation in which a lawyer displays intentional wrongful behavior and one in which he displays negligent behavior. As you'll learn, determining the cause of an act of intentional malpractice is important because the remedy for that malpractice may depend on its cause. Each of the following areas of potent claims—malicious prosecution, violation of civil rights, abuse of process, fraud, and libel/slander—may involve various forms of errant behavior.

Normally, people think of *legal malpractice* as an attorney's failure to act within the accepted standards of legal representation, resulting in damages to his client. However, unlike the topics covered in previous chapters, these classes of wrongs may not fit the scenario in which you, as a client, are injured by your attorney. Rather, malpractice as discussed in this chapter may refer to the acts of an attorney who represents your opponent in a dispute.

Legal malpractice insurance may not cover intentional acts of malpractice, frustrating the ultimate recovery of money damages. Be sure to confer with an attorney who specializes in legal malpractice representation to determine your course of action.

MALICIOUS PROSECUTIONS

Under Model Rule 3.1 "Meritorious Claims and Contentions" and under court rules, lawyers have the responsibility to not file frivolous or malicious lawsuits. A *malicious lawsuit*—or *malicious prosecution* as it is often referred to—is defined as an action begun with malice and without probable cause to believe that the allegations can be sustained. In other words, a lawsuit that is begun for the sole purpose of harassment can be considered malicious if it were known at the outset that the allegations could not be proven. As mentioned in the discussion of F.R.C.P. Rule 11 on page 45, regardless of what a client may have told his lawyer prior to the drafting and filing of a suit, a lawyer can get sued for malicious prosecution if the lawsuit is deemed false and malicious. Note that sanctions can be levied not only on your attorney but also upon you equally should the court rule that your case should never have been filed. In this instance, you may have a suit against your attorney based on negligence or incompetence in preparing the lawsuit improperly, for giving you bad advice to file suit in the first place, or for not knowing the state of the law or procedures properly.

For a malicious prosecution case, one must prove the following elements:

1. The institution or continuation of original judicial proceedings, either civil or criminal.

2. By, or at the instance of, the defendant.

3. The termination of such proceedings in plaintiff's favor.

4. Malice in instituting the proceedings.

5. Want of probable cause for the proceeding.

6. The suffering of injury or damage as a result of the action or prosecution complained of.

Possible causes of action in a lawsuit for malicious prosecution include:

1. Absence of probable cause in a case filed on your behalf by your lawyer. This would be a lawsuit against your attorney for wrongfully advising you to sue in the original action.

2. Presence of malice can be established by a lawyer's bringing a case against you when the facts show you should not have been sued in the first place. This is a case of a lawyer's intentional act of malpractice.

3. Just as a legal malpractice action for negligence is a "case within a case," in a malicious prosecution action, one must prove the first case was maliciously filed in the first place.

4. If your attorney negligently advised you to bring an initial action against a party that wins in the first case, and you are subsequently sued in a second action for malicious prosecution, your attorney may be liable for exposing you to this liability. Alternatively, another opposing attorney may be liable personally for taking part in a malicious case against you. In addition to case law (discussed in Appendix C), the Federal Rules of Civil Procedure (governing all U.S. Federal Courts) and many state rules of procedure may make an attorney personally responsible for paying legal fees for bringing a "frivolous" or meritless action.

VIOLATION OF CIVIL RIGHTS

Violation of civil rights is not normally associated with acts of legal malpractice that your attorney could commit against you. Attorneys may violate others civil rights, however, by doing the following:

- Sexually harassing employees, clients, or other female associates (Title VII).

- Underpaying staff or failing to pay overtime wages (Fair Labors Standards Act).

- Illegally discriminating against prospective or present employees (Section 1983).

- Prosecutors can cause a defendant to be wrongfully arrested or prosecuted, under color of state law (Section 1981).

Civil rights law includes federal and state law concerning equal treatment in public accommodations, voting, employment, housing, administration of welfare, social security, and more. When a lawyer practices in the area of civil rights, he may have stepped into a minefield filled with potential issues for a possible legal malpractice claim. The procedures involved in dealing with such laws as Title 7 of the U.S. Code (employment), Americans with Disabilities Act (ADA), Family Medical Leave, and the Federal Labor Standards Act are complex and confusing. In some instances, cases in these areas must deal with federal, state, and local law. Because these laws may appear to be inconsistent or contradictory, the prosecution and/or defense of actions may be difficult at best, and, at worst, an invitation for a malpractice claim if an attorney does not know the intricacies of this ever-changing area of law.

Attorneys can violate your civil rights by getting unauthorized interception of your private information, by violating provisions of the Fair Debt Collections Practice Act, or by extorting you. Extortion is not limited to having a bill collector break your knees if you do not pay. Legally, extortion is the threat of prosecuting someone criminally (bringing charges against you) in exchange for a financial benefit on the part of the threatening person. If an opposing attorney does this to you, this would be malpractice, though not in the traditional sense.

ABUSE OF PROCESS

Abuse of process is often confused with *malicious use of process* (or prosecution). While these two concepts are close in meaning and in language, they are entirely different. An abuse of process is to misuse the legal system for an ulterior motive. Malicious use of process, on the other hand, is to use the system properly but without sufficient reason. (Refer to the case *Westland Development Co, Inc. et al. v. Kenneth T. Romero, et al.*, 117 N.M. 292; 871 P.2d 388; 1994 N.M. App., in which an appellate judge provides a succinct understanding of the differences between the two concepts in the court's decision. The court found that the distinction between abuse of process and malicious use of process was useful for preventing jury confusion.)

Examples of abuse of process include the excessive or forceful execution on a judgment; attachment (or taking of) property other than property involved in the litigation or in an excessive amount; oppressive conduct in connection with the arrest of a person or the seizure of property; and extortion of excessive sums of money. (This does not mean that extortion of small sums of money is okay.)

The law in Florida provides for a three-day notice demanding back rent prior to an eviction action. That notice must be placed on the demised premises. If a lawyer desires to obtain entry more quickly than three days (assuming the rent were not brought current) and were to skirt that process, it would be an example of abuse of process.

An attorney can be liable for violations of the Fair Debt Collections Practices Act for overly aggressive tactics against a debtor.

FRAUD

Fraud is defined by *Black's Law Dictionary* as "an intentional perversion of the truth for the purpose of inducing another in reliance upon it to part with some valuable thing belonging to him [or her] or to surrender a legal right." Examples of attorneys' fraudulent actions include, but are not limited to, the following:

- Stealing from clients.

- Using trust funds for personal use.

- Misleading a client as to the status of a case, or the attorney's past or present involvement with the client's adversary.

- Misleading a client for personal gain of the attorney or another client.

- Charging an excessive fee when the attorney knows, because of his superior legal knowledge, that very little legal work will be required. For example, if a lawyer knows that an insurance company would almost automatically tender or offer the policy limits for an accident because of extensive client injuries (regardless of the presence of an attorney), it would be fraudulent for him to claim that the case was difficult and obligate the client contractually to pay a large contingency percentage on a routine matter.

An attorney may fraudulently represent to a client that he is qualified to undertake representation merely to get the initial fee. He may then refer the case to another attorney when the case becomes too difficult for him to handle or he may simply plan to accept the best settlement rather than take the case through the full litigation process. Another fradulent act is for an attorney to set up a company or real estate venture at the expense of his client without advising the client to seek the services of an independent attorney. Attorneys have actually written themselves into wills, onto deeds, and into corporations, and have taken money out of trust funds. Some have even married elderly clients to inherit their property! Necessity is the mother of invention, and the ways an attorney can commit fraud on a client are limited only by the ingenuity of the bad attorney. Be sure to stay involved in *all* aspects of your case or legal matter. Demand paper backup, including financial records of trust account deposits. Learning whether or not an attorney you wish to hire is in good standing by contacting the bar association and asking for references is a good first step in avoiding becomming a victim of an attorney's act of fraud.

The Supreme Court of the United States established the essential elements of actionable fraud as follows: "(1) [A] false representation or concealment of a material fact; (2) reasonably calculated to deceive; (3) made with intent to deceive; (4) and which does, in fact, deceive; (5) to the hurt of the injured party." See *Vail v. Vail*, 233 N.C. 109, 113, 63 S.E.2d 202, 205 (1951). However, "constructive fraud differs from active fraud in that the intent to deceive is not an essential element, but it is nevertheless fraud though it rests upon presumption arising from breach of fiduciary obligation rather than deception intentionally practiced." See *Miller v. First Nat'l Bank*, 234 N.C. 309, 316, 67 S.E.2d 362, 367 (1951). "Where a relation of trust and confidence exists between the parties 'there is a duty to disclose all material facts, and failure to do so constitutes fraud.'" See *Vail* at 114, 63 S.E.2d at 206.

LIBEL/SLANDER

Libel is defined as any written false or malicious statement (including pictures) about another person. However, if an angry lawyer were to become to zealous, for instance, in his repudiation of a former client, he might libel the client by telling the world the lawyer's bill did not get paid or that the client refused to meet his obligations to third parties. In such a case, you might have the grounds for a malpractice action against your former lawyer.

It is more probable that during the course of a legal action, a statement that could be considered libelous might be included in an allegation in a lawsuit. If that happens and you are accused of libel, your attorney must take responsibility and solve the problem since he is the knowledgeable team member in the legal action. Solving the problem may be as simple as withdrawing the written statement, making a public apology, or having to come up with something of greater value, money perhaps, to settle the damages. Statements that are injurious to another person or entity should not be made if they are not true. If a statement or claim can be proven as *true* regardless of how hurtful or damaging, it is not considered libel. Also, statements in judicial proceedings are generally privileged from being defamatory in the legal sense.

11.1. CASE IN POINT
The Reluctant Helper

Mary needed to finish a paper for graduate school and asked her boyfriend Bill to help her type the paper, which was due the following morning. Bill agreed. Mary's mother, Sally, was out that evening, so the plan was for Bill to sleep over. Normally, Mary and her mother, Sally, shared the loft bedroom, which had two twin beds.

As it turned out, Bill wasn't much help to Mary, and he went to bed early. Not wanting Mary to have to crawl over him while he was sleeping, Bill took the outside bed, closest to the edge of the loft. (There was no railing on the loft.)

During the night Bill got up to use the downstairs bathroom, but he didn't get very far. He fell off the edge of the loft. Bill filed a claim for $150,000 against Mary's homeowner insurer for his injuries and discomfort. The claim was denied. So Bill hired an attorney who filed a complaint against Mary and her mother, the owner of the apartment. However, by summary judgment, the court took Sally out of the case. Mary was still the defendant.

The case was called for trial in late August, but Bill had been planning to move out of town that week and asked his lawyer to postpone the trial. The attorney believed he could get a continuance—a court-approved delay—for the trial so he gave Bill the go-ahead to move. Unfortunately, the judge in the case did not agree with the idea of continuance, and the attorney was forced to take a voluntary dismissal—a lawyer's agreement to accept a court-ordered dismissal. The attorney failed to inform his client of the voluntary dismissal. About six weeks later, Bill sent a letter to his lawyer, asking him to reschedule the court date for sometime in November.

Despite the fact the attorney did not have a pending case for his client (he had not yet refiled the case), he led Bill to believe that the case simply had to be rescheduled.

The law in North Carolina provides one year to refile a case that has been voluntarily dismissed. Sadly for Bill, the lawyer did not refile until four days past the deadline, resulting in the second case's dismissal with prejudice—meaning the case could not be refiled. The judge granted summary judgment for both Mary and Sally, and the case was over. Bill would not collect any money for his unfortunate accident.

Bill filed a malpractice suit against his former lawyer and the firm he was associated with. The complaint alleged four primary causes of action: 1) negligence, 2) fraud, 3) breach of fiduciary duty, and 4) breach of contract. In the simplest terms: negligence, because the lawyer missed deadlines; fraud, because the attorney had lied to his client; breach of fiduciary duty because the lawyer did not carry out his responsibility to his client; and breach of contract because he had reneged on his agreement to do the job for which Bill had hired him.

To substantiate his claim for legal malpractice against the attorney, Bill's malpractice attorney hired as witnesses two expert licensed attorneys who had handled at least fifty personal injury cases. The expert witnesses testified that Bill "could have or might have obtained a judgment or settlement" had the case gone to trial. However, the attorney was now claiming that Bill did not have a case to begin with, so the trial judge was not convinced of the malpractice claim. The trial judge granted the attorney's request for a summary judgment in his favor. Bill lost again.

Bill and his new counsel appealed the trial court's decision. The justices of the North Carolina appellate court looked at the circumstances of Bill's claim of malpractice as well as that of his original claim against Mary and her mother. They determined that in a malpractice case against a lawyer, the plaintiff must prove the following three things:

1. The original claim was valid.

2. It would have resulted in a judgment in his favor.

3. The judgment would have been collectable. (In this case, *provable*, as the

homeowner's insurance policy most likely covered the type of negligence and damages claimed by Bill.)

The appeals court ultimately found that the attorney was, in fact, negligent. Next, the judges turned to the subject of fiduciary duty and fraud. The appeals court pointed to the Supreme Court's ruling that set the standard for actionable fraud as follows:

1. False representation or concealment of a material fact.

2. Reasonably calculated to deceive.

3. Made with the intent to deceive.

4. To the detriment or harm of the injured party.

A North Carolina court stated, "Where a relation of trust and confidence exists between the parties there is a duty to disclose all material facts, and failure to do so constitutes fraud." Bill's lawyer certainly did not disclose the facts to him. The appellate judges also found that the attorney was guilty of fraud because he failed to disclose the denial of the continuance and voluntarily dismissed the case but claimed that the case was still active and that the trial was to be reset.

And finally, as to breach of contract, the court found that a contract had been signed by attorney and client that read in part: ". . . the attorney will represent the client in bringing and prosecuting to a conclusion such action as may be required to enforce client's right as a consequence of damages [the fall form Mary's loft] sustained. . ."

Although the appellate court said, "[the] likelihood of prevailing on the original case is a question of fact in this case for determination by a jury," the court found that a contract did exist between Bill and the attorney and that it was breached by the attorney. Bill won the appeal; he was free to go back to the trial court and pursue his malpractice claim.

11.2. CASE IN POINT
The Lying Lawyer

A woman gave birth prematurely to twin daughters at "hospital A." Both children were born with birth defects. The twins were immediately transferred to "hospital B" where they both underwent surgery. The first twin died approximately one week later.

The parents then filed a medical malpractice suit against hospital B on the first twin's behalf and received a $6 million default judgment when the hospital's lawyer failed to appear at a court hearing. Later, the attorney for the parents ("attorney A") settled the default judgment for $70,000 without his clients' approval.

A little less than a month later, the surviving twin died. In December of the following year, the parents hired an attorney ("attorney B") to file a legal malpractice claim against attorney A for settling the default judgment without their consent and also to pursue a medical malpractice claim against hospital B for the second twin's death.

The new attorney settled the legal malpractice claim against attorney A for $400,000, with the parents' consent. Meanwhile, the statute of limitations ran out on the medical malpractice claim. The suit had not been filed. The parents then sued attorney B for legal malpractice because he failed to file the medical malpractice action for the second twin's death within the two-year statute of limitations. The parents also sued attorney B for unconscionable action under the Deceptive Trade Practices-Consumer Protection Act (DTPA), a Texas law, because he affirmatively represented (wrongfully lied) to them that he had filed the suit and was actively prosecuting the medical malpractice claim. Finally, the parents also alleged in their suit that attorney B "wrongfully misrepresented himself, breached the contract of employment, and was negligent." The parents further alleged that the attorney's "unconscionable action or course of action" violated the DTPA.

Though the parents lost the case in the lower court, it was finally resolved at the state Supreme Court level.

The parents asserted that attorney B acted unconscionably in representing that he was actively prosecuting their medical malpractice claim for the second twin's death, when in fact he was not.

Since the DTPA statute does not require a plaintiff (in this case, the parents) to prove the "suit within a suit" element—that is, the strength of the underlying case—when suing an attorney under Texas law, the parents only had to present some evidence of attorney B's unconscionable action.

The Texas law also allows that "[a] consumer may maintain an action where any of the following constitute a producing cause of economic damages or damages for mental anguish . . . any unconscionable action or course of action by any person." Under well-established case law, plaintiffs must present "direct evidence of the nature, duration, and severity of their mental anguish, thus establishing a substantial disruption in the plaintiff's daily routine." From the plaintiffs' testimony, the state Supreme Court ruled that the mother met that threshold of anguish. The court held that mental anguish damages are actual damages recoverable at common law for some common law torts. Therefore, the parents did not have to first prove that they suffered economic damages in order to recover mental anguish damages; they only had to present some evidence of mental anguish.

In sum, the court found that there was some evidence that the attorney's conduct caused the parents a high degree of mental pain and distress that a jury could consider. The court stated that it was confident that the trial judge would explain to the jury that they would need to make a distiction between the mental anguish the parents suffered because of their daughters' deaths (which was not compensable in this suit) and the mental anguish they may have suffered because of the attorney's actions, for which the parents may be compensated.

Thus, the court held that the deliberate and wrongful lies of the attorney who said he filed a suit when, in fact, he did not were actionable by his clients under the provisions of the Texas Deceptive Trade Practices-Consumer Protection Act. The parents would have their day in court.

CONCLUSION

It may seem unthinkable that a lawyer would deliberately perpetrate an act of malpractice on a client, but it does happen. When you hire a lawyer, you expect him to be honest in all of his dealings with you and to carry out on your behalf whatever legal tasks you have put before him. If you find out that your legal case or matter has been damaged because of your attorney's deliberate wrongful actions, you've been harmed in the worst possible way. It may be necessary to claim a number of wrongs by your former lawyer in the hopes that one will stick.

The next chapter covers one of the most contentious area of the attorney-client relationship, the question of fees. A thorough understanding of this subject may help prevent a breakup of an otherwise good relationship with your chosen counsel.

12

A Question of Fees

Three friends were returning home from a round of golf when tragically their car was struck head on by a tractor trailer. They died instantly. Shortly after the accident, the three professionals stood before St. Peter—it was their judgment day.

St. Peter asked the first man, "What did you do for a living and how old are you?" The reply was straightforward: "I am an accountant, and I gave as much of my time to charity as possible. I am fifty-two." The second fellow was asked the same questions. "I am fifty-seven and spent my life as a teacher." St. Peter turned to the youngest of the three inductees and asked him what he did and how old he was. The remaining individual, the most dapper of the three, looked right at St. Peter and said, "I am a lawyer, and I am forty-seven years old."

St. Peter said not a word, but motioned for the accountant to ascend the golden stairs to Heaven. Then he motioned to the teacher and sent him up to Heaven as well. When he turned to the lawyer, St. Peter asked, "Are you certain of your age?" The lawyer answered, "Of course I am." St. Peter frowned and pointed toward the flaming path to hell. "I'm sorry," he said to the shocked gentlemen, "but copies of your financial records indicate that you are much older than you claim. According to your billable hours, you are eighty-two years old."

Jokes like this one permeate our society and for good reason. The question of fees is one of the most contentious elements of discussion and discord between lawyers and clients. Unfortunately, the system lawyers use to bill their clients—the billable hour—is a major part of the problem. You may be surprised to learn that lawyers have been using time records as the primary element of the legal bill for only about forty-five years. Before then, billing practices were very different. This chapter discusses the evolution of the legal fee, the repercussions of the billable hour, and alternatives to this system. You'll also learn what the ABA has to say on the subject of legal fees.

BILLING PRACTICES OF YESTERYEAR

According to William G. Ross in *The Honest Hour* (Carolina Academic Press, 1996), during the Roman Empire, people who performed legal services often worked for free in order to achieve public recognition by "pleading the case of their clients." The Romans, however, gradually began to pay a stipend to those pleading their cases or speaking on their behalf despite a 204 B.C. statute that "prohibited anyone from accepting money or a gift for pleading a case." Later, around A.D. 41–54, the emperor Claudius provided recognition to the legal profession by "establishing a graduated scale of maximum compensation" for services rendered by lawyers.

During the Middle Ages in England, lawyers' fees were regulated by the kingdom. By the 1600s, however, this was replaced by a market-based scheme in which many factors were taken into consideration. According to Wilfred Prest in *Lawyers in Early Modern Europe and America* (Holmes & Meier Publishers, Inc., 1981), these factors included "the amount of the matter in dispute, the labor of the serjeant [feudal servant in battle], his value as a pleader in respect of his [learning], eloquence and repute and lastly the usage of the court."

The American colonies initially used England's same business practices and legal system until around the 1640s, when Virginia deviated from England's billing system by adopting a fixed fee for the services of an attorney. According to Ross, other colonies, including Massachusetts, New Hampshire, New York, North Carolina, and Pennsylvania, went to the same fixed fee for litigation system.

Generally speaking, in the United States, each side bears their own legal fees. This is referred to as the *American rule*. Also generally speaking, in England, the losing party pays the attorney's fees of the winning party in addition to damages. This is known as the *English rule*.

In "Lawyer's Tightrope: Use and Abuse of Fees," Louis P. Contiguglia and Cornelius E. Sorapure, Jr., provide an example of what American lawyers charged in the early nineteenth century: New York's legal fee statute prescribed, "25 cents for serving a declaration, $1.25 for arguing a special motion, $1.50 for attending a trial of a case, and $3.75 for arguing an appeal."

By the mid 1800s, American courts began to recognize that lawyers should collect larger fees than those provided in the fee statutes, and most states began to repeal the rigid fee laws. In some cases, "task-based billing" replaced the fee schedules set by county bar associations. This system allowed lawyers to charge a set fee for a specific job—perhaps more for a real estate closing and less for a business contract.

In 1908, the American Bar Association formally approved the *contingency fee*, which was especially suited to poor people. The contingency fee allowed an attorney to participate in the outcome of a case—to take a percentage of monies collected in a winning case—in lieu of an upfront legal fee. This billing practice became known as "the poor man's key to the courthouse," since a person with a strong case and a certainty of the outcome could obtain legal representation without having to lay out money.

By the 1930s and 1940s, the state bar associations began to set fee schedules for lawyers in particular jurisdictions. These fees were not mandatory because the associations were aware that requiring a certain fee might violate the antitrust laws. Antitrust laws protect trade and commerce from unlawful restraints and monopolies or unfair business practices, and state statutes on price-fixing—that is, setting prices for products and services that transcend an industry or professional standard—could run a foul of the federal antitrust laws.

In a salient quote in *The Honest Hour*, famed attorney Simon Rifkind provides some insight into billing practices before the era of the infamous billable hour:

> . . . the only cases in which we kept time records were those for which the fee was established by the court. How did we bill? Billing was a fine art. We asked ourselves the question, "What have we accomplished for the client?" When we were successful, we were very well paid.

THE BILLABLE HOUR

What changed the fee system and the genteel lawyer's evaluation of what she had accomplished before deciding on the amount to charge? The answer lies in a decision of the United States Supreme Court in the case of *Goldfarb v. Virginia State Bar*, 421 U.S. 773 (1975). In this case, which took years to make its way to the Supreme Court, the court ruled that minimum fee schedules violated the antitrust laws. The court found that providing all lawyers in a jurisdiction with a fee schedule amounted to price-fixing. By the 1960s, attorneys began working on a billing system that ". . . converts time into dollars," as stated by Joel A. Rose in the article "Simplified Timekeeping and Billing Management" in the Spring 1975 issue of the *Journal of Legal Economics*. The "value for services" concept was out, and the blank timesheet was in!

The problem with charging for legal services based on a time record is that "it diminishes the incentives for expeditious work and rewards incompetence and inexperience," as stated by William Ross in *The Honest Hour*. Ross also says "the billing procedures used by most large firms . . . invite attorneys to commit the 'perfect crime.'"

To make more money, a lawyer only has to increase his "billable hours." The system provides an inherent conflict between a client's need for expeditious work and a lawyer's need to expend more hours to make more money. It's almost impossible to determine if an attorney has padded his bill. Many lawyers will react negatively to a request to substantiate the hours on their timesheets. The timesheet, which was created to control the inventory of time, is now the inventory itself. Instead of selling results, lawyers now sell what they record on timesheets.

In certain segments of the business of law, there seems to be a conscious attempt not only to "milk" clients for additional billable hours but also to perform unnecessary procedures and employ unnecessary personnel on a matter or case. Some experts believe that this sort of practice is responsible for the growth of the business of law or what is popularly called our *litigious society*. In the opinion of some experts, there is compelling evidence that a direct relationship exists between the increase in the business of law and the length and complexity of litigation. In simple terms, more work generates more profits for lawyers.

REVIEWING THE LEGAL BILL

It's important to carefully scrutinize a bill once it is rendered. This is especially important in complicated matters and with billing statements from large law firms. (See "Billed for Work Not Done?" on page 121 for some advice regarding a suspect bill.)

In *Simburg, Ketter, Sheppard & Purdy, L.L.P. v. Olshan*, 109 Wash. App. 436 (1999), the court found that "there is an issue of fact as to whether [the lawyer] sufficiently communicated the basis or rate of its fees . . . the [lawyer] did not make a full revelation of its billing practices." In other words, did the lawyer actually tell the client how his fee was calculated at the time the bill was negotiated for settlement? In this case, the lawyer actually admitted "changing the hourly rates slightly for one attorney during the representation." If a bill reflects rates for staff lawyers or other personnel that have changed arbitrarily when the bill is drawn, how can a client review such a bill based on a prior price schedule, written or oral?

Billed for Work Not Done?

Every bill you receive should be checked for accuracy. Honest mistakes occur. These may be due to a simple human oversight or computer error. Legal bills are no exceptions. These bills may be complex and difficult to understand. There may be a number of areas that create billing confusion: errors based on the level of service and the applicable billing rate (junior partner vesus senior partner); case law research measured against the attorney's learning a field of law she purported to know when the client signed; or bills for clerical work billed as legal fees.

You must not be afraid to ask questions about anything you do not understand. Nor should you be intimidated by a jargon-filled answer. Make sure you don't stop asking questions until you know what each charge is for. Also, make sure that your billing conforms to the type of billing you and your lawyer had originally agreed upon (see Table 12.1 on page 126).

Should you feel that you have been deliberately charged for work not performed by your lawyer, your grounds for action may fall under a number of legal areas depending on the facts involved with the overcharge. These may include intentional acts of malpractice (see Chapter 11), client relations errors (see Chapter 10), or breach of fiduciary duty (see Chapter 6). Judges do not support a lawyer's attempt to collect for work not performed. See page 36 in Chapter 3 for one court's opinion on the subject.

Here are some common abuses and the corresponding bar rule that address the issue and appropriate case law:

1. Violation of Rule 1.15 (a) (4): amount of the fee involved and the result obtained.

   The *Model Rules* state, "Failing to perform legal services or performing only minimal services, yet demanding a substantial fee that is disproportional to the result, is unreasonable." *The Florida Bar v. Road* 633 So. 2d 7 (1994) and *Kershner v. State Bar of Texas* 879 S.W. 2d 343 (Tex Ct. of App. 1994).

2. Violation of Rule 1.5 (a) (1): "A lawyer's fee shall be reasonable."

   (1) ". . . the time and labor required, the novelty and difficulty of the questions involved, and the skill required to perform the legal service properly." Two factors that are to be considered in the reasonableness of a lawyer's bill are:

   a. Different rates for clerical and legal work.

   b. Charges for file organization and the deliveries should be included in a lawyer's hourly fee. *Spicer v. Chicago Bd. Options Exch. Inc.* 844 F Supp. 1226 (N.D. Ill 1993).

3. Violation of Rule 1.1: This rule does not permit a lawyer to "charge for their own learning curves." Learning on client's time, prior to the case strategy or fee basis agreed upon with the client, is born out of selfishness for the sole purpose of determining whether a contingency fee is potentially more profitable than another fee basis. *Norman v. House Auth. of Montgomery* 836 F2d 1292 (11th Cir. 1988). A lawyer needs to have training to justify the same rate as a specialist, *United States v. Self* 818 F supp. 1442 (D. Utha 1992), and related cases.

In the case cited on page 120, the Washington Court of Appeals noted the following in its opinion:

> . . . the billing statements do not show the hourly rate for each attorney and staff person, but merely the total services billed in each statement. . . . Attorney fee arrangements that violate the Rules of Professional Conduct (RPC) are against public policy and are unenforceable by the courts. RPC 1.5 (b) requires an attorney to communicate the basis or rate of the fee, in writing, upon request by the client. . . . Professional misconduct in billing attorney fees may be grounds for denying attorney fees.

The Washington Supreme Court justices made it clear that "It is within the trial court's discretion to decide what impact, if any, lawyer misconduct will have on a claim for attorney's fees." This only helps, of course, if your case regarding a bill dispute is heard by a judge. If you are not in court against your former attorney for malpractice or for any other issue stemming from of a lawyer's representation of your matters, you may need to rely upon whatever help you can get from the your state bar association's fee dispute arbitration (if your state has one). Armed with the lawyer's disclosure information—that is, written justification or explanation—regarding the bill in question, it may be possible to conduct negotiations with your attorney to reach, in legal terms, an accord and satisfaction of the bill. The State of Washington court explains the concept of *accord and satisfaction settlement*, this way:

> An accord and satisfaction requires that there be a bona fide dispute; an agreement to settle that dispute; and performance of that agreement. In addition, when a fiduciary [the lawyer] claims accord and satisfaction with a principal [the client], there is a fourth requirement, namely, evidence of an express agreement made upon *full revelation*. [Emphasis added.]

WHAT THE ABA HAS TO SAY ABOUT FEES AND EXPENSES

All-important Model Rule 1.5 "Fees" covers the relationship between attorney and client with regard to legal fees. This rule, updated by the ABA Ethics 2000 Commission, appears below in its entirety.

Rule 1.5. Fees

(a) A lawyer shall not make an agreement for, charge, or collect an unreasonable fee or an unreasonable amount for expenses. The factors to be considered in determining the reasonableness of a fee include the following:

(1) the time and labor required, the novelty and difficulty of the questions involved, and the skill requisite to perform the legal service properly;

(2) the likelihood, if apparent to the client, that the acceptance of the particular employment will preclude other employment by the lawyer;

(3) the fee customarily charged in the locality for similar legal services;

(4) the amount involved and the results obtained;

(5) the time limitations imposed by the client or by the circumstances;

(6) the nature and length of the professional relationship with the client;

(7) the experience, reputation, and ability of the lawyer or lawyers performing the services; and

(8) whether the fee is fixed or contingent.

(b) The scope of the representation and the basis or rate of the fee and expenses for which the client will be responsible shall be communicated to the client, preferably in writing, before or within a reasonable time after commencing the representation, except when the lawyer will charge a

The Problem With Value for Services

It is not always possible to determine if you are getting the service a lawyer is capable of giving. In other words, if you buy a house with a certified appraisal, you have a reasonable chance of knowing that you got what you paid for. But with a lawyer, the determination of value for services is not always known at the time the services are rendered. Such a determination may even be made at a much later date—for example, after losing a case, you find out that your attorney neglected to do something that might have made a difference in the outcome. In that situation, you might value the attorney's services at zero or approaching that number.

regularly represented client on the same basis or rate. Any changes in the basis or rate of the fee or expenses shall also be communicated to the client.

(c) A fee may be contingent on the outcome of the matter for which the service is rendered, except in a matter in which a contingent fee is prohibited by paragraph (d) or other law. A contingent fee agreement shall be in a writing signed by the client and shall state the method by which the fee is to be determined, including the percentage or percentages that shall accrue to the lawyer in the event of settlement, trial or appeal; litigation and other expenses to be deducted from the recovery; and whether such expenses are to be deducted before or after the contingent fee is calculated. The agreement must clearly notify the client of any expenses for which the client will be liable whether or not the client is the prevailing party. Upon conclusion of a contingent fee matter, the lawyer shall provide the client with a written statement stating the outcome of the matter and, if there is a recovery, showing the remittance to the client and the method of its determination.

(d) A lawyer shall not enter into an arrangement for, charge, or collect:

(1) any fee in a domestic relations matter, the payment or amount of which is contingent upon the securing of a divorce or upon the amount of alimony or support, or property settlement in lieu thereof; or

(2) a contingent fee for representing a defendant in a criminal case.

(e) A division of a fee between lawyers who are not in the same firm may be made only if:

(1) the division is in proportion to the services performed by each lawyer or each lawyer assumes joint responsibility for the representation;

(2) the client agrees to the arrangement, including the share each lawyer will receive, and the agreement is confirmed in writing; and

(3) the total fee is reasonable.

The phrase *fair and reasonable* is often refereed to in the business of law and by the ABA. The ABA issued commentary to Model Rule 1.5 regarding what is considered "fair and reasonable." There are six relevant statements that may be considered individually; not each statement will be relevant in every instance. They are as follows:

1. [In the matter of expenses] "A lawyer may seek reimbursement for the cost of services performed in-house, such as copying, or for other expenses . . . such as telephone charges, either by charging a reasonable amount

to which the client has agreed in advance or by charging an amount that reasonably reflects the cost incurred by the lawyer."

2. " . . . lawyer's customary fee arrangements . . . states the general nature of the legal service to be provided, the basis, rate or total amount of the fee and whether and to what extent the client will be responsible for any costs, expenses or disbursements in the course of the representation."

3. "Contingent fees, like any other fees, are subject to the reasonableness standard . . . [and] a lawyer must consider the factors that are relevant under the circumstances . . . [and] applicable laws may impose limitations on contingent fees."

4. "A lawyer may accept property in payment for services such as an ownership interest in an enterprise . . . [but the fee] may be subject to Rule 1.8(a) because such fees often have the essential qualities of a business transaction with the client."

5. " . . . a lawyer should not enter into an agreement whereby services are to be provided only up to a stated amount when it is foreseeable that more extensive services will be required, unless the situation is adequately explained to the client."

6. Prohibited contingent fees, "when payment is contingent upon securing of a divorce or upon the amount of alimony or support or property settlement to be obtained."

FEE AGREEMENTS

The ABA's Center for Professional Responsibility in Reporter's Explanation of Changes (to the Model Rules) per the 2000 ethics meeting recognizes that it is important for a client to keep in mind "that a statement about fees should include a corresponding statement of what the lawyer is expected to do for the fee." In the midst of trying to solve a problem or get a deal accomplished, we often forget that a lawyer is a hired employee by the client, and that she is working for the person or entity who is paying the bill. Therefore, a lawyer should do what the client asks as long as it is not illegal, improper, or frivolous, maintaining at all times the client's best interest (and not only the lawyer's pocketbook). Any discussion of fees should include what the lawyer will do for the fees. It is best to have this in writing, although a verbal agreement will do.

To help avoid a dispute over a bill, a fee agreement should be fashioned at the start of a relationship with a lawyer—and if possible, not on an hourly basis. There are many types of fee agreements that do not give a lawyer a blank check or a blank timesheet. In the words of loss prevention experts Professor Gary A. Munneke and Anthony Davis, Esq., in *The Essential Formbook*, "Any billing method that does not depend exclusively on time spent as a *measure of value* provides an incentive for efficiency and early resolution of the matter being handled." Some alternative billing systems are shown in Table 12.1 below.

TABLE 12.1 ALTERNATIVE BILLING SYSTEMS	
ADVANTAGES	DISADVANTAGES
Fixed or Flat Fee	
The fee for services is agreed upon at the start.	The scope of work will be limited. It may be difficult to define exact parameters of service—that is, what the lawyer will do or is expected to do—due to possible unexpected occurrences.
Contingency Fee	
The fee is based upon a percentage of the dollar proceeds obtained through a victory or settlement. An expense cost may be charged during the course of the case.	This is a bit of a gamble. The fee is the same no matter how much work the attorney puts in to it. She may make big money for little work, or may make very little money for a large amount of work.
Fixed Fee Plus Hourly Rate	
This allows for fee negotiation. You agree upon the work done and/or hours expended for a fixed fee. Additional work is done at an agreed upon hourly rate.	The billable hour is still part of the equation.
Fixed Fee Plus Usually Lower Contingency Fee	
This creative billing plan offers the best of both worlds. The client and lawyer share the risk as well as the reward, but guarantees the lawyer can begin representation on a more difficult case.	The parameters of service and contingencies must be well defined to work.
Percentage of Recovery	
A modified contingency fee; the fee is based on a sliding percentage of the dollar proceeds obtained through a victory or settlement. An expense cost may be charged during the course of the case.	The deal may be difficult to agree on—that is, how much the fee should be and what percentage of recovery the lawyer will get.

ADVANTAGES	DISADVANTAGES
Availability-only Retainer	
The lawyer agrees to be paid a fixed amount for a set period of time to answer questions, offer legal counsel, and perform minor legal work. This keeps high-level expertise close at hand. Your lawyer is always available to you.	The amount agreed on may not bring expected results or benefits. The lawyer may not provide you with an adequate amount of time and may take shortcuts.
Unit Billing	
Each type of legal procedure or task has a fixed fee. Such fees can be negotiated.	This may not provide you will the highest level of service.
Relative Value	
The fee is open-ended and may be based on expertise, experience, and reputation. Service fees are also broken down by level of employee participation—that is, partner, associate, paralegal, and so on.	Establishing a base schedule is complicated. It combines number of hours, fixed fees, and value billing—billing is based on what is accomplished and by whom.
Reverse Contingency	
Similar to a contingency fee, but the fee is based on a percentage of the amount the lawyer saves the client. This involves risk sharing.	You pay a percentage of savings achieved based on the lawyer's projection of fees at the outset. Fees may be subject to significant changes based on outcome.
Lodestar*	
The hourly rate can go up or down based on criteria as set by a court other than time spent.	This billing method may encourage inefficiency. It is very complicated and discourages early settlements.

*The Lodestar method of legal billing was established by the federal court system. To determine the Lodestar, the hours spent are multiplied by a reasonable billing rate per hour. That amount is then multiplied by a factor set by the court, for example, 1.4, 1.7, 3.0, or 0.8, to recognize factors other than time spent—that is, uncertainty of payment, collection difficulties, and so on. For an example of how Lodestar works, refer to 487 F.2d 161 (3rd Cir. 1973).

Regardless of the method chosen, the costs of legal services have risen out of proportion to other costs in society. By eliminating a lawyer's incentive to use time (or the blank timesheet) to generate income, a client can take a giant step into the arena of legal-fee cost containment. The place to start is the engagement letter.

The Engagement Letter

Most people are familiar with employment agreements or contracts for work. An engagement letter is similar to that of an employment agreement. An engagement letter is usually prepared by the lawyer you are retaining. It indicates what the job will be and how much will be paid to get the task accomplished. Another item that should be included in the engagement letter, but often isn't, is the time frame for getting the work done.

In addition to a lawyer's boilerplate copy about what she is not responsible for, the engagement letter will attempt to spell out what the lawyer is supposed to do, the cost and expected expenses, and the result desired. Look at the engagement letter as *your* engagement of a lawyer, not as her engagement of you.

The Cost of Legal Research

Because legal research is a necessary part of any legal matter, it is a valid billable activity. However, if a lawyer conducts research simply to determine the economic value of a case to her, billing the client for that time borders on fraud. Moreover, if the theory of the case has not yet been determined—that is, the applicable statute, case law, or evidence needed is not available—any research by the lawyer falls into the category of "learning on the client's time." This violates Model Rule 1.5.

Also, the ABA states as a section heading in the *Annotated Model Rules of Professional Conduct,* Third Edition, that "Unintelligible Bills Can Be Voided." Bills sometimes contain simple statements like "research," "planning," or "review documents." This language is so vague that courts have disallowed all or most of the hours billed for such activities because there is no way for the court to determine their purpose. In the case of legal research, a lawyer could simply provide the court with copies of the cases on point to substantiate her claim for research time.

Unbundling of Legal Services

To avoid being billed for legal services you do not need or for things you can handle yourself, you might want to explore the practice known as *unbundling of legal services.* The unbundling concept allows you to purchase certain legal services from a lawyer just as you might do in other areas of commerce. For instance, if you want to file a suit to collect money from a nonpaying customer, you might hire an attorney to draw a complaint. Then you would make your own court appearance. The lawyer uses her expertise on your behalf, but then you use your own expertise regarding the facts of the case in court. The advantage of this method is clear. You pay for only what you need. However, once you walk out of the lawyer's office, you are on your own. You'll either sink or swim based on your ability to act pro se in the court system. If you decide to do this, be sure to gain some expertise first. A good starting place is Chapter 7.

If you do retain a lawyer to author papers for you, you must tell the court. The ABA has, what seems on the surface, to be an inconsistency when it comes to its prohibition on lawyers' ghostwriting. By revealing the "ghost," the prohibition should not apply. However, this is a very new area of law and should be checked with your jurisdiction's bar association.

Unbundling of legal services can also be used in the purchase of a home. An attorney would review and/or prepare all of the documents in her office. She would also do the title search on your behalf. Then you would attend the closing on your own behalf to save the cost of her appearance at the closing. If you have any legal questions during the closing, you can reach your attorney by phone, assuming you have made such arrangements beforehand.

Until 2001, unbundling of legal services was one of those self-serving rules that kept a lawyer on the clock throughout the entire case—regardless of whether she was needed. A lawyer was forbidden by the ABA to take on a case that she did not bring to conclusion. The public outcry over the cost of legal services forced the bar association to finally give in. In 2002, the ABA's house of delegates changed two simple concepts in Rule 1.2 "Scope of Representation and Allocation of Authority Between Client and Lawyer" that allowed lawyers to sell specific tasks to a client. First, the word *objectives* was replaced by the word *scope* with regard to a lawyer's representation of a client. When the *objectives* of representation are limited, drawing a complaint, for example, is not the objective; winning the lawsuit is the objective. However, when the *scope*—the breath of the subject—is limited, representation may be for the drawing of a complaint only, for example, not for a full-blown case that is to be brought to conclusion. The other change to Rule 1.2 provides for *informed consent* (to do the task requested) instead of needing consent after consultation, which a client might be charged for. The simple assertion by a client that she knows the risk may suffice to meet the new informed consent standard.

These few words, which permit lawyers to unbundle their services, represent an important change in our legal system. Professor Russell Engler, this author, and many influential people in the legal arena fought for this change. Prior to this rewording, it was improper, and possibly illegal, for a pro-se litigant to purchase unbundled services from a lawyer for use in court.

As the population at large becomes more familiar with the option to purchase unbundled services and takes advantage of this option, this change may exert downward pressure on the cost of legal services.

THE RETURN OF CLIENT'S FILES
UPON TERMINATION OF REPRESENTATION

When a client breaks off the relationship with her attorney, two major concerns are whether or not the former attorney can keep the client's file and whether or not the client has to pay her legal fees before the file is returned. If you have ever been in the middle of a pitched legal battle and a fee dispute erupts between you and your lawyer, you are aware of how troubling the issue of the return of your files and/or legal documents can be. Not even the American Bar Association has an answer to clarify these important issues. According to ABA ethics hotline attorney Patrick Sean Ginty, the ABA will issue an "opinion on topic" in the near future. In any event, as you've learned, matters that relate to the relationship between you and your attorney, such as this one, are usually a matter of state law. Ultimately, it may be the attorney who has to make the final decision to return your documents or not. The more detailed "answer" is stated in Model Rule 1.16 "Declining or Terminating Representation":

> Upon termination of representation, a lawyer shall take steps to the extent reasonably practicable to protect a client's interests, such as giving reasonable notice to the client, allowing time for employment of other counsel, surrendering papers and property to which the client is entitled and refunding any advance payment of fee or expense that has not been earned or incurred. The lawyer may retain papers relating to the client to the extent permitted by other law [which differs from state to state].

Take note of the contradictory phrases "surrendering papers and property" and "retain papers relating to the client," and you will understand the confusion over whether or not a lawyer can keep a client's file. To make matters more confusing, certain states provide for attorney's liens and/or retaining liens (applicable to lawyers) to secure payment of unpaid legal fees upon wrongful termination in some states. In Oregon, for instance, the attorney's lien law (87.430 attorney's possessory lien) states:

> An attorney has a lien for compensation whether specially agreed upon or implied, upon all papers, personal property and money of the client in the possession of the attorney for services rendered to the client.

In other words, in Oregon, a lawyer can legally keep your property. The law goes on to say that such money, papers, and property may be retained until "the lien created by this section [of the law], and the claim [the lawyers unchallenged claim] based thereon, is satisfied . . . "

Until the ABA gets around to the sticky question of a lawyer's right to withhold client materials (until they are paid as they see it) or there is an underlying ethical rule obligating lawyers to return all client materials at the cessation of representation, we may have to rely on the practical side.

Practically speaking, an attorney who is fired by a client or who withdraws will deliver the file or copy to the client, but will impose a lien on any of the proceeds of the case. In other words, the client cannot escape paying the fee ultimately.

There seems to be a greater preponderance of ethical rules and requirements, overall, that in practice, the Oregon-type lien notwithstanding, attorneys will return client's materials at the end of representation, especially when a trial is ongoing or about to begin. If the dispute arises at a time when a fee is outstanding and the matter is not before a court, or otherwise not time sensitive, then the client may be in a position of having to settle the fee before getting her materials returned by the lawyer.

12.1. CASE IN POINT
The Nonpaying Insurance Company

When a client discovers that value for services has not been provided, the courts recognize the client's right to pursue a claim for malpractice and an abatement of the charges for work that, in reality, is worthless. This is shown in the following case of a law firm that sued an insurance company for not paying its bill. The reason the insurance company refused to pay its bill was because the law firm did not do what the client wanted the lawyers to do: that is, win the case and reduce the possible damages against it.

The insurance company retained a large law firm to represent them in a legal matter. The lawyers lost the case and wanted payment for what they considered was *value for services*. The insurance company told the appellate court that the services were of *no* value.

The insurance company was not a stranger to litigation. It had faced many court challenges regarding their decisions to pay or to not pay claims and how much to pay. The president of the insurance company stated in his affidavit that he had requested that the attorneys call certain witnesses to the stand, but that they had ignored his request and neither produced nor attempted to produce such countervailing testimony. The president of the insurance company went on to detail the other items that his lawyers failed to do in his lost case, in which the adverse verdict against the company was $13 million.

So, these lawyers took on a case from a professionally knowledgeable client, refused to follow their instructions, lost the case, and contributed to the assessment of a high-dollar judgment against their client. Then they had the nerve to demand payment. The insurance company planned to file a malpractice case against their former law firm. You may want to consider doing the same thing if your attorney fails to follow instructions, providing that you know the law.

12.2. CASE IN POINT
Lawyers Protecting Themselves

R.T. Company disputed a bill of several hundred thousand dollars from its law firm and would not pay the bill. The client claimed that its attorneys defamed the company before the closing of an acquisition business transaction with another corporation. The client company also claimed that its law firm committed fraudulent conduct and interfered with its business dealings. The law firm countered with a breach of contract counterclaim and a host of other defenses. Also, the law firm refused to return the client's files and non-work product documentation, claiming an attorney's retaining lien under state law for the unpaid bill. Clearly, this is a case in which the attorney-client relationship had broken down!

R.T. Company sued in U.S. District Court, asking the court to determine the amount of the law firm's attorney's fee lien. The judge held that this was not a matter for a federal court to determine, since federal courts are of limited jurisdiction. The federal court held that all of the proceedings belonged in the state court since the fee dispute concerned "questions of interpreting the fee agreement. . . . work related to post-closing [acquisition] disputes and . . . work related to the underlying lawsuit, assessing the value of services provided by the attorneys and the reasonableness of the time spent and the amounts charged; and claims of malpractice."

So, as a result of the litigation between R.T. Company and their law firm, the district court "ordered the parties to come to an agreement by which [the client] could have access to its client file [in the possession of its former lawyer] in exchange for its posting of security as against obligations allegedly outstanding [to it lawyers]." This was a fair decision. It provided the client with its file while requiring the client to post enough money to cover the legal fees should the law firm prevail in state court.

12.3. CASE IN POINT
An Honest Dollar for an Honest Day's Work

In one estate dispute, two law firms that had agreed to split a court-awarded legal fee were forced to reduce their excessive $100,000-plus legal bill on a relatively simple estate matter.

Doris died in May, approximately one month after her husband, Bernard. Their wills, for the most part, were probated together. Both wills named Charles (Bernard's son and Doris's stepson) and a family friend, Sam, as coexecutors. Charles and his sister, Diana, were the only beneficiaries.

Sam retained firm "A" as counsel to represent him in his capacity as coexecutor and Charles retained firm "B." The two law firms agreed that fees would be split equally and would not exceed the amount that one firm would charge for performing all services relating to the probate of the wills. The estimated legal fees were presented to the Surrogate's Court for the court's approval. During the course of the probate proceedings, the law firms increased their estimate as a result of problems that had arisen in connection with the probate of Bernard's will.

The Surrogate's Court, in a decision relative to the requested amount of legal fees in the case, recognized that a delay in the administration of the estates was due in large part to a dispute over stock options, and nothing more. The Surrogate's Court noted that "[e]xcept for the tax audit and resulting proceeding in the Tax Court no unusual or extraordinary legal services were required in this estate." Then, the Surrogate's Court, on behalf of the beneficiaries of the estate, awarded legal fees of only $42,500 (including fees paid on account) plus disbursements of $314. The fees were much less than the law firms had asked for. The two law firms appealed to the appellate court.

The justices of the appellate court said in their opinion on the case, "It is by now well-settled that the . . . [Court] bears the ultimate responsibility to decide what constitutes reasonable legal compensation." And quoting from a precedent regarding the calculation of what a lawyer should be paid, "In general, the court in determining the justice and reasonableness of an attorney's claim for services should consider the time spent, the difficulties involved in the matters in which the services were rendered, the nature of the services, the amount involved, the professional standing of the counsel and the results obtained." The court did not increase the fees as awarded by the lower court.

CONCLUSION

The safest and most trouble-free way to engage the services of a lawyer is to have a written contract—an engagement letter for the attorney's services after a careful selection process. The engagement letter should spell out the task, the payment, and the type of fee schedule as stated in this chapter. If a fee dispute erupts between you and your lawyer in the midst of your case or legal matter and you fire your attorney, be aware that she may be able to hold on to your files until payment is received or until you arrive at some other agreement. While charging too much is not a crime, as you learned in this chapter, you do have some recourse if your attorney has failed to provide adequate representation or bills you excessively.

If your attorney has caused damage to you or your case, the next and last chapter will give you some idea how to get some satisfaction and possibly recover some of your losses.

13

Getting Even—
Making a Malpractice Claim

The ideal attorney-client relationship is one of mutual trust, communication, and hopefully success in or with the project or dilemma that brought you together in the first place. If it appears that you have chosen the "wrong" lawyer, it may be wise to retain other counsel. If you discover your error early in the relationship, you can probably avoid damages. However, if you do not discover your mistake until your lawyer's actions (or lack thereof) have damaged you, your case, or your matter, you may want to consider taking legal action against your lawyer.

This chapter is designed to arm you with the tools to pursue compensation for your errant lawyer's misdeeds, miscalculations, or mistakes. If a full-blown malpractice case is not possible, you may at least get some satisfaction by filing a bar complaint.

FIRING YOUR LAWYER

Before going into battle with your former trusted counsel, take the following steps:

1. Send a certified letter, return receipt requested, to your lawyer, that clearly outlines and details the reasons why you are discharging him. Make a demand for any case materials or other property that you may need for an ongoing matter.

2. Wait till you receive the receipt for the certified mail so that you can be sure your attorney has received your letter. You can then follow up with a phone call to your attorney.

3. Call your local bar association and request the appropriate form for making a complaint against your lawyer. (See "Filing a Bar Complaint" on page 138.) File the complaint.

If the bar does not remedy your complaint by taking action, or if you do not come to a compromise with your lawyer, you are ready to review the *causes of action* that you might use in a legal malpractice lawsuit. Begin by taking the following quiz.

CAUSE OF ACTION QUIZ

You may feel you have many reasons to file a lawsuit against your attorney, but you must have one or more legal reasons, or causes, for the court to recognize the validity of your lawsuit. Take this quiz to determine if you have a cause of action—fact(s) that give you a right to judicial relief. Ask yourself the following questions and keep a record of the answers. These answers will come in handy if you find a lawyer who is willing to take on your malpractice case.

1. Does your case fall within the statute of limitations? How much time has elapsed from the time that you knew or should have known about your attorney's act or acts of malpractice? Is there still time within your state's statute of limitations to file a legal malpractice suit? (See Appendix D.)

   If your answer to this question is "no," it's too late to file a malpractice claim. Skip the remaining questions and read the following section "Filing a Bar Complaint." If nothing else, your complaint will be a permanent stain on your former lawyer's file.

   Also, know that it may still be possible to pursue a claim for breach of contract, fraud, or breach of fiduciary. Be sure to discuss these possible options with your legal counsel.

2. Did you suffer a real and tangible loss by an attorney who you formally retained to act on your behalf? If so, how much? Was your pride hurt or did you actually lose money or property? You must have a tangible loss to prevail against your lawyer.

   To have a valid legal malpractice claim, an attorney-client relationship must have been present. An action for other causes of action, such as malicious interference and other claims, may be possible if the attorney-client relationship is not available to you. Once again, be sure to discuss your options with legal counsel.

   You and the lawyer may see things differently (and this is one reason lawyers protect themselves when declining representation). You may have been under the impression that he was still acting as your attorney or that his advice at the initial meeting (absent a non-engagement letter, or formal refusal) was detrimental to your matter or that certain ethical boundaries were crossed by the lawyer in his discussion with you or even that certain propriety information was divulged. There could be a host of other causes of action against the lawyer other than a strict legal malpractice claim.

3. Is your complaint regarding a litigation matter? Did the litigation go badly because of your attorney's actions or failure to act? If so, how much or what did you lose?

4. Is your complaint regarding a business matter that was handled poorly and caused you a monetary loss? If so, how much did you lose?

5. The answers to the following questions are very important, so be honest with yourself. Did you do whatever you could within reason to support your lawyer in the proper handling of your legal matter, including:

   a) provide documentation when asked?

   b) show up when you were supposed to? For example, did you attend scheduled meetings and appear in court when you were supposed to?

   c) tell the complete truth and nothing but the complete truth to your attorney with regard to your legal matter?

   d) follow your lawyer's instructions after agreeing to them?

6. Was there a conflict of interest with another client in the law firm that your lawyer did not disclose that damaged your case?

7. Is (or was) your lawyer in business with you or someone close to you? Did it affect your legal position or case?

8. Was there a conflict of interest—business or personal—that caused the rift between your lawyer and you (or the case)?

9. Based on what you have read in this book, what area of malpractice do you think your former lawyer committed?

10. Do you have documentation and/or a court record that will back up your side of the story?

If you have answered "yes" to number 1 and to one or more of the other questions, there's a good chance you have a valid malpractice claim. The balance of this chapter will help you through the various steps necessary to prosecute a claim against your lawyer for malpractice.

FILING A BAR COMPLAINT

If you do not have sufficient evidence to file a malpractice claim or if the statute of limitations has expired, your best chance to "get even" is by filing a complaint with your state bar association, if you haven't already done so. (Also, when planning to file a malpractice claim, it's a good idea to initially document your claim by filing a complaint.)

Regardless of the outcome, a bar complaint stays on a lawyer's record for the balance of his career. While it may be of little solace, filing the complaint may help you overcome some of the emotional hurt caused by your once-trusted lawyer. Also, your former lawyer will have to take the time to respond to the complaint to get himself off the hook. Since lawyers cannot bill themselves, the time a lawyer takes to respond to a complaint is money out of his pocket. Knowing this may give you some satisfaction. Also, if other complaints have been lodged against the lawyer's record, some disciplinary action may be taken.

Most state bar organizations will have a complaint form available. Call you local state bar association and ask them to send you one. You may even be able to download the form from the Internet. The complaint form will most likely request the following information:

1. Date of the complaint.

2. Your name, address, and telephone number.

3. The name, address, and telephone number of the attorney against whom you're filing the complaint.

4. A detailed description of what your complaint is, when and where the incident(s) occurred, why you went to the attorney, and any other pertinent information about your complaint. Some forms may ask if you are now represented by counsel in the matter of the complaint.

If your local state bar association does not have a special form, compose a letter that contains all of the above information. Type the word "COMPLAINT" a few inches below the letterhead so that your reason for sending the letter is apparent. Be sure to type your complaint so that it is clear and legible. Take care to avoid misspellings and other glaring grammatical errors. A presentable document will be taken more seriously than a poorly drafted, sloppy one.

Be aware that a copy of your complaint will be provided to your former attorney. This form may be considered public record depending on the bar association and may, therefore, be available for public inspection.

EVALUATION AND PREPARATION
OF YOUR LEGAL MALPRACTICE CLAIM

Assuming that your complaint falls within the statute of limitations, simply filing a bar complaint will not get your money back or right the wrong caused by your attorney. The remedy to recoup your losses is a full-fledged malpractice claim. The following steps will guide you in evaluating the strength of your claim and will help in its preparation.

1. Examine Your Claim

The first step is to examine your claim in light of the "Cause of Action Quiz" on page 136 with an expert or experts if possible. Examining your claim doesn't stop there, however. With regard to a claim for legal malpractice, the Supreme Court of Ohio justices said:

> A standard of proof [is necessary] that requires a plaintiff [you] to prove to a virtual certainty that, but for the defendant's [your lawyer or law firm] negligence, the plaintiff would have prevailed in the underlying action [case], in effect immuniz[ing] most negligent attorneys from liability.

So don't expect smooth sailing. It will be tough. You will need to evaluate your proof for the "but for" test. The "but for" test means that you will have to show that you would have won, or possibly would have won, your case *but for* your lawyer's acts of malpractice. If you would have lost your case hands down without question, then your malpractice case cannot possibly prevail.

Although the conventional wisdom, as indicated above, is a strict interpretation of the "but for" test, some state court judges see the test as too strict and damaging to an injured client. In *Vahila et al. v. Hall et al.* (674 N.E. 2d 1164), the Ohio justices bring out several points to consider when evaluating a lost case due to legal malpractice:

> We reject any finding that the element of causation in the context of a legal malpractice action can be replaced or supplemented with a rule of thumb requiring that a plaintiff, in order to establish damage or loss, prove in every instance that he or she would have been successful in the underlying matter [the original case] giving rise to the complaint. This should be true regardless of the type of representation involved. In fact, one legal authority has severely criticized imposing such a burden on [the "but for" obligation] victims of legal malpractice.

The Ohio justices further stated:

A standard of proof that requires a plaintiff to prove to a virtual certainty that, but for the defendant's negligence, the plaintiff would have prevailed in the underlying action, in effect immunizes most negligent attorneys from liability. No matter how outrageous and morally reprehensible the attorney's behavior may have been, if minimal doubt exists as to the outcome in the original action, the plaintiff may not recover in the malpractice action [using the but for standard]. Except in those rare instances where the initial action was a "sure thing," the certainty requirement protects attorneys from liability for their negligence.

On the subject of the necessity to have a trial within a trial, to prove *but for my attorney's negligence I would have won,* the court discusses the pitfalls for a damaged client of that approach to prove legal malpractice citing as its legal authority *The Standard of Proof of Causation in Legal Malpractice Cases* (1978), 63 Cornell L.Rev. 666, 670–671:

[additionally] stringent standards of proving "but for" require the plaintiff to conduct a "trial within a trial" to show the validity of his underlying claim. A full, theoretically complete reconstruction of the original trial would require evidence about such matters as the size of jury verdicts in the original jurisdiction. For example, an experienced attorney could testify that juries in that jurisdiction typically award verdicts of x dollars in similar cases. But such evidence is too remote and speculative; the new fact-finder must try the merits of both the malpractice suit and the underlying claim to make an independent determination of the damage award. The cost and complexity of such a proceeding may well discourage the few plaintiffs otherwise willing to pursue the slim chance of success. Other problems await those who do proceed with the "trial within a trial." For example, the attorney in the original action may have negligently failed to pursue the discovery that would have insured success. If the results of that same discovery are now necessary to prove the merit of the underlying claim—and the passage of time has precluded obtaining that information—the attorney by his own negligence will have protected himself from liability. In such a case, the more negligent the attorney, the more difficult is the plaintiff's task of proving causation.

The Ohio court points out another problem with the established principle of "but for," which is what might have happened if a settlement opportunity had presented itself. The Justices addressing this matter, said:

A strict "but for" test also ignores settlement opportunities lost due to the attorney's negligence. The test focuses on whether the client would have won in the original action. A high standard of proof of causation encourages courts' tendencies to exclude evidence about settlement as too remote and speculative. The standard therefore excludes consideration of the most common form of client recovery.

And this, in this author's opinion, would make a strict reliance on the "but for" principle very unfair to a damaged client. In their decision, the Ohio court justices stated:

Accordingly, we hold that to establish a cause of action for legal malpractice based on negligent representation, a plaintiff must show (1) that the attorney owed a duty or obligation to the plaintiff, (2) that there was a breach of that duty or obligation and that the attorney failed to conform to the standard required by law, and (3) that there is a causal connection between the conduct complained of and the resulting damage or loss. We are aware that the requirement of causation often dictates that the merits of the malpractice action depend upon the merits of the underlying case. Naturally, a plaintiff in a legal malpractice action may be required, depending on the situation, to provide some evidence of the merits of the underlying claim. However, we cannot endorse a blanket proposition that requires a plaintiff to prove, in every instance, that he or she would have been successful in the underlying matter. Such a requirement would be unjust, making any recovery virtually impossible for those who truly have a meritorious legal malpractice claim.

It's important to note, however, that the Ohio court's decision represents only one of fifty states. While their decision would seem fair to any individual or entity pursuing a legal malpractice claim, it is important to check statutes, case law, and bar rules in each and every state where a legal malpractice action is contemplated. Also, a different standard may be applied to a civil case than to a criminal one.

2. Document Your Claim

In addition to the letter in which you fired your lawyer, discussed earlier, document your claim by formally notifying your former counselor what he did wrong and the damage it caused you. Send a certified letter, return receipt requested, to your former attorney outlining your concerns and what the attorney did to damage you. Inform your former lawyer that you wish to be compensated for your losses and explain what you want. The letter should be typed and look as professional as possible if you want to be taken seriously. If you do not get an answer within a reasonable amount of time (about two to three weeks), send a second letter also by certified mail, return receipt requested, indicating your intention to sue for legal malpractice.

These letters will serve to document your complaint. You can be sure that your former lawyer is also documenting his position. If the case goes to arbitration, mediation, or before a judge, you may be called upon to prove that you made your lawyer aware of your feelings and made a demand in writing.

3. Obtain Legal Counsel

If your former legal counsel will not cooperate with you to resolve the matter, you may need to find a lawyer who is willing to file a legal malpractice suit on your behalf. Finding an attorney to represent you in a legal malpractice case can be very difficult. (See the Resources section for some helpful websites.)

If you cannot find an attorney who is willing to take on your case, you can represent yourself in the matter. See Chapter 7 for some advice and read the section "Filing Suit and Prosecuting the Case Pro Se" on page 144. Remember that in most jurisdictions individuals acting pro se cannot represent a corporation, even if the individual is a sole shareholder. So, if your grievance is on behalf of your corporation, you will have to find an attorney who is willing to handle your case. However, in some jurisdictions, such as Florida, a corporation may be permitted to operate in small claims court without an attorney. Therefore, if your state allows access to its small claims court by a corporation, it may be possible to file a malpractice claim on behalf of the corporation in that forum.

4. Find Expert Witnesses

To prove your claim, you will need to find an expert witness or perhaps several expert witnesses. Any claim that might be considered *standard of care*—what would normally be expected from an attorney under a given set of circumstances—will need expert testimony to prove to the court and jury (if it is, in fact, a jury trial) that the work was not done in a professional manner. You will need a witness such as a practicing lawyer who can establish under oath and under cross-examination that your former lawyer did a bad job on your behalf. Also, if a speciality of law is involved in your underlying case, you will need a lawyer in a similar specialty to refute your former lawyer's position. You can be sure that these witnesses will charge handsomely for their time and expenses, including transportation, hotel charges, meals, and possibly legal research.

All of this aside, lawyers who are witnesses may be reluctant to testify against a peer. If a lawyer testifies against another in the same jurisdiction, that lawyer may fear retaliation. If you wish to have an expert lawyer testify on your behalf, try to find one who practices outside the jurisdiction of the defendant attorney.

Other experts may include economists, appraisers, and others knowledgeable of the area of law involved.

5. Investigate Your Attorney's Malpractice Coverage

Investigating your attorney's malpractice coverage would normally be the next step. However, it is necessary to first file a lawsuit in order to obtain the legal right to use the rules of civil procedure for discovery—that is, the stage of litigation that allows each side to obtain information, documents, and other materials to help them determine and ready the facts of the case. File the lawsuit, hold discovery, and then with the information regarding the parameters of your former lawyer's malpractice insurance now in hand, it becomes a simple matter to ask the court for *leave to amend*—to make changes in the text of your complaint. In the early stages of a lawsuit, judges almost always grant a motion to amend the pleadings.

If your attorney is insured, look into the parameters—the areas of coverage—of the policy. Does it exclude fraudulent acts by the insured and are there other exclusions that you should be aware of? Once you have a working knowledge of the insured's policy, you will want to amend your complaint to reflect the cause or causes of action that are covered under the insurance policy.

If your former attorney is not insured and you win the malpractice case, collection may be problematic. You may find helpful information in *How and When to Be Your Own Lawyer* (Avery Publishing, 2000), specifically the chapter on civil enforcement (collecting a judgment).

Despite the hardships, law books are filled with legal malpractice cases published from appellate court decisions. So, if you lose your case, be prepared to take it to the appellate level for another chance. If you have a strong case, it may be necessary to get out of the jurisdiction of the old boys and girls club in order to prevail.

FILING SUIT AND PROSECUTING THE CASE PRO SE

If you cannot find a lawyer who is willing to take on his peers, your only option is to go it alone by filing the suit and prosecuting the case pro se. Once again, you may find the book *How and When to Be Your Own Lawyer* helpful. While it doesn't specifically address suing your attorney for malpractice, it will help you apply the information in this book, and specifically in this chapter, to your current pursuit for justice.

POSSIBLE CAUSES OF ACTION

The cause of action in your complaint must be strong enough to pass muster when your opponent tries to tell the judge that the complaint should be dismissed because there is no cause of action. A well-drawn and researched complaint with a *valid* cause or causes of action should get you past the attempt to dismiss the case for lack of *cause*. However, in a legal malpractice case, the number of causes of action open to you is limited. These are discussed below.

Negligence as a Cause of Action

Negligence is perhaps the single-most pleaded cause of action in legal malpractice cases. The definition of *negligence* in *Black's Law Dictionary* is "Damages due generally through a breach of duty or care or negligent action." On its face, this definition seems to be suited to legal malpractice claims. In a legal malpractice case, negligence would have to be shown to be the proximate cause of the damage. Negligence, in the legal sense, is itself a tort—an injury or damage not involving a contract. Because so many fee agreements (if such a document even exists between a client and his attorney) are lacking the details or specifics of the attorney's duties, it becomes necessary to rely on a non-contract cause of action to pursue the malpractice action, such as negligence, in those instances.

The law is fluid and ever changing to meet the needs of our society. In recent years, the pendulum is swinging toward the belief that a violation of the bar rules provides evidence of negligence. So, in order to develop evidence of negligence in the proof stage of your malpractice case, it may be necessary to determine which of the bar rules your lawyer violated and present that (along with appropriate evidence of each violation) to the judge. It's also a good idea to include some case law that supports the use of violations of bar rules as evidence of negligence with the overall presentation in your direct case. And, of course, this is where you expert testimony comes in.

In the case of *Vahila et al. v. Hall et al.* the Supreme Court of Ohio justice's opinion indicates why experts are so important to proving a lawyer guilty of malpractice. The majority states:

> . . . we hold that to establish a cause of action for legal malpractice based on negligent representation, a plaintiff must show (1) that the attorney owed a duty or obligation to the plaintiff [the client], (2) that there was a breach of that duty or obligation and that the attorney failed to conform to the standard required by law, and (3) that there is a causal connection between the conduct complained of and the resulting damage or loss.

How do you prove your former attorney "failed to conform to the standard required by law"? You use the facts and expert testimony. Your expert should be a practicing attorney with as many years of experience as possible and a pillar of the community. A retired judge or law professor would be best.

Breach of Contract as a Cause of Action

If a written agreement was executed between your lawyer and you, and your lawyer took money from you and did not perform the work as indicated in the document, you have a clear-cut breach of contract suit. The breach of contract would be your cause of action in your legal malpractice claim. Your complaint would then spell out what was paid, what you believe was to be accomplished by the lawyer, and what was not done.

Perhaps even more important, a suit on breach of contract grounds could be used to get around the relatively limited statute of limitations on legal malpractice claims under certain circumstances. In general, the statute of limitations for suing for breach of contract is longer than those set for suing for legal malpractice.

Remember, in order to sue for breach of contract, a written agreement between you and your attorney must exist. Alternatively, you must be able to prove that a verbal agreement or contract *existed* between you and your attorney. For example, if you can show that the attorney performed some of the work that he verbally agreed to, but did not carry out the remainder of the work required to resolve your case or matter, it may be possible to move forward with your claim.

Fraud as a Cause of Action

Fraud is an intentional perversion of the truth for the purpose of inducing an individual or entity to rely upon it and consequently part with or lose something valuable or surrender a legal right—in other words, fraud is detrimental reliance. To be a fraud, elements must include false representation and damage as a result of the misrepresentation.

While negligence is an act of omission, fraud is an act of commission—meaning that it is intentional. Malpractice insurance usually doesn't cover a lawyer's fraudulent acts.

In general, the statute of limitations for suing for fraud is longer than those set for suing for other acts of legal malpractice. For instance, in a California case, the state's quoted statute of limitations states in part, "An action against an attorney for a wrongful act or omission, other than for actual fraud . . . shall be commenced within one year."

Unjust Enrichment as a Cause of Action

Unjust enrichment—when one party underhandedly gains an advantage at the expense of another—is a doctrine with roots in equity. It is firmly established in our society that one person should not be permitted to unjustly enrich themselves at the expense of another. This principle has become embedded in our legal system, as well.

Often, the nondisclosure of facts or information for personal monetary gain is considered unjust enrichment. For example, a lawyer might know that an insurance company has a policy of paying an almost automatic $100,000 to settle difficult claims. Rather than take the matter to court on behalf of the client or discuss options with the client, the lawyer might think to himself, *We can get $100,000 on this case, so I'm not going to risk a trial.* This lawyer may get a contingency fee without doing a stick of work, and the client would lose any chance of a larger recovery.

Specific Performance as a Cause of Action

Specific performance is a requirement to carry out an agreed upon task or tasks. Those tasks may be required to be carried out under court order by a judicial decision if not done by the previously agreeing party willingly or previous to the court order.

This cause of action differs from negligence because it cannot be claimed that what was not done was accidental or that the attorney was not aware of the need for the task to be carried out. When a cause of action is for specific performance, the plaintiff is seeking the court's order to enforce the terms of a breached agreement.

Breach of Fiduciary Duty as a Cause of Action

While breach of fiduciary duty is a subspecies of the general category of legal malpractice in many jurisdictions, it comes in many colors and forms and may or may not necessarily fall into the definition of legal malpractice. It may be actionable on its own.

The release or use of someone's personal information garnered from his medical records improperly is a breach of the fiduciary responsibility, or duty, of a lawyer. If a lawyer represents an individual whose information was improperly used by the lawyer, it may be actionable both as legal malpractice and as a breach of the fiduciary duty. Some other acts of breach of fiduciary duty include being involved with a client personally and/or sexually to the detriment of the legal representation; being involved with a client in business and using information to the client's detriment; disclosing confidential information; engaging in any conflict of interest; stealing client's money from a trust account; and disloyalty, in any form, to the client's detriment.

Misrepresentation as a Cause of Action

Taken in the legal sense, the word *misrepresentation* is related to fraud, but differs due to the facts involved and the degree of damages, if any. In general, *misrepresentation* is considered "the giving of an untrue or misleading idea."

Under Model Rule 4.1 "Truthfulness in Statements to Others," lawyers have the duty to be truthful to others when dealing on a client's behalf. According to the rule, misrepresentations can also occur "by failure to act."

The bar looks at misrepresentation as a violation of the rules and the practice of law—a violation that must be dealt with severely. In the case of *Harold B. Peek, a Member of the Bar of the District of Columbia Court of Appeals* (565 A.2d 627; 1989 D.C. App.), a lawyer was given an extra period of suspension due to misrepresentation: ". . . the Board [on Professional Responsibility] reasoned that, because of the added element of misrepresentation involved, respondent's transgressions warranted a stiffer penalty than the thirty days assessed. . . ."

Exaggerating one's experience and ability (puffery) is not usually a serious matter, although it is blatantly dishonest. For instance, a warehouse worker might try to pass himself off as a former warehouse manager to get a better position elsewhere—maybe even without causing serious damage to the company that hires him. However, when a professional does the puffing—or perhaps even worse, lies about his credentials—then it may be considered misrepresentation. If a lawyer misrepresents his experience and ability, he could damage a client's case. If due to that misrepresentation, a client retains the attorney and legal malpractice occurs during the course of the case, the client may have yet another cause of action known as *fraud in the inducement*.

Other Causes of Action

Depending on the type of law that is involved in the underlying case, there are many other causes of action that may be pleaded in a claim for legal malpractice. These may be researched in a "cause of action" manual, which can be found in most well-stocked law libraries.

DETERMINING THE STATUTE OF LIMITATIONS

Each state's statutes may pose obstacles in the pursuit of "getting even." For instance, in the case of *Gomez v. Burlington Northern Railroad Co.*, the justices cited the Indiana statute known as the Personal Injury Representation Act. That law limits and dictates the process of pursuing a malpractice case in the field of personal injury. Therefore, it's important for you to check your state's laws on, and in the field of, your legal malpractice claim against your former counsel to be sure you have covered all the bases. You can be sure your former attorney is doing the same. Don't let lack of knowledge or time spent on legal research ruin an otherwise good case. Time is not on your side. See Appendix D for the statute of limitations pertaining to legal malpractice.

PREPARING YOUR COMPLAINT

The preparation of a well-drawn and thorough complaint is important to the integrity of your case. If you are proceeding pro se, you need to bone up on the subject of drafting a complaint and inscribing in it the various applicable causes of action available to you in the particular set of facts of the case, as discussed above.

As mentioned several times, *How and When to Be Your Own Lawyer* is a good place to start. Then, with the basic understanding of using a law library gleaned from Appendix C, begin your research. (By the way, you can also ask the local clerk of the court to search for other cases of legal malpractice filed against your attorney. If such a case exists, you may be able to hire the attorney handling that case or make a copy of the complaint in that case.)

WHAT TO EXPECT NEXT

Once the complaint is well crafted to include all of the possible causes of action in your legal malpractice case against your former lawyer, it needs to be filed at your local courthouse and served on the lawyer and/or his firm. Whatever the outcome, your lawyer will not be happy when the sheriff deputy serves him with your complaint. Your former attorney will then have the prescribed amount of time in your jurisdiction to answer your complaint. Along with the summons and complaint, serve on the attorney written interrogatories (questions) that ask him to identify his legal malpractice insurance company, limits, policy number, and also for him to produce an actual copy. The rules of discovery require him to do so just like any other defendant in a lawsuit.

Your next task is to prove the allegation, or allegations, asserted against your lawyer. Documents, witnesses, and a full range of discovery will be helpful to prove the causes of action you allege in your compliant. Often, information garnered in discovery—such as the parameters of any malpractice insurance carried by your lawyer and/or his firm—will make it necessary for you to ask the court for *leave to amend* your complaint.

After discovery is complete and the time to gain information has elapsed, most courts will hold a scheduling conference to prepare both sides for trial, and a date will be assigned to your case. That's when you'll finally have *your* day in court against your errant lawyer.

CONCLUSION

When a professional, such as a lawyer, doctor, or accountant, damages a client, the reaction may be especially intense. This is because professionals have a special place in our society. Public expectations are much higher for those in such professions. Their years of training and greater compensation reflect the responsibilities they have agreed to take on. It is precisely because of these high expectations that when something goes wrong, those most affected may be propelled into a unique degree of frustration and, in some cases, rage. However, we use the term "getting even" not as retribution, punishment, or vengeance, but in the literal sense—to gain back what is lost.

Getting even, however, may not always be as easy as you might wish. The legal system is a labyrinth of rules, statutes, and common law or case law. It is hard to beat a lawyer at his own game. However, trying may be worthwhile if the monetary value of the claim is sufficient and if the facts and documentation are on your side. A successful legal malpractice case against a lawyer can be an immense source of satisfaction.

If, however, the dollar amount is not substantial and the proof is not sufficient to launch full-blown litigation against the lawyer (and his firm), you may want to consider pursuing the bar complaint route. At the very least, knowing that your complaint against a lawyer will remain part of the record will be provide some degree of "getting even."

In Closing

If you've been damaged by your lawyer's conduct or believe you have been treated unfairly, hopefully this book has provided a positive outlet for your frustration and anger. Certainly, the information contained within this book will empower you to pursue possible remedies. With your new understanding of the complexities of legal malpractice law, the playing field may be leveled just enough to help you get back what you have lost. And with your new understanding of the statistics of legal malpractice, the specifics of lawyers' mistakes, and how to possibly accomplish getting even if you have been damaged, you will relieve yourself of some of the frustration that accompanies an unsatisfactory lawyer-client relationship.

The legal cases discussed in this book and others like them have helped shape the law as it is known and practiced today. These cases should provide you with a better understanding of our legal system and the judicial views on the subject of legal malpractice. Hopefully, you have also gained an inkling of why the legal profession has acquired such a bad reputation in modern times.

Gerald E. Curry, lawyer and "good family guy" (as described by his neighbor), was shot as television cameras rolled just outside of the Van Nuys Courthouse in California. (According to the *Los Angeles Times,* the reporters who were present just happened to be in the vicinity.) Mr. Curry was being targeted by William Strier—the losing party in a recent hearing on the matter of a "special needs" trust. Mr. Curry had been successful in limiting the amount of funds Mr. Strier was permitted to use from the trust. Enraged by Curry's win and its impact on him, Mr. Strier approached Curry outside the courthouse and began pumping bullets into the lawyer. As Curry took cover behind a tree, video cameras captured the moment. Though critically wounded, the lawyer survived the incident.

Shakespeare's line "The first thing we do, let's kill all the lawyers" was one of the first "lawyer jokes" to find an audience. Unfortunately, Mr. Strier took the statement seriously. This quote, as well as all of our modern-day lawyer jokes, are indicative of how Americans feel about the legal profession in this country. Perhaps this hostility stems from a litigious society trapped by its own ever-increasing misuse of the legal system to settle, arbitrate, and pursue every one of life's problems by legal means. Perhaps it is the glut of legal scoundrels who are all too willing to offer their services— at almost any price.

Once drawn into the web of litigation, most clients are not schooled enough in the law to deal with a situation that turns sour—to know if it is the complexity of the case, the facts or missing facts, the law or statutes, an act of malpractice, or even worse, a lawyer's deceit that interfered with a favorable outcome. According New York Supreme Court Appellate Division Justice J. Hopkins:

> The recipient of the [lawyer's] service is necessarily at a disadvantage to question the reasons for the tactics employed or the manner in which the tactics are executed. . . . The client is hardly in a position to know the intricacies of the practice [of law] or whether the necessary steps in the action have been taken. For better or for worse, the client must depend on his [or her] attorney to pursue litigation diligently and according to the rules.

This black hole of legal knowledge and total dependence on lawyers by most clients also adds to the frustration level, especially when their attorneys do not succeed for them, cheat them, or even over bill them. Up to this point, there has been limited outlet for this rage. Certainly, shooting a lawyer is no solution. Take heart. The information offered in this book provides you, the damaged client, with the means to right a wrong.

It is my sincere hope that you have gained a clear understanding of the legal community's professional responsibilities and that you use this book as a tool to refocus your frustration. I also hope that once you have acted upon the information in this book, you will understand when to let go of the resentment and anger you feel. By continuing to hold on to this rage, you truly become the losing party.

In closing, I wish you wise counsel, fair judges, and good luck.

Glossary

abandonment. Unjustified refusal by an attorney to attend to and communicate with his or her client.

abstract. A synopsis or description of the history of ownership of real property, including the deeds and other instruments leading to title in the present owner.

acknowledgment. As used in a document, confirmation of the truth or veracity of the content of the document with a signature that may be sworn to. In the general sense, confirmation or admission to the authenticity or correctness of a set of facts.

action. A term used to describe the underlying circumstances that justify and establish the basis for filing a lawsuit. It may also be used to denote a lawsuit.

actionable. A term that describes a set of circumstances that may be considered the basis for legal relief or for filing a lawsuit.

ad litem. Latin for "for the purpose of the suit." For example, a person appointed specifically to perform a limited function within a particular lawsuit would be designated guardian ad litem.

administrative law and procedure. An area of law enacted by a governmental body, usually establishing board or commission, which is granted the power to impose rules, regulations, and procedures affecting a relatively narrow area of activity, such as the Federal Communications Commission or the Food and Drug Administration.

advance. To make forward progress in a legal case, toward resolution or trial.

affirmative defense. New matter that constitutes a defense to a charge that has been asserted in a complaint; it must be raised in the answer to the complaint.

alternative dispute resolution. Methods of resolving conflicts without resorting to the court system, such as conciliation, mediation, and arbitration.

amended complaint. A version of a complaint that corrects faults, errors, and omissions in an original complaint.

answer. The formal written statement made by a defendant stating the defense. The answer is used by the defendant to resist the plaintiff's allegations of fact, or to confess to the facts and allege new information to avoid the plaintiff's attempt to win on facts presented.

appeal. Review of a lower court's decision by a higher court, usually available as a matter of right from final orders and certain other rulings if filed within the prescribed time period. Times for filing an appeal are usually ten or twenty days, depending on the nature of the order being appealed.

appellate. Relating to a legal appeal from a decision of a lower court or from alternative dispute resolution, as appellate court. The appellant is the party appealing the lower court's judgment; the appellee is the opposing party in the appeal.

arbitration. The assignment of a dispute to an impartial third party chosen by the parties to the dispute, who have agreed in advance to abide by the arbitrator's decision rendered after a hearing.

attestation. Execution (signing) of a document as a witness.

attorney's lien. A situation in which an attorney retains or keeps a portion of a client's money or property until fees and costs have been paid. It is permitted only in some jurisdictions.

bar grievance. A complaint filed against an attorney with the municipal or state organization monitoring or regulating attorneys.

board certified. A designation earned by an attorney based on specialized experience and licensure after passing a certification examination.

breach of duty. An attorney's improper handling of a client's matter.

brief. A written summary of the facts, laws, and arguments of a position in a lawsuit; appellate brief.

burden of proof. The obligation of a particular party to establish a sufficient level of proof in a lawsuit.

case law. Jurisprudence; the law as set forth in past written decisions of judges and appellate courts; available in state and federal reporters.

case within a case. Refers to the burden facing a client to prevail in a legal malpractice case; a client that sues his or her former lawyer for legal malpractice must prove that the original case that was lost or dismissed would have been won but for the negligence of the attorney.

causation. The act or omission of an attorney that leads to the dismissal of a client's case or results in damage to a client without any other intervening act, without which the client's loss would not have occurred.

certiorari. Review of a lower court's or an administrative agency's decision by a higher court at the discretion of the court when an appeal as a matter of right is unavailable. Petitions for certiorari are generally subject to strict filing deadlines.

citation. Written reference to statutes, cases, texts, articles, and opinions that are authorities for the subject matter under discussion.

civil contempt. Usually applied to a willful failure to comply with a court order, such as an injunction or an order to appear at a deposition or other judicial process as directed by the court. Punishment for civil contempt may be a fine or imprisonment; the object of such punishment is ultimate compliance with the court order.

claims bar date. Deadline for submission of claims in cases such as bankruptcy, receivership, or probate.

competent. As to an individual, one who is legally capable; qualified to act in a legally acceptable capacity—for example, to draw a will, to be served in a lawsuit, or to testify.

complainant. The party that initiates a lawsuit.

complaint. The original pleading or paperwork filed within a jurisdiction, by which a legal action is commenced. The document sets forth a statement or claim for relief, and usually contains (1) a short statement of the reasons the court has jurisdiction, (2) a short statement showing why the pleader is entitled to a favorable decision, and (3) a demand for judgment to which the pleader feels entitled.

constructive notice. Legal fiction by which one is charged with the knowledge of matters, such as legal requirements or documents filed in the public records, even without actual knowledge.

contingency fee. A method of payment of an attorney's fee in which the fee itself and the amount of the fee is dependent on the outcome of the litigation.

continuance. Postponement or adjournment of a legal proceeding (such as a session, hearing, or trial) to a later date or time.

corporation. A form of legal entity or business authorized under state law in which ownership is vested in shareholders, and liability is limited to the amount each shareholder has invested in the company.

costs. The out-of-pocket expenditures involved in a lawsuit, usually other than attorneys' fees. Certain costs are awarded to the party that prevails in the action. Costs usually include filing fees, court reporter fees, witness fees, sheriff fees, and expert fees. In a foreclosure action, you will see abstract and title fees, and so on.

counterclaim. A claim asserted by a defendant in opposition to or as a deduction from the claim of the plaintiff. Counterclaims are either compulsory or permissive. If compulsory, a pleading should state any claims that, at the time the pleading is served, the pleader has against any opposing party's claim. (That is, of course, if the court has jurisdiction and the matter is not subject to other litigation at the time.) If permissive, a pleading may state in a counterclaim only claims against an opposing party not arising out of the transaction or occurrence that is the subject of the opposing party's claim. *Counterclaim* is the generally accepted term for offsets and setoffs.

court reporter. One who takes down in shorthand or other code the testimony of witnesses, questions and answers of the attorneys, and comments of the judge, for use in appellate proceedings or other review; a stenographer.

criminal contempt. An action that may be construed as obstruction of justice. Conduct directed against the dignity and authority of the court (see civil contempt).

cross-claim. A claim by one party against any other party with the same designation named in a particular lawsuit. The claim must arise out of the transaction or occurrence that is the subject of either the original action or of a counterclaim relating to any property (or dispute) that is the subject of the original action. Cross-claims involve parties with the same designation (plaintiff or defendant) in the litigation, whereas counterclaims involve parties on opposite sides.

damages. An amount of value that is claimed or intended as compensation or reparation for a loss or injury.

de facto. Latin for "in fact." Used to indicate the acceptance of a fact despite that it is legally or otherwise not so.

declaratory judgment. An order declaring the rights, status, and obligations of the parties; often sought by insurance companies as means of determining there is no coverage prior to trial of cases in which they would otherwise have a duty to provide a defense.

default. An omission of that which ought to be done. Specifically, the omission or failure to perform a legal or contractual duty, to observe a promise, or to discharge an obligation.

default judgment. When a party against whom a judgment is asked of the court fails to answer or otherwise defend the action, that party is in default and a judgment by default may be entered by the clerk of the court.

defendant. The person or entity in a lawsuit named by the plaintiff as being responsible. The defendant has certain rights and obligations in a lawsuit.

deposition. The process of taking oral testimony under oath, recorded by an officer of the court, and used as discovery along with interrogatories, request for admissions, and production prior to a trial or hearing.

direct case/case in chief/on direct. The initial presentation of the plaintiff's case during trial through the introduction of evidence to support his or her claim.

directed verdict. An order disposing of a case after presentation of evidence, based on absence of evidence to support a contrary outcome.

discharge. In a bankruptcy case, an order that releases the debtor from prior debts. Some debts may be excepted from discharge but may require filing of a complaint objecting to discharge or dischargeability within a specified time frame.

disclosure. An obligation of an attorney to make known to a potential client possible conflicts of interest in the representation.

discovery. The stage of litigation that allows each side to obtain information, documents, and other materials to help them determine and ready the facts of the case.

docket. The court's calendar of legal activities or the court's record of individual documents filed within a particular case.

doctrine of laches. The legal principle by which a person who knows what he or she must do to assert a claim or right, but who neglects or omits to do so within a reasonable period of time, is considered to have surrendered that right or claim.

domestic relations. An area of law that pertains to the legal rights and obligations involving marriage, divorce, alimony, equitable distribution, and related issues.

duces tecum. See subpoena.

duty. An obligation or legally recognized requirement of conduct imposed on a person for the benefit of another; refers to an attorney's obligation to a client, imposed by law or standard of the legal community.

easement. Right of access or other limited use of property by someone other than an owner or tenant; may arise by the recording of subdivision plat, express grant, or reservation in a recorded document, by implication, or by prescription (use over an extended period of time).

ejectment. An action to restore to a person or entity entitled to it the possession of a premises or property.

election of remedies. Acceptance of one legal remedy that acts to bar another inconsistent remedy. For example, rescission of a contract would preclude a suit for damages for breach of that contract.

equity. Justice administered by applying standards of fairness rather than formal rules and regulations.

estoppel. When a party is prevented from raising a particular issue or claim, or where an issue or claim has been conclusively resolved and a party is charged with direct knowledge that the matter was so resolved.

et al. Latin for "and others."

et seq. Latin for "and the following."

evidence. Documents, testimony, and other forms of proof, whether written or unwritten, that demonstrate the truth of a litigant's statements or position.

ex parte. Latin for "for one party." A term for a judicial proceeding or hearing that is held at the request of one party without notice to the other party, and that results in the issuance of an order or other judicial decree.

excusable neglect. An understandable mistake warranting relief from default or other sanction.

exhibit. A document or thing used as evidence in a legal proceeding.

failure to prosecute. Lack of record activity in a case warranting its dismissal.

family law. Similar to domestic relations, but also refers to child custody and child support, adoption, guardianships, and trust law.

fiduciary. An individual who has accepted legal responsibility to act in a representative or responsible capacity for another.

filing. The deposit or delivery of pleadings or other legal instruments to a public official's central filing office such as the clerk of the court.

final judgment. A judgment is considered final when it determines the rights of the parties to an action and disposes of all the issues involved so that no future action of the court will be necessary to determine the entire controversy. The final judgment leaves nothing for the court to do in a case except to carry out the judgment. It is from this judgment that appeals are born.

fraud. Perpetration of some deceitful act or trickery upon another to cause him or her to part with some property or legal right.

headnote. A summary of a legal issue placed ahead of the actual text of the case opinion or ruling in a reporter, or report, of the case.

hearing (nonlegislative). A proceeding of relative formality before a magistrate, judge, hearing examiner, or administrative law judge, without jury, dealing with issues of fact or law. Witnesses may be heard and evidence may be presented in much the same manner as at trial. The session may terminate in a final order on the issues in question.

in personam. Latin for "against or about a person." Having control or jurisdiction over an individual.

in re. Latin for "concerning," "regarding," "in the matter of."

in rem. Latin for "against or about a thing." A term used to refer to a proceeding or action involving tangible things or property.

injunction. Court order directing or prohibiting certain acts; may be entered temporarily while a case is pending in order to preserve the status quo pending the final outcome in the case, or as a permanent injunction at the conclusion of a case; generally not available if a judgment for money damages would be an adequate remedy.

insurance. An agreement by an insurance company to indemnify another from loss or other damage.

interrogatories. One method of discovery in which a party is required to answer under oath written questions.

involuntary dismissal. Dismissal of an action by the court over the plaintiff's objection; often based on failure to comply with the rules or a court order, or failure to plead claim on which relief can be granted.

joint and several. A term used to describe liability where one or more parties may be liable either individually or all together.

judgment. The final decision of a court, rendered in written form.

judgment on the pleadings. Order disposing of a case prior to trial because one side's own allegations establish that one side is entitled to prevail as a matter of law.

judicial notice. Recognition by a judge that a given fact is true, for the purpose of acceptance as evidence during trial, especially when it is generally well known but would be unduly time-consuming and difficult to prove formally.

jurisdiction. The authority by which courts and judicial officers take cognizance of and decide cases, or the legal rights by which judges exercise their authority. This term encompasses the power and authority of a court to hear and determine a judicial proceeding, and the power of a court to rule concerning the subject matter in a given case. Also, the geographic area in which a court has authority, and the types of cases it has authority to hear.

jury instructions. The explanation of the law given to the jury by the judge at the beginning and end of a case as to how the jury is to deliberate and render its decision.

jury verdict. The final decision of a jury on matters of fact submitted to it for determination in a trial.

laches. Equitable doctrine barring stale claims, particularly where a delay in bringing the claim has been unfairly prejudicial to the defendant.

law library. A place (public, private, or educational) in which law-related books are kept for use; consists of statutes, case law, treatises, codes, law reviews, legal periodicals, journals, legal newspapers, and Internet-related research via computer and information technology.

lawsuit. A civil action or proceeding filed for the recovery of damages or other relief.

legal description. Portion of deed or other instrument that identifies the affected real property, usually by reference to a recorded plat or by "metes and bounds," the dimensions established by a survey.

legal malpractice insurance. A policy of insurance that indemnifies an attorney for damages assessed or awarded against him or her in favor of a client based on the attorney's legal neglect.

legal negligence. The failure on the part of an attorney to act with the requisite skill and ability possessed by other members of the legal community on behalf of a client that causes actual damage to the client.

lien. A legally recognized encumbrance or security interest attaching to a property.

malfeasance. Intentional wrongdoing, such as a breach of trust.

misfeasance. Wrongful performance of a lawful act.

mitigation of damages. Limitation on further damages that could occur when damages and injury have already occurred. All parties should exercise reasonable care to limit further damage or injury.

motion. A formal request from a party to a lawsuit (or his or her attorney) asking the court for a particular rule or order.

motion for rehearing. Motion asking the court to reconsider a final ruling based on matters it may have overlooked or misapprehended; if timely filed (usually within ten days of order), generally suspends finality of the order sought to be reheard.

motion in limine. Motion before trial to prevent any mention of irrelevant or unduly prejudicial evidence.

motion to dismiss. A motion requesting that a complaint be dismissed by the court, usually based on the theory that either the complaint has been drawn incorrectly or that the complaint fails to properly set forth a claim upon which relief can be granted.

nonfeasance. Omission of an act that ought to be performed.

nonjoinder. A proper party to a lawsuit who has not been previously joined, either as a plaintiff or a defendant. That party is subject to being joined upon proper motion and service.

novation. The act of substituting a new agreement for a prior agreement. Where there is an existing contract, debt, or obligation and the terms of the agreement evidencing that contract, debt, or obligation are materially changed or restated without releasing the original contract, debt, or obligation.

on point. Closely analogous; an earlier case that addresses the same issues and situation involved in a current suit is said to be on point.

order. A ruling, directive, mandate, or command issued by a judge, usually in written form.

party. One of the opposing persons or entities in a legal or judicial proceeding; also a person or entity that has entered into a contract or agreement.

perjury (civil). A false statement under oath or affirmation, usually involving an official or court proceeding.

permitted exceptions. Matters of record affecting title to real property, such as easements or restrictive covenants of record, which are specifically excepted from coverage under a policy of title insurance.

personal injury. An injury to a person's body; with reference to a legal action, a type of lawsuit involving injury to a person arising out of contract or tort law.

personal jurisdiction. Power of court to exercise authority over a particular person or entity; usually limited to parties located in or having substantial contacts with the state or federal district in which the action is brought.

petition. A formal, written application to a court requesting action on a matter. Also, a formal written request addressed to a governmental body. The right to petition for redress of grievances is protected by the First Amendment to the Constitution.

petitioner. The party that starts an equity proceeding or the party that takes an appeal from judgment. In legal proceedings that are initiated by petition, the person against whom action or relief is sought, or the person or entity who opposes the petition, is called the *respondent*.

plaintiff. A person or entity who brings a legal action; a complaining party seeking remedial relief for damage or injury to rights. The plaintiff has certain rights and responsibilities in a lawsuit, such as presenting the case first and summing up first. The plaintiff also pays the court filing fees to start the lawsuit.

pleadings. Documents that contain the formal allegations of the parties to a lawsuit, including the complaint, the answer, counterclaim, cross-claim, third-party complaint, and their respective answers. The Rules of Civil Procedure establish which documents are pleadings.

precedent. The results of cases that have been tried and decided. The rulings and rationales from previous cases are often used in deciding later cases, particularly where no statute directly addresses the situation at issue.

preponderance of evidence. Evidence that is more convincing and holds greater weight than the evidence offered in opposition.

pro se. Appearing for, or representing, oneself in a court proceeding without the formal assistance of an attorney.

probate. The formal procedure used to establish the validity, correctness, or truth of a will. Wills are generally required to go through this process in a probate court, which uses a set of laws or rules often called *the probate code.*

proximate cause. That action or inaction that directly results in injury to another without any intervening cause, without which the injury or damage would not have occurred.

quash. To void, nullify, vacate, overthrow, or abate of (usually) indictments or original service in a civil lawsuit. To set aside an original action or pleading.

quit-claim deed. An instrument of conveyance that does not represent that the seller owns any interest in what is being conveyed, but conveys only whatever interest, if any, that he or she has.

ratio decidendi. Latin for "the reasoning behind the decision"; the reasoning or justification given by a judge, court, or tribunal for its decision.

real estate contract. A written agreement entered into by buyers and sellers of land or other interest in realty, setting forth the terms such as price, description, time limits, costs of the transactions, contingencies to close, notices, remedies and damages for default, choice of forum, and other terms.

real property. Land and permanent attachments on the land that cannot be moved.

recording laws. Statutes under state law that provide for the filing method of instruments affecting title to real estate and the priority given to certain instruments in the event of a dispute over ownership of land.

recusal. Refers to a motion to disqualify a judge based on bias or prejudice; the act of removing a judge, voluntarily or involuntarily, from hearing a case to avoid the appearance of an impropriety or because of bias or prejudice alleged by one or both parties.

release. A written agreement in which one or both parties to a dispute voluntary abandon a right or claim against another in exchange for consideration or resolution of the dispute; can refer to the act of giving up such a right or claim.

replevin. A statutory action intended to return or retrieve specific goods or property to the rightful owner, where another party has wrongfully retained the property.

reporter. A volume or set of volumes, usually continually updated copies of court or administrative law decisions. Usually found in law libraries.

res judicata. Latin for "the thing has been judged." The principle of law that holds that once a matter is judicially decided, it is finally decided.

rescission. Order rescinding a contract and restoring parties to previous condition, usually based upon fraud or a mistake.

respondent. The party in an equity action, similar to a defendant in a civil action, who makes an answer to an equity action. In appellate actions, the respondent is the party that is against the appeal (the appellee).

restrictive covenants. Restrictions on use or ownership of real property recorded in the public records that bind each successor owner of the property.

retainer agreement. The contract between an attorney and client that sets forth the nature of the relationship, the scope of the lawyer's duties, and the method of compensation to be paid to the attorney.

scrivener's error. Minor error in a legal document, such as misspelling, transposition of digits, or typographical error, which can usually be corrected or overlooked if no one is misled or otherwise prejudiced.

setoff. In a situation in which a plaintiff is entitled to a recovery from the defendant but, in a separate matter, the defendant is owed money by the plaintiff, the amount owed by the plaintiff to the defendant. This may be deducted from the plaintiff's recovery.

slip and fall. A type of personal injury lawsuit in which a person or plaintiff sues for injuries sustained as a result of another's negligence that led to the plaintiff's losing balance on some defective condition in the defendant's flooring surface; also called *trip and fall*.

special warranty deed. An instrument of conveyance that does not represent that the seller owns any interest in what is being conveyed, but only that he or she is conveying whatever interest that he or she has and that he or she has not done anything to impair that interest.

specific performance. An order requiring a party to perform its obligations under a contract; generally not available if an award of money damages would be an adequate remedy.

statute. A law enacted by legislative process.

statute of limitation/limitation period. The period of time set forth by statutory law within which an action must be brought, and if not, the right to bring such action will be lost.

stay. The stopping of a judicial proceeding by order of the court. The suspension of or cessation of some designated proceeding.

stay of execution. The stopping or arresting of the act of executing on a judgment or other order of the court.

stipulation. An agreement between two or more litigating parties.

subpoena. A command to appear at a certain time and place to give testimony regarding a certain matter. A *subpoena duces tecum* requires the recipient to produce books, papers, and possibly other things related to the subject matter of the action, and usually to give testimony about the items requested.

summary judgment. A court order ruling on a claim, counterclaim, or cross-claim without trial, based on the court's determination that there is no issue of material fact to be tried. A party to a civil action may move the court for summary judgment in his or her favor on a claim, counterclaim, or cross-claim when he or she believes that all necessary facts have been settled and that the law is clearly on his or her side. Outside material, evidence, and affidavits may be used in support of this motion.

summons. Document utilized at the beginning of civil action. It is a means of acquiring jurisdiction over an individual or entity. When a complaint is filed, the court clerk issues a summons available for delivery to the marshal, sheriff, or a person specially appointed to serve it on those named. The following may be requirements for a summons: (1) signed by the clerk of the court; (2) be under the seal of the court; (3) contain the name of the court; (4) indicate the names of the parties; (5) be directed to the defendant; (6) state the name and address of the plaintiff's attorney or the plaintiff; (7) state the time within which rules require the defendant's appearance or response; (8) give notification that if the defendant fails to defend, judgment by default will be rendered against the defendant for the relief sought in the complaint.

survey. The map, drawing, or other description of land setting forth the land's boundaries and topographical characteristics; a requirement of purchasing real property to ascertain the amount of land being transferred and to confirm that no encroachments exist.

"Thing." An object or the subject matter of rights. All law relates to persons (persona), actions, or things (res).

third-party claim. A complaint filed by a defendant in an action against a person or entity not presently in the lawsuit (a third party) alleging that the party is or may be liable for all or part of the damages involved in the matter.

tolling. Suspension of running of limitations period for bringing suit, sometimes based on an act of defendant that hampered or prevented bringing a suit against him or her.

tort. An action arising from a violation of a duty, a civil wrong, or injury not involving a contract that is committed upon another person or property. A personal injury lawsuit is a tort action.

tort-feasor. A person who commits an intentional or unintentional act against another that causes mental or physical injury.

trial court. The tribunal in which the dispute is resolved by presentation of witness testimony and evidence before a judge or jury for determination; distinguished from an appellate court to which decisions of the trial court can be appealed and reviewed.

usurious. A rate of interest that is greater than that allowed by statute within a given jurisdiction.

venue. The particular city, county, state, or federal district in which a court with jurisdiction may hear and determine a case. Venue deals with the locality of a suit and relates only to the place where or territory within which either party may require a case to be heard.

voluntary dismissal. Dismissal of an action at the request of the plaintiff or its attorney. Generally, a plaintiff has an absolute right to dismiss without prejudice at any time before trial, but such a dismissal may create liability for court costs, and filing of another suit may be barred if the limitations period has run out.

waiver. The relinquishment, abandonment, or cessation of a right or interest that one possesses. Though generally an intentional, unilateral, or voluntary act, a waiver may occur unintentionally or involuntarily.

with prejudice. A term denoting a final order or judgment that is intended to be conclusive or dispositive as to the rights of the parties in the action, precluding the same party from bringing another lawsuit on the same subject. Such an order would require an appeal in the event of a dispute with its conclusion.

withdrawal. The action of an attorney's removing himself or herself or his or her appearance on behalf of a client.

without prejudice. A term for a type of dismissal of a case that is not meant as a final or dispositive declaration of rights or privileges in the action. The action may be refiled thereafter, assuming all other factors are suitable for refiling—for example, that the statute of limitations has not expired.

writ. The form of a court order requiring or directing a specific act or performance to take place.

writ of execution. A document issued by the court following an award of damages, which, when filed with the appropriate authorities, permits those authorities to seize and sell certain property to make payment toward the damages and any assessed costs.

APPENDIX B

Barrister Blunders—
A Guide to the Common
Errors Attorneys Make

Although there are many things that can go wrong during the course of a legal matter, some mistakes occur more often than others. This appendix discusses some of the more common blunders that lawyers commit in the various categories of legal representation. Well-informed clients are those clients who are aware of what their attorneys should be doing on their behalf and know the potential problems to be on the lookout for throughout the course of their legal matter.

REAL PROPERTY LAW

Real estate is a broad term that involves land and anything permanently attached to the land, such as a building. An attorney who specializes in real property law must be familiar with a great number of rules that deal with an even greater variety of situations. A client might want to purchase land, which could be residential (in the case of a home), commercial (in the case of a restaurant, office building, car wash, gas station, and so on), or industrial. Each of these purchases requires different skills and knowledge on the part of the attorney. Other situations might involve renting land to a tenant, renting land from another person (a leasehold space), or evicting a tenant for failure to pay rent. The list of possible real estate transactions and real-estate-related matters goes on and on; some are much more involved than others.

Disputes are not uncommon between buyers and sellers in real estate transactions. For example, one party to the transaction might contend that the other party did not honor its side of the bargain. A buyer might try to enforce its right to close on a deal that the seller is trying to renege on (frequently called *backing out of the contract*). Whatever the transaction or resulting dispute, an attorney's role is critical to ensuring that his or her client's interests are protected.

The following are some common errors that attorneys commit in the area of real property law:

❏ Failure to record a document prior to the purchase of property that would allow others to record another document on the property, thereby creating a cloud on title, which could result in loss of the property.

❏ Failure to record a uniform commercial code financing statement, thereby allowing assets to be sold to a third person without the payoff of the first loan.

❏ Failure to check city or municipal liens, requiring the purchaser to pay the previous owner's bills.

❏ Improper preparation of closing statement, resulting in more money paid by the client.

❏ Failure to check taxes prior to closing, resulting in the buyer's having to pay the seller's unpaid taxes.

❏ Failure to advise to order survey, or if ordered, failure to properly read and inspect, which might reveal encroachments or easements that could defeat the use of the property.

❏ Failure to properly prepare contract for sale.

FAMILY LAW

Generally speaking, family law refers to that branch of law or specialty involving matters such as adoption, guardianship, incompetence, annulment of marriages, divorce or dissolution of marriage, paternity, child support, alimony, division of assets, palimony, and community property issues. Obviously, a family law attorney must be familiar with a myriad of issues.

The following are some common errors that attorneys commit in this area of the law:

❏ Failure to properly prepare a financial statement required for divorces.

❏ Improper preparation of premarital settlement agreement or property settlement agreement, resulting in its being set aside in litigation.

❏ Failure to serve the party being sued.

❏ Failure to know the case law surrounding alimony, child support, modification proceedings, equitable distribution, claims for pensions, and increased assets.

❏ Failure to suggest or use expert witnesses such as child psychologists or forensic accountants.

BANKRUPTCY LAW

There are federal laws in the United States, generally under 11 United States Code, that govern and administer the procedures for the benefit and relief of debtors who are unable to pay their debts and obligations. Debtors may include individual persons or couples, partnerships, or corporations. Most commonly known avenues or relief to a debtor are Chapter 13 "Wage Earner"; Chapter 7 "Liquidation for a Person"; and Chapter 11 "Reorganization." Bankruptcy involves the collection of assets (possibly turning them over to a trustee), liquidation, and payments to creditors according to a priority schedule and according to strict time limits and procedures. Likewise, bankruptcy proceedings afford an opportunity for creditors, or those to whom debts are owed by the debtor, to protect their interests and to collect on the obligations owed them, if possible.

Bankruptcy lawyers may become involved in issues involving mortgage foreclosure, tax law, litigation of related civil disputes between debtor and creditor, preparation of schedules, lists and application petitions, or objections to discharge that are under strict time limits (much shorter than other statutes of limitations).

The following are some common errors that attorneys commit in this area of the law:

❏ Failure to prepare schedules and petition properly.

❏ Failure to attend initial meeting of creditors or court appearances set by a judge.

❏ Failure to advise on bankruptcy laws.

❏ Failure to file a claim in court against debtor on behalf of a creditor, resulting in its being overlooked or stricken.

PERSONAL INJURY LAW

In general, personal injury law is a subspecies of negligence law and refers to the recovery of money damages and compensation from responsible negligent parties or their principals and insurance companies for victims of an accident or wrongful act. Included in this field of law are situations involving car accidents, slip and fall injuries, products liability, medical or dental malpractice, intentional physical assaults and torts, premise liability, defective food ailments, and any other methodology by which one person is injured by the negligence or malfeasance of another.

Injured victims—or their survivors in the case of those plaintiffs that institute survivor actions or wrongful death cases—may recover for physical injuries; scarring; loss of limbs or eyesight; pain and suffering; loss of the ability to enjoy life; loss of past, present, or future earnings or earning capacity; future net accumulations; past, present, or future medical bills; and a host of other damages. For example, a person can recover the loss of consortium for injuries to his or her spouse. Consortium may involve the loss of finances or day-to-day affection.

The following are some common errors that attorneys commit in this area of the law:

❏ Failure to file a complaint within the statute of limitations period, resulting in loss of right to seek damages.

❏ Failure to name all responsible parties.

❏ Failure to serve all parties with the lawsuit in accordance with law.

❏ Failure to act diligently.

❏ Failure to obtain all insurance information, resulting in the inability to collect all collectible damages.

❏ Failure to advise of all offers made by opposition, including the danger of rejecting a reasonable offer that could later result in attorney's fees and costs being incurred for failure to accept the offer.

❏ Failure to obtain all available medical records.

❏ Failure to take all necessary discovery, such a depositions and request to produce.

❏ Failure to hire or disclose necessary expert witnesses for the particular matter within the proper time limits.

❏ Failure to claim all possible damages.

❏ Failure to prepare for trial, including jury instructions.

❏ Failure to file an appeal in a timely manner.

CRIMINAL LAW

Every country has developed a system in which those who violate a set of laws governing society's conduct are punished. Criminal law generally refers to the particular form of the administration of justice or penalties. Although there are federal crimes specifically set forth by federal law, the United States has deferred most of the administration of the penal codes to the various states. The laws and procedures, which are very specific, vary from state to state.

Criminal law involves the knowledge of criminal procedure, which details the rights afforded to a person and the requirements for the state or prosecution to charge a defendant with a crime and prove those charges. State statutes define crimes against persons, nature, or property, violence, and fraud as felonies (punishable by imprisonment of more than one year) or as misdemeanors (punishable by imprisonment of less than one year), depending on the severity.

Certain states allow jury trials for misdemeanors, while others do not. Defendants are entitled to confront their accusers, evidence, and witnesses against them and to be processed quickly (the right to speedy trial). Pretrial procedures and sentencing procedures exist to ensure due process is afforded to all.

The following are some common errors that attorneys commit in this area of the law:

❏ Failure to suppress evidence that was clearly wrong and clearly would have been suppressed if a timely motion were made.

❏ Failure to take discovery depositions, if allowable.

❏ Failure to interview witnesses.

❏ Failure to submit plea offer made by prosecution for client's consideration.

❏ Failure to advise client of minimum and maximum penalties.

❏ Failure to attend hearings, resulting in the issuance of an arrest warrant.

CORPORATION/BUSINESS LAW

The manner in which people or entities may engage in business is set forth in laws governing the formation and operation of corporations. The individual states and the federal government regulate business operations (for example, the products produced and how customers, creditors, and employees are dealt with), in general, to provide for the protection of the public.

Businesses and people who do business with one another are entitled to be treated fairly and predictably. In the event of a breakdown or dispute in the relationship, they can seek the power of the law through its courts to enforce their rights.

Business law involves knowledge of the technicalities of business formation or incorporation, the commercial rules that govern relationships within an industry or between entities, and litigation issues to enforce rights and duties if required.

The following are some common errors that attorneys commit in this area of the law:

❏ Failure to file annual reports when hired to do so, resulting in dissolution of the business.

❏ Improper preparation of articles of incorporation, bylaws, and/or notices of annual meeting.

❏ Failure to disclose conflict of interest that results when the board attorney represents the majority shareholder and corporation to the disadvantage of other shareholders.

❏ Failure to prepare offering circular in accordance with state or federal SEC requirements.

❏ Failure to advise in changes of industry standards or laws affecting the industry, when hired to do so.

LAW INVOLVING TRUSTS, ESTATES, AND WILLS

This area of law is very broad and involves the ownership, administration, and transfer of assets from one person or entity to another. This may involve the death or incapacity of a person. A person who is preparing for the orderly transfer of his or her wealth may want to do so in a way that minimizes adverse tax consequences to the fullest extent possible.

The manner in which such issues are handled may be very complicated and are governed by state laws of succession and wills (or even several states if properties are located in different jurisdictions) and are frequently overlaid with federal tax requirements.

This area of law subsumes issues of family law, real property law, corporate/business law, and possibly personal injury law. It covers creditor protection and the preservation of the rights of widows and survivors.

The following are some common errors that attorneys commit in this area of the law:

❏ Failure to properly prepare probate forms with court, resulting in the loss of assets.

❏ Failure to publish notices in newspapers, resulting in the filing of claims that could have been extinguished.

❏ Failure to object to an improper claim filed.

❏ Failure to record documents properly.

❏ Failure to obtain IRS and state tax authority clearances.

❏ Improper preparation of a will, resulting in the decedent's intentions not being carried out, thereby harming the heirs that would have inherited otherwise.

❏ Improper supervision of attestation of important documents such as a will or trust. Improper execution may result in a document's being determined void.

LITIGATION OF CIVIL CASE

The courts of all states provide for judicial proceedings to resolve controversies or disputes between parties. The disputes may concern actions for negligence, breach of contract, intentional torts or wrongs, accounting, breach of trust, quieting of title concerning real estate disputes, and so on. The way that a case may progress is usually set forth by the rules of civil procedure and other statutory requirements for each jurisdiction.

The anatomy of a civil case starts with the initial pleading, usually called a *complaint* or *petition,* which is filed by the plaintiff or petitioner. The defendant or respondent files an answer or motion to dismiss the matter based on technical grounds. Failure to file an answer on a timely basis subjects the defendant or respondent to entry of default, in which the court can enter a judgment in favor of the plaintiff due to the defendant's failure to respond (despite having been properly served). Myriad rules govern the method of service and a defendant's or respondent's response.

After the initial pleading stage, the parties are permitted to engage in the process of discovery, whereby they can learn of the other side's witnesses, evidence, exhibits, and case theories. Each side can ask the other written questions (interrogatories) or questions directly under oath in the presence of a court reporter (depositions). They can have their respective expert witnesses examine documents when permitted under the law or rules of civil procedure. And they can require the opposition to produce documents or other material that may reflect on the case.

Following discovery, the parties must comply with certain pretrial procedure rules, as well as rules that govern the trial. Trials may be jury or nonjury, depending on the issues or dispute involved. Following trial, the enforcement of a judgment and the procedures to appeal a decision are controlled by the rules of civil procedure.

The following are some common errors that attorneys commit in this area of the law:

❑ Failure to respond with written answer to complaint in court, resulting in default.

❑ Failure to comply with discovery obligations.

❑ Improper examination of witnesses at trial.

❑ Lack of preparedness for trial.

❑ Violation of court rules and pretrial orders.

❑ Failure to advise client of offers.

❑ Failure to attend mediation, resulting in the dismissal of the case.

❑ Improper jury instructions or failure to prepare jury instructions.

❑ Failure to advise of offer of judgment rule and its consequences.

❑ Failure to preserve objections at trial level.

❑ Failure to know substantive law on matters litigated.

❑ Failure to assert all defenses possible if being sued.

❑ Failure to assert all causes of action possible, if doing the suing (plaintiff).

❑ Failure to assert a counterclaim against the plaintiff.

❑ Failure to act on case within the statute of limitations.

APPENDIX C

Research—
Your Tool for Success

C an you imagine walking into your lawyer's office one morning to discuss your case and saying to your startled counselor, "By the way, in the case of Smith versus Jones brought before the Florida Fourth District Court of Appeals in 1994, the court found that . . . I believe Smith versus Jones is exactly on point with facts very similar to our case." Francis Bacon, the great English philosopher, essayist, and statesman, said, "Knowledge is power." With that kind of knowledge—understanding and using case law—spurting from your lips, your esteemed barrister will sit up and take notice. Your attorney might even do a better job representing you.

The law library is an important tool for enhancing your ability to research your case or to "get even," if necessary. This appendix explains how to use a law library. Dissecting its contents will help eliminate the intimidation caused by the sheer mass of material.

ABOUT THE LAW LIBRARY

For all things legal, the law library is the place to acquire knowledge. Although a law library may seem intimidating at first, knowing how to use it will give you immense power in understanding your legal matter. Moreover, it can be used as a tool to check on the work your lawyer is doing or has done. If you're not satisfied with the outcome of your case, you can use the library to research similar cases, or *cases on point*, to determine if the law was properly applied to the facts of your case. You might even find a case that shows that the judge was wrong about the law or how it was applied to the facts of your case and that an appeal should be considered. Or you may find that your attorney didn't do the necessary research and an action for malpractice may be in order.

When you understand the principle that "law" is the product of statutes plus the case law (as shown in Figure C.1 below), you will understand why you need to avail yourself of the vast amount of case law found within the law library. The statutes of any given jurisdiction may take up only a few shelves. The case-law section, however, may take up aisles and aisles of shelf space.

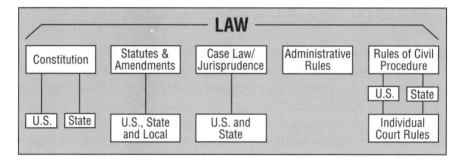

Figure C.1. The Elements That Make Up and Define the Laws

Authorities

In the practice of law, statutes, reported cases, court rules, opinions of the attorney general, and reported state court decisions are called *authorities.* The following are examples of authorities:

❏ State and federal constitutions

❏ State and federal statutes

❏ State and federal reported cases

❏ State and federal court rules

❏ Municipal ordinances and charters

❏ Opinions of the state and federal attorney generals

❏ Certain federal administration decisions: Securities and Exchange Commission, Federal Administrative Regulations/Code of Federal Regulations

❏ Federal labor law and administrative decisions

❏ Patent, trademark, and copyright citations and decisions

❏ Treaties and other international agreements

❏ Law reviews

❏ State bar rules or the *Model Rules of Professional Conduct*

What Is the Law?

To understand the fluidity of the law and what the term *law* actually means, let's examine what the law is and where it comes from. Law in the United States, for the most part, derives from three basic sources: statutes, decisions, and rules. Each of these is discussed below.

Statutes

Statutes are the written rules and regulations that regulate the transactions of life, enacted by our elected officials on a local, county, state, and federal level. These are the laws our legislators enact and must conform to the constitutions of both the United States and to the individual states' constitutions. The various statutes are then interpreted by the courts, often as a result of interactions with the executive and legislative branches of government. In reverse, a legislature may amend or override court decisions by changing laws or passing new laws. This process is ongoing, adapting our laws to the ever-changing needs of society.

Decisions—Precedents and Traditions (Case Law)

The court system determines exactly how the laws will be interpreted and applied to society at large. Almost every day, an appellate court somewhere in the United States is deciding an issue of law. This process of interpreting statutes and reviewing previous decisions, more than any other action by any branch of government, is responsible for the evolution, or fluidity, of the law. A statute enacted with good cause one day may not be valid the next day. A law enacted with all good intentions might be unconstitutional or even counterproductive to the needs of society. The result is a voluminous body of case law—precedents—that is a guiding light to others in their search for definitive answers to similar legal issues or questions. An attorney must research case law in order to be current on recent precedents and decisions.

Rules—Administrative Law and Procedures

Society has become so complex that another whole strata of law exists: rules, or administrative law and procedure. Certain governmental bodies, such as the Federal Communications Commission, the Federal Aviation Administration, and the Department of Transportation, have been empowered to create and enforce rules and regulations within the relatively narrow area of society that they control. Even the courts themselves propose and enforce rules and regulations that mandate procedure, form, and style within the justice system.

These rules affect the *practice* of law and change from time to time. A lawyer who is not up on the rules of a particular court system is operating in a vacuum and could get caught up in a procedural nightmare and lose a case on procedure alone.

The state legislature and congress codify common law, change and amend some existing laws, and enact new laws at each session. Appellate courts and the Supreme Court set precedent on a continuing schedule of decision-making. Individual court systems promulgate their rules as an ongoing function of the system. All these changes and additions are a staggering amount of *law* for the legal practitioner to digest. These changes represent the fluid nature of the law.

To make a legal case for your point of view by citing authorities, you must find authorities that deal with facts closely related to your set of facts—the circumstances of your case. Also, when possible, these should be cases that occurred in jurisdictions as close to *your* jurisdiction as possible. This is a very important point because judges tend to be more interested in cases or precedents that come from their own jurisdiction. Then, using the correct method of citing the authority (as indicated in a book on legal citation formats, such as *A Uniform System of Citation*, published by the Harvard Law Review Association), the information can be quoted in legal documents to make your point. Finding relevant authorities is where legal research comes in.

Figure C.2 on page 179 presents a typical case heading and front page from Lexis, the Internet legal research service. All of the legal research services, electronic as well as hardcopy, will present their reported cases in this form or a similar form. Case law is intriguing. Once you get into reading legal cases, you will find truth more fascinating than fiction.

THE CONTENTS OF A LAW LIBRARY

The material in most law libraries is divided into four sections: federal law, state and territorial law, specialty areas of the law, and general reference. (See Figure C.3 on page 180 for a diagram of a typical law library.) Let us consider each section of the library in turn.

Federal Law Section

The federal law section of most law libraries contains copies of the United States Constitution and annotated volumes of decisions that interpret the Constitution's provisions, complete with references, or citations, to cases that brought about those decisions along with explanatory notes and com-

CAROL D. COLEMAN, v. E. DONALD GURWIN, Defendant-Appellant.

Docket No. 94403

Supreme Court of Michigan

443 Mich. 59; 503 N.W.2d 435; 1993 Mich. LEXIS 1934

**May 5, 1993, Argued July 27, 1993, Decided
July 27, 1993, Filed**

PRIOR HISTORY: [***1] *195 Mich App 8; 489 NW2d 118 (1992).*

DISPOSITION:

Reversed.

CASE SUMMARY:

PROCEDURAL POSTURE: Defendant attorney appealed a judgment of the Michigan Court of Appeals, which affirmed a trial court's decision denying attorney's motion for a change of venue in plaintiff client's **legal malpractice** action.

OVERVIEW: Client filed her malpractice action against attorney alleging that in declining to represent her in a wrongful discharge action, he provided her with erroneous advice regarding the statute of limitations and that she was induced to forego a meritorious action. The lower court's decision was based on the trial court's finding that venue for client's malpractice action was proper in the county where the underlying wrongful discharge action arose. The court reversed, holding that venue for a **legal malpractice** action resided in the county in which the alleged malpractice occurred and not the county in which an underlying legal action would have resided. The court held that client could not sustain a cause of action for **legal malpractice** until she alleged all of the elements of that tort and that none of the parts of her cause of action for **legal malpractice** occurred in Wayne County. Attorney's alleged malpractice occurred outside of the county where the wrongful discharge occurred. For that reason, venue was improper in that county.

OUTCOME: The court reversed the lower court's judgment.

CORE TERMS: legal malpractice, venue, cause of action, malpractice, statute of limitations, cause of action arose, resides, wrongful discharge action, allegedly negligent, proximate cause, advice, underlying suit, attorney-client, meritorious, legislative intent, underlying action, place of business, legal action, causation, legal representation, wrongful discharge, resident, drafted, mailed

LexisNexis (TM) HEADNOTES - Core Concepts:

Civil Procedure > Venue > Individual Defendants
[HN1] See *Mich. Comp. Laws § 600.1629(1)(a)(i)*, Mich. Stat. Ann. § 27A.1629(1)(a)(i).

Civil Procedure > Venue > Individual Defendants
[HN2] Venue is proper where part or all of the cause of action arose.

Civil Procedure > Venue > Individual Defendants
[HN3] An action be instituted in a county where the defendant has some real presence such as might be shown by systematic or continuous business dealings inside the county.

Torts > Malpractice Liability > Attorneys
[HN4] In an action for **legal malpractice,** the plaintiff has the burden of proving: (1) the existence of an attorney-client relationship; (2) negligence in the legal representation of the plaintiff; (3) that the negligence was a proximate cause of an injury; and (4) the fact and extent of the injury alleged.

Torts > Malpractice Liability > Attorneys
[HN5] A plaintiff in a **legal malpractice** action must show that but for the attorney's alleged malpractice, he would have been successful in the underlying suit.

Figure C.2. Typical Malpractice Case Heading from Lexis. This is a printout, or page copy, of the results of legal research in the area malpractice law. (Any subject matter will look similar.) The first page of the case shows the case title. The names of the plaintiff and defendant (and/or appellant and appellee) are shown at the top of the page. This is followed by the particular court that heard the case, its citation number, and pertinent dates—that is, when filed and when decided. Most reporting services will provide the following: prior history, disposition, procedural posture, overview (short summary), outcome, core terms, and core concepts.

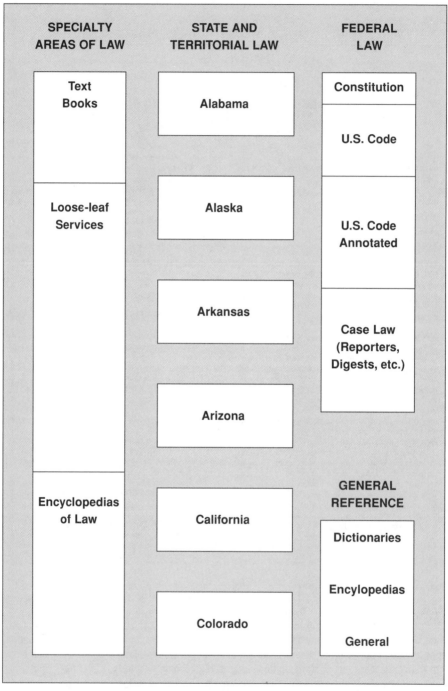

Figure C.3. Diagram of a Typical Law Library

ments. Next on the federal shelf is the United States Code, which is made up of approximately fifty volumes that contain all of the statutes enacted by Congress. These volumes are arranged by subject. The subjects are listed alphabetically in a fifty-volume index.

Alongside the United States Code, you will find an annotated version of the Code. It uses the same numbering system as the unannotated version, but this set also includes comments and references to court cases that have interpreted the particular statute. The annotation includes a brief summary of the important points of law. The entire set is indexed by subject in separate books.

By far, case law takes up the greatest amount of space in the federal section. The publication of federal court decisions falls into three categories: 1) United States Supreme Court, 2) United States Court of Appeals (13 Circuits), and 3) United States District Courts (96 Districts).

Because of the tremendous number of cases that have accumulated since about 1876 (when the reporting of cases began in the United States), it became necessary to create an organized system for recording the cases. One of the first systems used indexes or *digests* as they are called in the language of law. These books list each case by subject and provide a brief synopsis of the facts and findings of the case. Thus, the United States Supreme Court Digest is a complete indexed compilation of decisions of the United States Supreme Court system. The United States Court of Appeals Digest similarly indexes all the federal appellate court decisions.

The decisions themselves are printed in a set of volumes called *reporters.* The majority of decisions in federal cases are printed in a voluminous set of books called *Federal Reporter* (for appellate cases) and *Federal Supplement* (of selected district court cases). Table C.1 shows the types of cases and courts' decisions that are reported in these volumes.

Next in the federal section is a book known as the *Federal Rules of Civil Procedure* (FRCP), which contains the rules of court practice. Portions of the FRCP are often printed verbatim in the state's published rules, and then the state's rules will go on to indicate the state's own interpretation and/or requirements on the subject. When court decisions define and clarify issues involving civil procedure rules, these decisions are published in a set of reporters (originally in the *Federal Cases*). Since 1939, this set of books has been called *Federal Rules Decisions.* Many states have adopted all or part of these rules as their own court rules.

Thus, the Constitution (authority), the Code (law and statutes as enacted by Congress), the body of case law (decisions of the courts), and the

TABLE C.1. REPORTING OF FEDERAL COURT CASES	
FEDERAL REPORTER	**FEDERAL SUPPLEMENT**
U.S. Circuit Court	U.S. District Court
U.S. Commerce Court	U.S. Court of Claims
U.S. District Courts	U.S. Court of International Trade**
U.S. Court of Claims	Judicial Panel on Multi-District Litigation
U.S. Court of Appeals*	
U.S. Court of Customs and Patent Appeals	
U.S. Emergency Court of Appeals	
Temporary Emergency Court of Appeals	

Effectively, the reporting of federal cases is contained in one continuous set of volumes. However, there are different names assigned to the volumes for specific periods of time. The *Federal Reporter* picks up where a series of *Federal Cases* (West Publishing, 1894) leaves off; and the *Federal Supplement* picks up where a series called Volume 60, Second Series (West Publishing, 1924) leaves off.

*Formerly U.S. Circuit Court of Appeals
**Formerly U.S. Customs Court

courts' own rules and their interpretations are all found in the federal section of the law library. This complement of law books forms the basic tool for federal research.

There are, of course, additional useful volumes in the federal section. You will find that *Shepard's U.S. Citations* and *Shepard's Federal Citations* are extremely important to your legal research. (Their use is explained in the discussion of the volumes on state law in the library, but work the same way in federal research.) In addition to the Shepard volumes, the federal section will contain much of the following:

❑ Code of Federal Regulations

❑ Federal Register

❑ Bankruptcy Reporter

❑ Bankruptcy Digest

❑ Military Justice Reporter

❑ Opinions of the Attorney General

The following more specialized volumes will also generally be found in this section of the library.

❑ Civil Aeronautics Board Reports

❑ Interstate Commerce Commission Decisions

❑ Federal Trade Commission Decisions

❑ Federal Communications Commissions Decisions

❑ Federal Power Commission Decision

❑ United States Maritime Commission Reports

❑ National Labor Relations board Decisions

❑ Merit System Protection Board Decisions

❑ Occupation Safety and Health Review Commission Decisions

❑ Post Office Solicitor Opinions

❑ Securities and Exchange Commission Decisions

❑ Controller of the Treasury Decisions

❑ Treasury Decisions

❑ Immigration and Naturalization Administration Decisions

❑ Department of Interior (Indian Affairs) Decisions

❑ IRS

State and Territorial Law Section

The organization of the state section, which includes material for U.S. territories, parallels the basic organization of the federal section. The books are arranged in alphabetical order by state name, although the local statutes may be in a separate section.

In most law libraries, the available material on the home state far outstrips coverage of other states and territories. Using Florida as an example, here's what might be found in the home-state section of the law library.

Constitution of the State of Florida

Revised and amended, the constitution is published by the Florida Department of State and contains the constitution (indexed) without editorial comment or citations.

Florida Statutes (Laws)

Florida Statutes are published for each legislative session and are available from Florida's first General Assembly session in 1845 to the present, in their raw form, without commentary.

Statutes Annotated

The volumes of annotated statutes include the Florida Constitution with annotations and legal forms with comments. In these volumes, the laws and statutes are reprinted with annotations, using the same numbering system as in the *Florida Statutes*. They include notes on court decisions with points of law indicated, historical notes, law review commentaries on the subject, and other references, where applicable. Appropriate case listings and citations are included for the points of law, each of which is printed as an individual paragraph. The citations provide the case name and other pertinent information so you can find the case that played an important role in the interpretation of the statute. These volumes are indexed by subject in separate books to help you locate the appropriate section of the multivolume set of laws.

Court Rules

In Florida, for instance, court rules are published in one or more volumes. Most law libraries usually have the following items, among others:

❏ Evidence Code

❏ Rules of Civil Procedure

❏ Rules of Judicial Administration

❏ Rules of Criminal Procedure

❏ Worker's Compensation Rules of Procedure

❏ Rules of Probate and Guardianship Procedure

❏ Rules of Practice and Procedure for Traffic courts

❏ Small Claims Rules

❏ Rules of Juvenile Procedure

❏ Rules of Appellate Procedure

The individual court rule books make up the bible of every practicing attorney and judge, for the books describe the day-to-day conduct of the business of most court systems, including the federal system, circuit by circuit and judge by judge. (Also, if you are acting pro se, the appropriate rule book provides the information you may need to act in a professional manner. Most of this information can also be found on the websites of the individual courts.)

Case Law

Actual court decisions with editorial comments are provided in bound reporters. Each case appears with a heading that includes the plaintiff's name, case number, court name, and date (as shown in Figure C.2 on page 179). The editorial notes are divided into paragraphs relating to the points of law covered in the particular decision. Each specific point of law is assigned (in West Publishing's system of indexing and cross-referencing legal decision) a "key number." This key number can be used to locate other cases involving identical points of law throughout the West system. In addition to the key number, each point of law is numbered and codified with the same number placed in the body of the decision as a reference. This makes it possible to read the synopsis on the point of law and then quickly locate the specific words the court used regarding that point of law, eliminating the need to read the entire decision to find the court's opinion on a specific point.

Legal publishers put out continuous volumes of reporters that are geographically divided as follows:

❑ *The Atlantic Reporter,* which covers Connecticut, Delaware, Maine, Maryland, New Hampshire, New Jersey, Pennsylvania, and Rhode Island

❑ *The California Reporter*

❑ *New York State Reporter*

❑ *The Northeast Reporter,* which covers Illinois, Indiana, Massachusetts, New York, and Ohio

❑ *The Northwest Reporter,* which covers Iowa, Michigan, Minnesota, Nebraska, North Dakota, South Dakota, and Wisconsin

❑ *The Pacific Reporter,* which covers Alaska, Arizona, California, Colorado, Hawaii, Idaho, Kansas, Nevada, New Mexico, Oklahoma, Oregon, Utah, Washington, and Wyoming

❑ *The Southern Reporter,* which covers Alabama, Florida, Louisiana, and Mississippi

❑ *The Southwestern Reporter,* which covers Arkansas, Kentucky, Missouri, Tennessee, and Texas

Digests

These books provide an extraordinarily long index that describes, by subject, court cases that have been appealed. The digest itself is cross-referenced with a descriptive word index and a table of cases listing the plaintiff and defendant in all cases contained in the digest. To better understand the workings of the digest, see Figure C.4 for a typical listing.

Under the subject "landlord and tenant" and heading "possession, enjoyment, and use" is the topic or subheading of "right of entry and possession of tenant." Under that subheading, the digest describes a case that might have set a precedent on the subject of the listing. Cases may be similar, on point, relevant, or just helpful in understanding the application of the statute.

By finding the subject in its narrowest form possible in the digest, you can begin your research by reading the cases cited there. This listing opens the door to a particular avenue of research because all cases brought before the higher courts on appeal cite cases with precedents that they believe are in their favor and contain facts as close as possible to the case being argued. Reviewing these cases will lead to the next legal theory citing still more cases, and so on, all of which form the body of law on that particular subject. By following this line and not getting sidetracked by cases only marginally similar to yours, you should reach a conclusion—that is, you should accumulate a set of decisions that either prove or disprove your legal point.

Encyclopedia

A legal encyclopedia is similar to a digest except that it treats the subject as it might be treated in an entry in a general encyclopedia. It provides information, historical background, cases, and editorial comment on a particular subject of law. This is a good place for you to start your legal research.

Shepard's Citations

If you do any research in a law library, you will very quickly learn the name *Shepard. Shepard's Citations* is a system of case indexing that cross-references all reported cases and all existing points of law within those cases. In other words, *Shepard's Citations* provide the informational link between the case you are reviewing and other cases that have been cited by it or have some relevancy to it. Once you are familiar with the numbering system in a typ-

22 Fla D 2d—769 **LANDLORD & TENANT** ⇐129(2)

For references to other topics, see Descriptive-Word Index

specified right of way was not free from ambiguity, intent of parties was paramount consideration in determining whether words granting easement referred to width of way or were merely descriptive of property over which tenant might have way reasonably necessary to effectuate purpose of grant, and such intent would be ascertained by reference to surrounding circumstances.

Robinson v. Feltus, 68 So.2d 815.

⇐124(3)-125. *For other cases see earlier editions of this digest and the decennial digests.*

Library references

C.J.S. Landlord and Tenant.

⇐125. Tenantable condition of premises.

Library references

C.J.S. Landlord and Tenant § 303 et seq.

⇐125(1). In general.

Fla.App. 1981. There was no implied warranty on part of lessor that demised premises were safe or reasonably fit for occupation.

Alvarez v. DeAguirre, 395 So.2d 213.

Lessees could not bring on theory of breach of implied warranty, action against lessor owner for fire that started in electrical box behind kitchen stove allegedly due to faulty circuit breaker which caused overload.

Alvarez v. DeAguirre, 395 So.2d 213.

⇐125(2). Suitability of premises for the purpose for which they were leased.

Fla.App. 1980. Where mobile home was not readily transportable and was on blocks with wheels removed, intent of parties was to rent mobile home and slab for use as residence for period of indefinite duration, and mobile home was sufficiently affixed to ground with proper sewer and plumbing connections, mobile home was "real property," and not chattel, for purposes of determining whether landlord could be held liable for breach of an implied warranty that mobile home was fit for specific purpose.

Solomon v. Gentry, 388 So.2d 52.

Landlord is not liable to tenant for breach of implied warranty of fitness for specific purpose based on fire which broke out in mobile home and destroyed entire contents of home.

Solomon v. Gentry, 388 So.2d 52.

Fla.App. 3 Dist. 1982. When parties enter into a lease agreement with respect to a build-

(B) POSSESSION, ENJOYMENT, AND USE.

⇐126. Duty of tenant to take possession.

Library references

C.J.S. Landlord and Tenant § 307.

Bkrtcy.Fla. 1982. Where it was undisputed that premises were occupied and operated by wholly owned corporate shell created by debtor in Texas as convenience to satisfy legal requirement in that state, corporation name was trade name of all debtor's restaurants, funds and personnel involved in operation and all management control were provided by debtor, and landlord made no effort to disposess corporation as interloper, debtor, and not third party, occupied premises in question.

In re Interstate Restaurant Systems, Inc., 26 B.R. 298.

⇐127. Right of entry and possession of tenant.

Library references

C.J.S. Landlord and Tenant §§ 308, 309, 313.

Fla. 1942. Where broker pursuant to authority given by plaintiff leased plaintiff's residence to defendant on conditions stipulated by plaintiff, and put defendant in possession with aid of a key made by a locksmith when plaintiff's friend with whom he left key refused to deliver it to broker, defendant was not guilty of an "unlawful entry" on which plaintiff could maintain action for unlawful entry. F.S.A. § 82.01.

Caplan v. Burns, 6 So.2d 8, 149 Fla. 429.

Fla.App. 1979. Lessor may retain an interest in leased realty sufficient to permit releasing of the same property on a nonexclusive basis.

Century Village, Inc. v. Wellington, E, F, K, L, H, J, M, and G Condominium Ass'n, 370 So.2d 1244.

⇐128-129(1). *For other cases see earlier editions of this digest and the decennial digests.*

Library references

C.J.S. Landlord and Tenant.

⇐129. Actions for failure to deliver possession.

Library references

C.J.S. Landlord and Tenant §§ 314, 315.

⇐129(2). Pleading.

Figure C.4. Sample Digest Listing. Digests list cases, by subject matter, that have been appealed. Looking under the subject "landlord and tenant," you would find the subheading "right of entry and possession of tenant," and information referring you to the case of *Caplan v. Burns*.

🔑 127

🔑 127. Right of Entry and Possession of Tenant

Under Florida law, if you lease a residence from a broker who has the authority from the owner to make the deal on conditions stipulated by the owner and you had to break in or get a locksmith to let you in because the owner and/or broker could not or did not supply you with a key, you would not be guilty of unlawful entry.

F.S.A. §82.01—Caplan v. Burns, 6 S.2d 8, 149 Fla. 429.

"F.S.A." stands for Florida Statutes Annotated: "§82.01" means Section 82.01 of the Florida Statutes; the name of the plaintiff (Caplan) and the defendant (Burns) appear; "6 S.2d 8" is Volume 6 of the Southern Reporter, 2nd series, page 8; and "149 Fla. 429" refers to Volume 149 of the Florida Reporter, page 429.

The key number at the heading refers to the subject and is assigned by the editor of the volume. This number refers to all other references in the entire digest to the same point of law.

---

ical Shepard book, you will be able to trace forward the history of a case and similar cases up to the present through the entire court system. This is particularly important when you find a decision that supports your contention. Before you quote it in a memorandum of law—a written memorandum setting forth appropriate background, research, citations, and other authorities that support your position—"shepardize" the case to be sure that it was not modified or overturned at a later date. (See "Shepardizing" on page 193.)

Forms

Books and sets of forms for a given jurisdiction provide standard pleadings, practice, and specialized forms for use in that jurisdiction. If you are acting pro se, form books can be an essential tool. They may provide the outline of standard and accepted pleadings on hundreds of subjects, giving you an accepted plan of action to follow.

Readers' Guide to Periodicals

Readers' Guide to Periodicals can also get you articles on specific titles, legal treatises, and law review articles on the subject you are researching. Every legal article provides case citations.

Other Materials

There are several other categories of books in the home-state section that are worth pointing out. These include the following:

❑ Bar support publications

❑ Legislative history

❑ Miscellaneous texts

❑ Opinions of the Attorney General

❑ Special legal topics (from corporate law to environmental regulations)

This area of the state section may also have continuing education materials from the bar association for the state's bar members as well as hundreds of specialized publications on very narrow subjects of state law. They are certainly worth reviewing if you are dealing with one of those narrow specialties of the law, such as probate, juvenile, divorce, real estate, and worker's compensation.

The state section will obviously have a much fuller complement of law books on hand for the home state than for other states. Here's a typical listing of volumes contained in a Florida law library pertaining to New Jersey law.

❑ *New Jersey Constitution*

❑ *New Jersey Statutes Annotated* (including the Constitution)

❑ *New Jersey Court Rules* (with case synopses)

❑ *New Jersey Superior Court Reports,* which includes Appellate Division and Chancery Division (similar to equity)

Pocket Parts

It is impossible for any publisher to bring out bound volumes indexed and digested without a lengthy editorial process. Therefore, hardbound books are updated with soft-cover "pocket parts" (or occasionally loose-leaf pages) that are tucked away in the back of the hardcover volumes and updated periodically until new hardcover versions are available. It is essential to check these pocket parts for the most current information when working with a given set of law books. When I can't find the case I'm looking for, it usually means that I haven't checked the pocket part for that particular case or subject heading. More often than not, that is where I find the missing item.

❑ *New Jersey Law Digest*

❑ *Shepard's New Jersey Citations*

❑ The appropriate regional reporter (Some libraries put all regional reports in a separate section.)

While this complement of books may be smaller than that for the home state, the basic tools are certainly available for research and case preparation.

Specialty Areas of the Law Section

As shown in Figure C.3 on page 180, the specialty section of a typical law library contains textbooks, loose-leaf services—books produced in loose-leaf binders than can be easily updated on a weekly or monthly basis—and general and specific books on various subjects of the law. In this section, you'll find books on legal specialties such as tax law, probate, dissolution of marriage, and hundreds of other specialties.

General Reference Section

The general reference section in a typical library usually contains standard dictionaries and general encyclopedias, as well as references books, such as *Gray's Anatomy,* that you might find useful or necessary when working on a case. If you are acting pro se, you will find this section particularly valuable when it comes to learning about some of the unfamiliar terms and abbreviations used in the various areas of law. Meanwhile, to familiarize yourself with some of the abbreviations you may come across during the course of your legal research, see the inset "Some Common Legal Abbreviations" on page 191.

USING THE LAW LIBRARY

Before you attempt to use a law library, be aware of the relationship between some of the books described above. To show this relationship, let's research a hypothetical case. To do this, and with the permission of Thomson/West, we have preprinted (with our own annotations) several sections taken from various law books.

Sally Jenkins was injured in an auto accident. Although the defendant conceded liability, the issue of damages was brought to trial. At the time of the accident, Sally was entitled to receive Social Security and disability benefits (her disability was totally unrelated to the accident that was the sub-

Some Common Legal Abbreviations

Law books contain not only a vast amount of information, but a large and specialized collection of abbreviations as well. To do legal research effectively, you should become acquainted with the more commonly used abbreviations you will come across.

Administrat(ive,ion)	Admin	Federal	F., Fed
Appellate	App.	House of Rep.	H.R.
Associate	Assoc.	Institute	Inst.
Association	Assn.	International	Int'l
Board	Bd.	Law Journal	L.J.
Circuit Court (state)	Cir.Ct.	Law Review	L.Rev.
Circuit Court of Appeals	CirCt.App.	Municipal	Mun
Commission	Comm'n	North(ern)	N.
Commissioner	Comm'r	Securit(y, ies)	Sec.
Department	Dept.	Senate	S.
District	Dist.	South(ern)	S./
District Court (federal)	D.	Statute (federal)	U.S.C.
District Court (state)	Dist.Ct.	West(ern)	W.

Example of published sources:

Supreme Court Reporter	S.Ct.
Federal Reporter	F.2d
Federal Supplement	F.Supp.

ject of the damage claim). In addition to Sally's claim, her husband, who had lost a degree of consortium (love and affection) from his wife, claimed compensation for that loss.

The case went to trial and the Jenkins believed that the judge erred in his calculation of Sally's benefit income. The Jenkins appealed. The appellate court ruled in the Jenkins' favor and established a precedent. The appellate judge, in his opinion, cites the trial judge's interpretation of the statute known as §627.7372, "Collateral Sources of Indemnity." If you were involved in a similar situation, this is how you would trace the decision and the law.

Looking at Figure C.5 beginning on page 192, you can see that you would go to a *digest* and look up the subject. Finding the key number, you would then go to the volume containing that section (the section on damages) and look for the key number.

1 Begin in the *Digest's* index. Look up the general subject you are interested in, in this case, damages.

2 Under damages, find the specific situation that applies (benefits incident to injury), and locate the key number (60).

DAMAGES

References are to Digest Topics and Key Numbers

DAMAGES—Cont'd
MITIGATION—Cont'd
  Benefits incident to injury. Damag 60
  Breach of contract. Damag 62(4)
    For sale of goods. Sales 384(7), 418(7)
  Breach of contract for sale of goods. Sales 384(7), 418(7)
  Death actions. Death 91
  Discharged fireman. Damag 62(1)
  Dishonor of check—
    Payee's duty. Damag 62(1)
  Duty of person injured to prevent or reduce. Damag 62(1–4)
  Duty to prevent or reduce damage—
    Generally. Damag 62(1)
    Breach of contract. Damag 62(4)
      Buyer's duty to purchase similar property elsewhere. Sales 418(7)
      Seller's duty to resell goods. Sales 384(7)
  Discharged servant's duty to seek other employment. Mast & S 42

3 Go to the *Digest* volume that contains the subject Damages.

4 Under Damages, locate key number 60, and find the citation for the case.

DAMAGES ⬅62(4)

West's F.S.A. § 768.76.—Measom v. Rainbow Connection Preschool, Inc., 568 So.2d 123.
  Fla.App. 5 Dist. 1985. Collateral source statute [West's F.S.A. § 627.7372] expressing policy of state that injured person may not recover from tort-feasor such amounts as injured party has received from collateral sources is constitutional. —Amica Mut. Ins. Co. v. Gifford, 473 So.2d 220.
  Fla.App. 5 Dist. 1983. Amica Mut. Ins. Co. v. Gifford, 434 So.2d 1015, appeal after remand 473 So.2d 220.

⬅**60. Benefits incident to injury.**
  Fla.App. 1 Dist. 1985. Social security benefits and state retirement disability benefits to which plaintiff was entitled prior to injuries incurred in automobile accident, but which plaintiff first received following accident and which compensated plaintiff for damages not sustained or claimed in the accident, were not collateral to award of damages for injuries incurred in automobile accident, and thus, such benefits could not be deducted from damage award. West's F.S.A. § 627.7372. —Jenkins v. West, 463 So.2d 581.
  Fla.App. 4 Dist. 1983. Robert E. Owen & Asso-

Figure C.5. Tracing a Decision. To find a case that may be relevant to your own, there are five steps you need to follow. They are detailed above.

Once you find the case and have reviewed the synopsis and the facts seem to fit your situation, then review the statute (or statutes) that the case and the synopsis relied on. In this instance, you would turn to Statute §627.7372 in the *Annotated Statutes for the State of Florida*. (See Figure C.6 on page 199.)

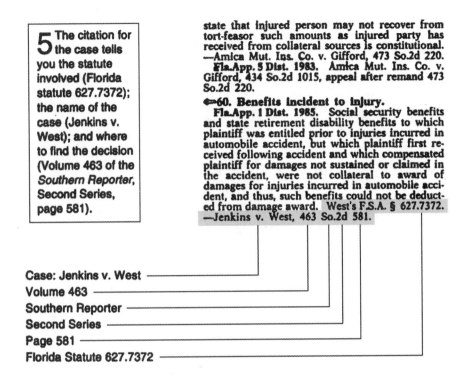

5 The citation for the case tells you the statute involved (Florida statute 627.7372); the name of the case (Jenkins v. West); and where to find the decision (Volume 463 of the *Southern Reporter, Second Series,* page 581).

state that injured person may not recover from tort-feasor such amounts as injured party has received from collateral sources is constitutional. —Amica Mut. Ins. Co. v. Gifford, 473 So.2d 220.

Fla.App. 5 Dist. 1983. Amica Mut. Ins. Co. v. Gifford, 434 So.2d 1015, appeal after remand 473 So.2d 220.

←60. Benefits incident to injury.

Fla.App. 1 Dist. 1985. Social security benefits and state retirement disability benefits to which plaintiff was entitled prior to injuries incurred in automobile accident, but which plaintiff first received following accident and which compensated plaintiff for damages not sustained or claimed in the accident, were not collateral to award of damages for injuries incurred in automobile accident, and thus, such benefits could not be deducted from damage award. West's F.S.A. § 627.7372. —Jenkins v. West, 463 So.2d 581.

Case: Jenkins v. West
Volume 463
Southern Reporter
Second Series
Page 581
Florida Statute 627.7372

To understand how the statute was applied and to review the details of the case that you are planning to cite in support of your own case, look at the actual record of the court case in the appropriate *reporter* that was cited in the digest and the annotated statutes (see Figure C.7 on pages 196–197). If you know the plaintiff's name, you can find a particular case in the digest simply by looking up the name in the alphabetical listing. (See Figure C.8 on page 198.)

Shepardizing

As you've learned, the law is fluid; decisions and interpretations continually change as new cases are brought before the courts. Cases may be reviewed and findings may be changed, affirmed, or reversed by higher courts. In order to be sure that the case or cases that you have found are the current renditions of the law and are reflective of the decisions being made, it is necessary to check the status of your research. *Shepard's Citations* is available for that task. The many volumes of *Shepard's Citations* contain tables of cases and references to any subsequent activity on the same subject within the court systems. Using Shepard will permit you to shepardize,

Research Plan

Since law involves both statutes and precedents, you need to research both to gain a thorough understanding of a particular legal matter. When you find a case with similar or the same set of facts as your situation, it is called *being on point*. A case on point may provide you with a treasure trove of information—that is, other cases on point, a judge's words explaining the statute and how it applies to the facts of the case, and possible other sources for additional research. The higher the court, the more weight the precedent will have. The following is a basic research plan:

1. Use a digest to look up the subject you wish to research.

2. Find the key number for the subject.

3. Go to correct volume of the digest containing that subject.

4. Look for the same key number.

5. Review the synopsis to establish if the facts seem to fit your case.

6. Look up the annotated statute that synopsis relied on.

7. If you are planning to cite that case, go to the appropriate reporter and review the case.

8. Shepardize the case to be sure that the information you found is current.

Having the ability to research case law will empower you. Through diligent research and study, the courts interpretation of the controlling statute(s) of your case will become clear and you will gain an understanding of the subject matter of your case. An understanding of the precedents surrounding your case will even allow you to do a better job of gathering evidence.

or review the current status of your research (see Figure C.9). These books are also useful for finding similar cases to the one you are Shepardizing.

To Shepardize a case—that is, to find out whether the decision you plan to cite was subsequently changed, affirmed, or reversed—follow the steps below.

1. Locate the correct set of *Shepard's Citations* for the type of authority you are working with: *United States Supreme Court Decisions, Federal Reporter, Federal Supplements, Regional Reports,* or *State Decisions.*

2. Be sure you have the correct volume numbers, as many of the Shepard's books have more than one volume; State volumes for states, case vol-

INSURANCE   **§ 627.7372**

627.7372. Collateral sources of indemnity

[See main volume for text of (1) and (2)]

(3) Notwithstanding any other provision of this section, benefits received under Medicare or any other federal program providing for a federal government lien on the plaintiff's recovery, the Workers' Compensation Law or the Medicaid program of Title XIX of the Social Security Act,[1] or from any medical services program administered by the Department of Health and Rehabilitative Services shall not be considered a collateral source.

Amended by Laws 1986, c. 86-220, § 70, eff. Oct. 1, 1986; Laws 1989, c. 89-203, § 1, eff. Oct. 1, 1989.

[1] 42 U.S.C.A. § 1396 et seq.

Historical and Statutory Notes

Laws 1985, c. 85-320, § 2, quoted the text of this section without making an amendment.

Laws 1986, c. 86-220, § 70, eff. Oct. 1, 1986, inserted in subsec. (3) "Medicaid program of Title XIX of the Social Security Act, or from any medical services program administered by the Department of Health and Rehabilitative Services".

Laws 1989, c. 89-203, § 1, eff. Oct. 1, 1989, in subsec. (3), provided that benefits received under Medicare or any other federal programs providing for federal government liens on plaintiff's recovery would not be considered a collateral source.

Law Review Commentaries

Florida's new collateral source rule. William A. Kebler and Steven L. Robbins, 64 Fla.B.J. 25 (Dec.1990).

No Fault Systems. Josephine Y. King (Winter 1984) 4 Pace L.Rev. 297.

————

Notes of Decisions

Compromise and settlement 6
Employee benefit plan 12
Future benefits 13
Insurance covering health, sickness, or income disability 2.5
Preemption 1.6
· Products liability 9
Purpose 1.5
Recovery from tortfeasor 14
Ships and shipping 10
Social security 11
Subrogation right of insurer 7

42 F.S.A.—5
1992 P.P.

Wrongful death 8

————

1. Validity

In truck driver's action against tire manufacturer for breach of implied warranty of mer-

2. Construction and application

Evidence of collateral source payments is allowed in motor vehicle injury cases only to establish set-off for damages awarded for same expenses under Florida law; thus, as long as plaintiffs do not seek recovery for expenses already covered by collateral source payments, evidence of those past payments is irrelevant to any issue before court. Shessel v. Murphy, C.A. 11 (Fla.)1991, 920 F.2d 784.

Under this section, evidence of disability payments to be received by personal injury plaintiff in future was not admissible. Shessel v. Murphy, C.A. 11 (Fla.)1991, 920 F.2d 784.

Defendant in personal injury suit arising from motor vehicle accident was properly precluded from introducing collateral source payments

Amount received by injured motorcyclist from insurers for past medical expenses could only be deducted against portion of verdict representing same item of damages, not against total verdict. Ganley v. U.S., C.A. 11 (Fla.)1989, 878 F.2d 1351.

Social security benefits and state retirement disability benefits to which plaintiff was entitled prior to injuries incurred in automobile accident, but which plaintiff first received following accident and which compensated plaintiff for damages not sustained or claimed in the accident, were not collateral to award of damages for injuries incurred in automobile accident, and thus, such benefits could not be deducted from damage award. Jenkins v. West, App. 1 Dist., 463 So.2d 581 (1985).

179

————

Figure C.6. Using an Annotated Statutes Volume. Annotated statutes volumes reprint statutes together with copies of relevant court decisions, law review commentaries, and other references. The case of *Jenkins v. West* is among a number of annotations given for Florida Statute §627.7372.

JENKINS v. WEST   Fla. **581**
Cite as 463 So.2d 581 (Fla.App. 1 Dist. 1985)

maintain life insurance for the benefit of his minor child.

Under the facts of this case and in light of the above authorities, we find that appellant is entitled to the insurance proceeds in question. The trial judge erred in refusing to impose a constructive trust as to those funds.

REVERSED.

WENTWORTH and THOMPSON, JJ., concur.

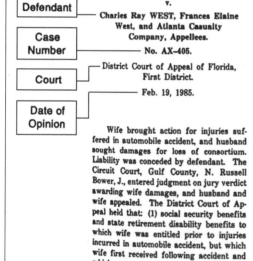

Plaintiff — Sally Clayton JENKINS, joined by her husband, Taylor Jenkins, Appellants,

v.

Defendant — Charles Ray WEST, Frances Elaine West, and Atlanta Casualty Company, Appellees.

Case Number — No. AX–405.

Court — District Court of Appeal of Florida, First District.

Date of Opinion — Feb. 19, 1985.

Wife brought action for injuries suffered in automobile accident, and husband sought damages for loss of consortium. Liability was conceded by defendant. The Circuit Court, Gulf County, N. Russell Bower, J., entered judgment on jury verdict awarding wife damages, and husband and wife appealed. The District Court of Appeal held that: (1) social security benefits and state retirement disability benefits to which wife was entitled prior to injuries incurred in automobile accident, but which wife first received following accident and which compensated wife for damages not sustained or claimed in the accident, were not collateral to award of damages for injuries incurred in automobile accident, and thus, such benefits could not be de-

ducted from damage award, and (2) husband was entitled to at least nominal damages, since husband offered substantial, undisputed evidence of loss of consortium, and since liability was conceded.

Reversed and remanded.

1. Damages ⟐=60
Social security benefits and state retirement disability benefits to which plaintiff was entitled prior to injuries incurred in automobile accident, but which plaintiff first received following accident and which compensated plaintiff for damages not sustained or claimed in the accident, were not collateral to award of damages for injuries incurred in automobile accident, and thus, such benefits could not be deducted from damage award. West's F.S.A. § 627.7372.

2. Damages ⟐=11
Husband, whose wife was injured in automobile accident, was entitled to at least nominal damages, since husband offered substantial, undisputed evidence of loss of consortium, and since liability was conceded.

———

Cecil G. Costin, Port St. Joe, for appellants.

Jack G. Williams of Bryant, Higby & Williams, Panama City, for appellees.

PER CURIAM.

On September 2, 1982, plaintiff Sally Jenkins was injured in an automobile accident for which defendant conceded liability. The issue of damages was tried to a jury. Loss of income, past or future, was not claimed.

Prior to this accident, plaintiff was under the care of an orthopedic surgeon for a previous disability. Her left kneecap was removed, and, pursuant to her doctor's advice, she retired from her employment. Plaintiff was totally disabled prior to the September 2, 1982 accident. Plaintiff began drawing social security in 1981 and applied for disability under the State retire-

Figure C.7. **Using a Reporter.** Reporters provide the actual records of court cases. The record of *Jenkins v. West,* found on page 581 of Volume 463 of *West's Southern Reporter, Second Series,*

ment program prior to the accident, but received her first payment in April of 1983, subsequent to the accident.

At trial, the court instructed the jury that any social security payments and State retirement program disability payments received by the plaintiff were collateral source payments which should be deducted from their overall verdict. The instruction was based on Section 627.7372, Florida Statutes (1981). We do not construe that statute to allow deduction for social security benefits and disability payments which preexisted the instant accident. Indeed, an interpretation which would allow such a deduction could render the statute subject to challenge on constitutional grounds.[1]

[1] We hold that social security benefits and state retirement disability benefits to which plaintiff is entitled prior to the instant injury which compensate plaintiff for damages not sustained or claimed in the instant injury, are not collateral to an award of damages for the instant injury. *See Transit Homes, Inc. v. Bellamy,* 671 S.W.2d 153 (Arkansas 1984).[2] The jury instruction was error; therefore, the award is reversed.

[2] As to the second point on appeal, we agree that the plaintiff Taylor Jenkins offered substantial, undisputed evidence of loss of consortium. *Hagens v. Hilston,* 388 So.2d 1379 (Fla. 2d DCA 1980); *Albritton v. State Farm Mutual Insurance Company,* 382 So.2d 1267 (Fla. 2d DCA 1980); *Webber v. Jordan,* 366 So.2d 51 (Fla. 2d DCA 1978); *Shaw v. Peterson,* 376 So.2d 433 (Fla. 1st DCA 1979). Therefore, since liability was conceded, he is entitled to at least nominal damages. A zero verdict cannot stand.

For the foregoing reasons, the case is reversed and cause remanded for a new

trial on all damages consistent with this opinion.

BOOTH and SHIVERS, JJ., and TILLMAN PEARSON (Ret.), Associate Judge, concur.

---

1. Constitutional vulnerability on this or any other ground is not at issue in this appeal.

2. In *Transit Homes, Inc. v. Bellamy,* 671 S.W.2d 153 at 160 (Ark.1984), the Arkansas Supreme Court explained:
   We do not think the court erred in allowing appellants credit for the $1,257 which the

Earlier court decision (precedent) the judges may have relied on. Precedent affirmed.

This court's holding (the decision).

allows you to review the details of the case. Reviewing the record of the case, one finds that the appellate court reversed the lower court's decision, citing the precedent *Transit Holms v. Bellamy.*

```
Jenkins v. Wainwright, CA11 (Fla), 763    Jennings v. State, FlaApp, 106 So2d 99.    JEPSCO Bldg. Mi
  F2d 1390.—Crim Law 394.1(3);  Jury        —Crim Law 518(1), 531(3).                   atwick Steel Lat
  33(2.1);  Witn 198(1), 372(1).          Jennings v. State, FlaApp 2 Dist,  419        BR 122.  See JEP
Jenkins v. Wainwright, CAFla, 488 F2d       So2d 750.—Crim Law 394.4(3).                Inc. In re.
  136, cert den 94 SCt 2620, 417 US 917,  Jennings v. State, FlaApp 3 Dist,  457      Jepsen v. Florida
  41 LEd2d 222.—Hab Corp 45.2(4).           So2d 587.—Crim Law 867.                     Fla, 754 F2d 924.
Jenkins v. Wainwright, Fla, 322 So2d      Jennings v. Stewart, FlaApp, 308 So2d         46(12).
  477.—Courts 207.1, 475(1);  Crim Law      611.—App & E 204(7).                      Jepsen v. Florida
  1210(4);  Hab Corp 44.                  Jennings v. U. S., CAFla, 391 F2d 512,        Fla, 610 F2d 13
Jenkins v. Wainwright, Fla, 285 So2d        cert den 89 SCt 154, 393 US 868, 21         Fed Civ Proc 160
  5.—Crim Law 1216(2).                      LEd2d 136.—Arrest 68(1);  Crim Law        J. E. R. v. State, F1
Jenkins  v.  West,  FlaApp 1 Dist,  463     317, 412.1(2).                              Infants 212.
  So2d 581.—Damag 11, 60.                 Jennings v. Wainwright, CAFla, 486         Jerabek v. Heckler,
Jenkins v. Wilson, FlaApp, 397 So2d         F2d 1041, cert den 94 SCt 2614, 417         —Social S 140.20,
  773.—Work Comp 1565.                      US 913, 41 LEd2d 218.—Hab Corp 85.       Jerabek v. U. S., C.
Jenkins, State ex rel., v. Maginnis, Fla-   4(1).                                       Embez 44(1).
  App, 254 So2d 11.  See State ex rel.    Jennings Const. Corp. v. C. H. V. Inv.     Jergens v. C.I.R., U
  Jenkins v. Maginnis.                      Corp., FlaApp, 386 So2d 290.—Judges         US 784, 88 LEd
Jenkins Trucking, Inc. v. Emmons, Fla,      32.                                         F2d 497.
  207 So2d 278.—App & E 483.
```

Figure C.8. Using a Digest's Index. If you know the name of the plaintiff in a case in which you are interested, you can locate the digest listing for it by looking up the plaintiff's name in the alphabetical listing.

umes for cases, and so on. Also, be sure you have the correct volume for the date of your case—more than one volume may be needed depending on the date of the authority you are shepardizing.

3. Use the correct table of citations. You must use the correct series (reports of cases are sometimes found in several different series). If the case you are working with does not appear in the table, you might have the wrong series.

Computerized Research

With today's extensive use of computers, much of today's legal research can be performed on several key websites. (See the Resources section on page 215.) The information provided by these websites and others like them can save you a trip to a law library.

In particular, the websites of LexisNexis and Westlaw provide vast research databases as well as access to many other publications such as newspapers and periodicals. Other specialized legal websites are also available. Many of these online research services also provide their databases on CD-ROMS.

Although working from your own computer is more convenient than traveling to a law library, it is important that you learn how to use the traditional method of legal research in case you do not have access to a legal research website or if a computer is unavailable. And while online legal research services greatly enhance and streamline the ability to research the law, the costs for their use may be high.

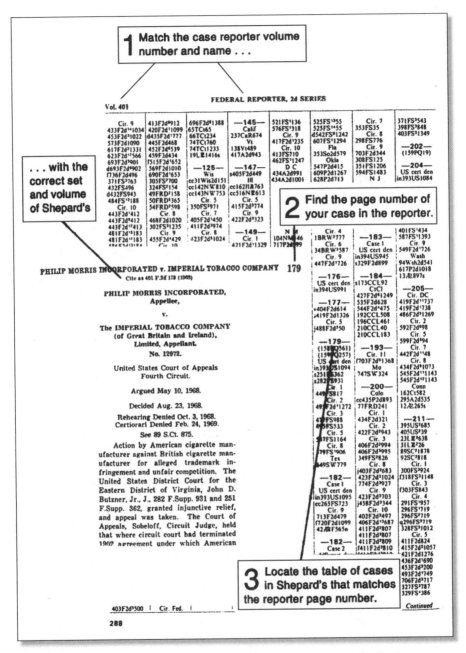

Figure C.9. Shepardizing a Case. To find out whether the decision you plan to cite was subsequently changed, or reversed, follow the steps detailed above.

4. To conduct a thorough research job, you must *shepardize* in the tables for all parallel citations, as well as in the principal citation. For example, for *Wisconsin Reports, Second Series,* the parallel reporter is *Northwestern Reporter, Second Series* (Wisconsin cases).

5. Once you have found the correct table of citations, look for the volume number you are sheypardizing.

6. Once you have found the correct volume(s) and the correct page(s) containing the volume number of the case reporter that has your case, find in the table the page number of your case. Then review the citations listed under it. Citations in parentheses indicate parallel cases. It is important to check the abbreviations listed in the front of each Shepard volume to completely understand the citations. For instance, raised letters refer to head notes in the case you are reviewing, which means a particular point of law can be found in a case with the same head note. When attempting to shepardize a particular point of law, this can be extremely helpful.

When you are using the results of your legal research in a legal memo, brief, or pleading, use a legal form book to help you write the citation correctly, as mentioned under "Authorities." The basic form for a citation contains the following information: the name of the case; published sources, if any; a notation that indicates the court; year or date of decision; and subsequent history, if any.

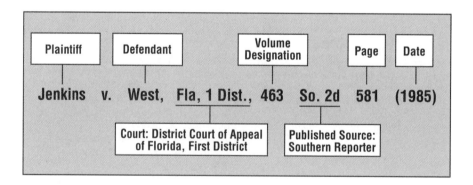

One important caveat: Courts may overrule part of cases or entire cases. Don't rely totally on Shepard; instead, retrieve and read the authority cited. There are many nuances in the law that may or may not apply to your case, and cryptic numbered codes cannot transmit them.

APPENDIX D

Statute of Limitations Applicable to Legal Malpractice

The Statute of Limitations establishes a time limit, or cut-off date, in which a former client can bring a legal malpractice case against his or her lawyer. Beyond the statute of limitations cut-off date, a person will not be able to sue his or her former lawyer even in a clear case of the lawyer's negligence. When a lawyer is on the receiving end of such a lawsuit, he or she will usually try to get the case dismissed due to the statute of limitation. Before filing a legal malpractice action, check your jurisdiction's statue of limitation under the cause of action you wish to use. In some instances, it may be possible—if the time limit has expired on the cause of action you were going to use—to switch tactics and use a cause of action that has not yet expired. For instance, unjust enrichment in a specific state may have a longer period in which an action may be brought than fraud as a case of action. Keep in mind that any cause of action that you wish to pursue in related matters may have different statutes of limitation. So the sooner you move on a case, the better.

The following is a state-by-state guide to the statute of limitations. (The symbol § is legal shorthand for the word *section*.) Keep in mind that the law is fluid and always changing, so check your appropriate current statutes before filing a lawsuit.

ALASKA

Under Section 09.10.070: actions for torts, for injury to personal property, for certain statutory liabilities, and against peace officers and coroners to be brought in two years.

ALABAMA

Under Section 6-5-574(a): two years.

ARIZONA

Under A.R.S. Section 12-542 (2003) and Section 12-542: injury to person; injury when death ensues; injury to property; conversion of property; forcible entry and forcible detainer; two-year limitation, except as provided in § 12-551, there shall be commenced and prosecuted within two years after the cause of action accrues, and not afterward, the following actions:

1) For injuries done to the person of another including causes of action for medical malpractice as defined in § 12-561.

2) For injuries done to the person of another when death ensues from such injuries, which action shall be considered as accruing at the death of the party injured.

3) For trespass for injury done to the estate or the property of another.

4) For taking or carrying away the goods and chattels of another.

5) For detaining the personal property of another and for converting such property to one's own use.

6) For forcible entry or forcible detainer, which action shall be considered as accruing at the commencement of the forcible entry or detainer.

Legal malpractice actions are subject to the two-year statute of limitations for tort claims set forth in this section, and accrue when 1) the plaintiff knows or reasonably should know of the attorney's negligent conduct, and 2) the plaintiff's damages are ascertainable and not speculative or contingent. (*Kiley v. Jennings, Strouss & Salmon,* 187 Ariz. 136, 927 P.2d 796 [Ct. App. 1996]).

ARKANSAS CODE ARCHIVE DIRECTORY

Under A.C.A. Section 16-56-105 (2002): actions with limitation of three years. The following actions shall be commenced within three years after the cause of action accrues:

1) All actions founded upon any contract, obligation, or liability not under seal and not in writing, excepting such as are brought upon the judgment or decree of some court of record of the United States or of this or some other state.

2) All actions for arrearages of rent not reserved by some instrument in writing, under seal.

3) All actions founded on any contract or liability, expressed or implied.

4) All actions for trespass on lands.

5) All actions for libels.

6) All actions for taking or injuring any goods or chattels.

CALIFORNIA

Under CA Code 340: one year from discovery, or four years from date of act or omission, whichever occurs first.

COLORADO REVISED STATUTES

Under C.R.S. 13-80-102 (2002): general limitation of actions, two years.

1) The following civil actions, regardless of the theory upon which suit is brought, or against whom suit is brought, shall be commenced within two years after the cause of action accrues, and not thereafter:

   (a) Tort actions, including but not limited to actions for negligence, trespass, malicious abuse of process, malicious prosecution, outrageous conduct, interference with relationships, and tortuous breach of contract; except that this paragraph (a) does not apply to any tort action arising out of the use or operation of a motor vehicle as set forth in § 13-80-101 (1) (n);

   (b) All actions for strict liability, absolute liability, or failure to instruct or warn;

   (c) All actions, regardless of the theory asserted, against any veterinarian;

   (d) All actions for wrongful death.

   (e) Repealed.

   (f) All actions against any public or governmental entity or any employee of a public or governmental entity for which insurance coverage is provided pursuant to article 14 of title 24, C.R.S.;

   (g) All actions upon liability created by a federal statute where no period of limitation is provided in said federal statute;

   (h) All actions against any public or governmental entity or any employee of a public or governmental entity, except as otherwise provided in this section or § 13-80-103;

   (i) All other actions of every kind for which no other period of limitation is provided;

   (j) All actions brought under § 42-6-204, C.R.S.;

   (k) All actions brought under § 13-21-109 (2).

CONNECTICUT

Under Conn. General Statute: two years for mistake in title search, but in no event more than ten years.

DELAWARE

Under Section 8106: actions subject to three-year limitation.

No action to recover damages for trespass, no action to regain possession of personal chattels, no action to recover damages for the detention of personal chattels, no action to recover a debt not evidenced by a record or by an instrument under seal, no action based on a detailed statement of the mutual demands in the nature of debit and credit between parties arising out of contractual or fiduciary relations, no action based on a promise, no action based on a statute, and no action to recover damages caused by an injury unaccompanied with force or resulting indirectly from the act of the defendant shall be brought after the expiration of three years from the accruing of the cause of such action; subject, however, to the provisions of § 8108–8110, 8119 and 8127 of this title.

DISTRICT OF COLUMBIA

Under Section 12-301: limitation of time for bringing actions. Except as otherwise specifically provided by law, actions for the following purposes may not be brought after the expiration of the period specified below from the time the right to maintain the action accrues:

3) for the recovery of damages for an injury to real or personal property, three years.

FLORIDA

Under FSA 95-11(4): two years.

GEORGIA

Legal malpractice: in a legal malpractice action filed subsequent to the running of the four-year statute of limitations, where there was no evidence giving rise to factual merit in plaintiff's claim that the limitations statute was tolled due to fraud, and where there existed no justifiable issue of law as to such claim, the trial court erred in denying defendant attorney's motion for attorney fees. (*Brown v. Kinser*, 218 Ga. App. 385, 461 S.E.2d 564 [1995]).

Under Section 9-3-96, Tolling of Limitations for Fraud of Defendant: If the defendant or those under whom he claims are guilty of a fraud by which the plaintiff has been debarred or deterred from bringing an action, the period of limitation shall run only from the time of the plaintiff's discovery of the fraud.

HAWAII

Under HRS Section 657-1 (2003), Division 4, Courts and Judicial Proceedings, Title 36, Civil Remedies and Defenses and Special Proceedings, Chapter 657. Limitation of Actions, Part I, Personal Actions, § 657-1: six years.

IDAHO

Under Idaho Code 5-219(4): two years.

ILLINOIS

Under Section 13-214.3: two years/six years from discovery.

INDIANA

Under Ind. Code 34-4-19-11: two years.

IOWA

Under Section 614.1. Period: actions may be brought within the times herein limited, respectively, after their causes accrue, and not afterward, except when otherwise specially declared:

2) Injuries to person or reputation—relative rights—statute penalty. Those founded on injuries to the person or reputation, including injuries to relative rights, whether based on contract or tort, or for a statute penalty, within two years.

KANSAS

Under K.S.A. Section 60-512 (2002). Chapter 60, Procedure, Civil, Article 5, Limitations of Actions, Personal Actions and General Provisions, 60-512: actions limited to three years. . . . 27, 28 (1988). "Legal Malpractice—The Elusive Statute of Limitations," . . .

KENTUCKY

Under Section 411.165. Liability of Attorney for Professional Negligence:

(1) If any attorney employed to attend to professional business neglects to attend to the business, after being paid anything for his services, or attends to the business negligently, he shall be liable to the client for all damages and costs sustained by reason thereof.

(2) If any attorney employed to attend to any professional business receives his fee and does not attend to the business, he may be sued and made to refund the fee.

Under Section 413.245. Actions for Professional Service Malpractice:

Notwithstanding any other prescribed limitation of actions which might otherwise appear applicable, except those provided in KRS 413.140, a civil action, whether brought in tort or contract, arising out of any act or omission in rendering, or failing to render, professional services for others shall be brought within one (1) year from the date of the occurrence or from the date when the cause of action was, or reasonably should have been, discovered by the party injured. Time shall not commence against a party under legal disability until removal of the disability.

LOUISIANA

Under La. Code 9:5605(B): one year/three years from discovery.

MAINE

Under MRSA 753-A: six years.

MASSACHUSETTS

Under Chap. 765: three years.

MICHIGAN

Under Mich. Code 600.5805: two years.

MONTANA

Under Mont. Code 27-2-206: three years from discovery/maximum ten years.

MARYLAND

Under MD Courts and Judicial Proceedings Code Ann. Section 5-101 (2002): three-year limitation in general.

A civil action at law shall be filed within three years from the date it accrues unless another provision of the code provides a different period of time within which an action shall be commenced.

MINNESOTA

Under Stat. Section 541.07 (2002): two- or three-year limitations.

Except where the Uniform Commercial Code, this section, § 148A.06, 541.05, 541.073, or 541.076 otherwise prescribes, the following actions shall be commenced within two years:

1) for libel, slander, assault, battery, false imprisonment, or other tort, resulting in personal injury, and all actions against veterinarians as defined in chapter 156, for malpractice, error, mistake or failure to cure, whether based on contract or tort; provided a counterclaim may be pleaded as a defense to any action for services brought by a veterinarian after the limitations period if it was the property of the party pleading it at the time it became barred and was not barred at the time the claim sued on originated, but no judgment thereof except for costs can be rendered in favor of the party so pleading it.

MISSISSIPPI

Under MISS. Code Ann. Section 15-1-29 (2003): limitations applicable to actions on accounts and unwritten contracts.

Except as otherwise provided in the Uniform Commercial Code, actions on an open account or account stated not acknowledged in writing, signed by the debtor, and on any unwritten contract, express or implied, shall be commenced within three years next after the cause of such action accrued, and not after, except that an action based on an unwritten contract of employment shall be commenced within one year next after the cause of such.

MISSOURI

Under Section 516.120: within five years:

1) All actions upon contracts, obligations or liabilities, express or implied,

except those mentioned in § 516.11, and except upon judgments of a court of record, and except where a different time is herein limited:

4) An action for taking, detaining, or injuring any goods or chattel, including actions for the recovery of specific personal property, or for any other injury to the person or rights of another, not arising on contract and not herein otherwise enumerated;

NEBRASKA

Under NEB. Statute 25-222: two years/maximum ten years.

NEVADA

Under NEV. Statute 11.207: four years.

NEW HAMPSHIRE

Under NH Statute 508.4: three years.

NEW JERSEY

Under Section 2A:14-2. 2 years; actions for injuries to person by wrongful act

Every action at law for an injury to the person caused by the wrongful act, neglect or default of any person within this state shall be commenced within two years next after the cause of any such action shall have accrued.

§ 2A:53A-26. "Licensed person" defined. As used in this act, "licensed person" means any person who is licensed as: c) an attorney admitted to practice law in New Jersey;

N.J. Stat. Ann. § 2A:53A-27 required malpractice claims to be supported by an affidavit of merit from another attorney.

N.J. Stat. Ann. § 2A:53A-27 applies to any action for personal injuries, wrongful death or property damage resulting from an alleged act of malpractice by a licensed person. An attorney admitted to practice law in New Jersey is one of the professionals defined by the statute as a "licensed person." N.J. Stat. Ann. § 2A:53A-26c.

NEW MEXICO

Under Section 37-1-4. Accounts and Unwritten Contracts; Injuries to Property; Conversion; Fraud; Unspecified Actions: Those founded upon accounts and unwritten contracts; those brought for injuries to property or for the conversion of personal property or for relief upon the ground of fraud, and all other actions not herein otherwise provided for and specified within four years.

NEW YORK

Six-Year Statute

Under Section 213: actions to be commenced within six years—where not otherwise provided for; on contract; on sealed instrument; on bond or note, and mortgage upon real property; by state based on misappropriation of public property; based on mistake; by corporation against director, officer or stockholder; based on fraud

The following actions must be commenced within six years:

2) an action upon a contractual obligation or liability, express or implied, except as provided in section two hundred thirteen-a of this article or article 2 of the Uniform Commercial Code or article 36-B of the general business law;

Under CPLR Section 213(2), there is a six year statute of limitations on an action for legal malpractice based on an attorney's failure to commence a trespass action, since such an action is one for failure to exercise due care in the performance of a contract, seeking recovery for damages.

Three-Year Statute

Where plaintiff fails to commence action to recover damages on legal malpractice claim within three years of accrual of cause of action, and seeks to rely on six-year contract statute of limitations to protect that claim, damages will be limited to those damages recoverable for breach of contract; to extent that legal malpractice claim seeks damages different from or greater than those customarily recoverable under breach of contract claim, three-year period of CLS CPLR § 214(6) will govern.

NORTH CAROLINA

Under N.C. Gen. Stat. Section 1-15 (c): four-year statute of repose and three-year statute of limitations.

NORTH DAKOTA

Under ND Cent. Code 28-01-18(3): two years.

OHIO

Under Section 4705.06. Liability of Attorneys; Prosecution: if a suit is dismissed for the nonattendance of an attorney at law practicing in any court of record, it shall be at his costs, if he has not a just and reasonable excuse. He shall be liable for all damages his client sustains by such dismissal, or any other neglect of his duty, to be recovered in any court of record. Such attorney receiving money for his client, and refusing or neglecting to pay it when demanded, shall be proceeded against in a summary way, on motion, before any court of record, either in the county in which the judgment on which such money has been collected was rendered, or in the county in which such attorney resides, in the same manner and be liable to the same penalties as sheriffs and coroners are for money received on execution.

Under Section 2305.11. Time Limitations for Bringing Certain Actions:

A) An action for libel, slander, malicious prosecution, or false imprisonment, an action for malpractice other than an action upon a medical, dental, optometric, or chiropractic claim, or an action upon a statute for a penalty or forfeiture shall be commenced within one year after the cause of action accrued, provided that an action by an employee for the payment of unpaid minimum wages, unpaid overtime compensation, or liquidated damages by reason of the nonpayment of minimum wages or overtime compensation shall be commenced within two years after the cause of action accrued.

OKLAHOMA

Under 12 Okl. St. Section 95 (2003). Limitation of Other Actions:
Civil actions other than for the recovery of real property can only be brought within the following periods, after the cause of action shall have accrued, and not afterward:

3) Within two years: An action for trespass upon real property; an action for taking, detaining, or injuring personal property, including actions for the specific recovery of personal property; an action for injury to the rights of another, not arising on contract, and not hereinafter enumerated; an action for relief on the ground of fraud—the cause of action in such case shall not be deemed to have accrued until the discovery of the fraud.

OREGON

Under ORS Section 12.110 (2001): actions for certain injuries to person not arising on contract; action for overtime or premium pay; action for professional malpractice; effect of fraud or deceit; action for injuries to person arising from nuclear incident.

1) An action for assault, battery, false imprisonment, or for any injury to the person or rights of another, not arising on contract, and not especially enumerated in this chapter, shall be commenced within two years; provided, that in an action at law based upon fraud or deceit, the limitation shall be deemed to commence only from the discovery of the fraud or deceit.

PENNSYLVANIA

Under 42 Pa.C.S. Section 5524 (2002): two years.

The following actions and proceedings must be commenced within two years:

7) Any other action or proceeding to recover damages for injury to person or property which is founded on negligent, intentional, or otherwise tortuous conduct or any other action or proceeding sounding in trespass, including deceit or fraud, except an action or proceeding subject to another limitation specified in this subchapter.

RHODE ISLAND

Under RI Statute 9.1-14.3: three years.

SOUTH CAROLINA

A negligence cause of action arising or accruing prior to April 5, 1988, must be commenced within six years after the person knew or by the exercise of reasonable diligence should have known that he had a cause of action. S. C. Code Ann. Sections 15-3-530–535 (Supp. 1995).

Limitation on actions commenced under Section 15-3-530(5): except as to actions initiated under § 15-3-545, all actions initiated under § 15-3-530(5) must be commenced within three years after the person knew or by the exercise of reasonable diligence should have known that he had a cause of action.

Under Section 15-3-530: within three years—

1) an action upon a contract, obligation, or liability, express or implied, excepting those provided for in § 15-3-520;
2) an action upon a liability created by statute other than a penalty or forfeiture;
3) an action for trespass upon or damage to real property;
4) an action for taking, detaining, or injuring any goods or chattels including an action for the specific recovery of personal property;
5) an action for assault, battery, or any injury to the person or rights of another, not arising on contract and not enumerated by law, and those provided for in § 15-3-545;

S. DAKOTA

Under SC Code 15-4-14.2: three years.

TENNESSEE

Under TENN. Code 28-3-104: one year.

TEXAS

Under Tex. Ci v. Prac. & Rem. Code Section 16.003 (2002): two-year limitations period.

a) Except as provided by § 16.010 and § 16.0045, a person must bring suit for trespass for injury to the estate or to the property of another, conversion of personal property, taking or detaining the personal property of another, personal injury, forcible entry and detainer, and forcible detainer not later than two years after the day the cause of action accrues.

UTAH

Under Utah Code Ann. Section 78-12-25 (2003): within four years.

An action may be brought within four years:
1) upon a contract, obligation, or liability not founded upon an instrument in writing; also on an open account for goods, wares, and merchandise, and for any article charged on a store account; also on an open account for work, labor or services rendered, or materials furnished; provided, that action in all of the foregoing cases may be commenced at any time within four years after the last charge is made or the last payment is received;

VERMONT

Under 12 V.S.A. Section 511 (2003): a civil action, except one brought upon the judgment or decree of a court of record of the United States or of this or some other state, and except as otherwise provided, shall be commenced within six years after the cause of action accrues and not thereafter.

VIRGINIA

Under Va. Code Ann. Section 8.01-246 (2003). Personal Actions Based on Contracts:

Subject to the provisions of § 8.01-243 regarding injuries to person and property and of § 8.01-245 regarding the application of limitations to fiduciaries, and their bonds, actions founded upon a contract, other than actions on a judgment or decree, shall be brought within the following number of years next after the cause of action shall have accrued:

2) In actions on any contract which is not otherwise specified and which is in writing and signed by the party to be charged thereby, or by his agent, within five years whether such writing be under seal or not;

4) In actions upon any unwritten contract, express or implied, within three years.

VIRGINIA FIDUCIARY LIABILITY

Under Section 26-5. Liability for Losses By Negligence or Failure to Make Defense: if any fiduciary mentioned before in this chapter, or any agent or attorney at law, shall, by his negligence or improper conduct, lose any debt or other money, he shall be charged with the principal of what is so lost, and interest thereon, in like manner as if he had received such principal.

If any personal representative, guardian, conservator, curator, or committee shall pay any debt the recovery of which could be prevented by reason of illegality of consideration, lapse of time, or otherwise, knowing the facts by which the same could be so prevented, no credit shall be allowed him therefor.

WASHINGTON

Rev. Code Wash. (ARCW) Section 4.16.080 (2003)

RCW 4.16.040(1) provides: "The following actions shall be commenced within six years:

1) An action upon a contract in writing, or liability express or implied arising out of a written agreement.

n26 [HN6] RCW 4.16.080(3) provides: "The following actions shall be commenced within three years: . . .

3) Except as provided in RCW 4.16.040(2), an action upon a contract or liability, express or implied, which is not in writing, and does not arise out of any written instrument.

WEST VIRGINIA

Under W. Va. Code Section 55-2-12. Personal Actions Not Otherwise Provided For: every personal action for which no limitation is otherwise prescribed shall be brought: (a) within two years next after the right to bring the same shall have accrued, if it be for damage to property; (b) within two years next after the right to bring the same shall have accrued if it be for damages for personal injuries; and, (c) within one year next after the right to bring same shall have accrued if it be for any other matter of such nature that, in case a party die, it could not have been brought at common law by or against his personal representative.

WISCONSIN

Under Wis. Statute Section 893-53: an action to recover damages for an injury to the character or rights of another, not arising on contract, shall be commenced within six years after the cause of action accrues, except where a different period is expressly prescribed, or be barred.

WYOMING

Under Wyoming Statute 1-3-107: two years.

Resources

American Bar Association (ABA) Legal Research Selected Starting Points
www.abanet.org/lawlink/home.html
Provides links to other legal research and information resources on the Internet. Updated as new sites appear.

Cornell Law School Legal Information Institute (LII)
www.law.cornell.edu
Offers legal documents and information including: Supreme Court decisions; U.S. Code; U.S. Constitution; Federal Rules of Evidence; Federal Rules of Civil Procedure; recent decisions of the New York Court of Appeals; and information about federal, state, foreign, and international law.

FindLaw
www.findlaw.com
An index to many legal sources.

LawGuru.com
www.lawguru.com/search/lawsearch.html
Access to over 360 legal search engines.

Lexis-Nexis
www.lexis-nexis.com
Subscription on-line legal research service that is fast and efficient, though expensive. Gives you access to an excellent legal library. Lexis-Nexis also provides data bases for news and business research.

Martindale-Hubbell Lawyer Locator
http://lawyers.martindale.com/marhub
Allows you to search for lawyers anywhere in the United States and Canada. You can search by attorney name, firm name, type of practice, and other criteria.

Meta-Index For U.S. Legal Research
http://gsulaw.gsu.edu/metaindex
Offers judicial opinions, including those of the U.S. Supreme Court, Federal Circuit Courts, and U.S. Bankruptcy Court; legislation, including U.S. Code (through the House of Representativies Internet Law Library) and House and Senate

bills; and the Congressional Record; Code of Federal Regulations; and links to other legal sources.

Westlaw

www.westlaw.com

Offers a subscription legal research service that, although expensive, gives you an excellent legal library at your fingertips. Thomson/West (on the Web at www.west.thomson.com) is also a major publisher of legal books on CD/ROM and traditional printed books.

West Legal Directory

www.wld.com

Provides profiles of more than 800,000 lawyers and law firms, in addition to profiles of international counsel, corporate counsel, and U.S. government attorneys.

World Wide Legal Information Association (WWLIA)

www.wwlia.org/diction.htm

Free access to a legal dictionary written in plain English (but without legal citations).

References

ABA 27th National Conference on Professional Responsibility, Conference Book, ABA Center for Professional Responsibility, 2001, Miami, Florida.

Annotated Model Rules of Professional Conduct, Third Edition. Chicago, Illinois: Center for Professional Responsibility, American Bar Association, 1996.

Annotated Model Rules of Professional Conduct, Fifth Edition. Chicago, Illinois: Center for Professional Responsibility, American Bar Association, 2004.

Blacks Law Dictionary. St. Paul, MN: West Publishing Company, 1991.

Contiguglia, Louis P., and Cornelius E. Sorapure Jr., *Lawyer's Tightrope: Use and Abuse of Fees,* 41 Cornell L.Q., 683, 690 (1956), citing N.Y. 2 Rev. Stat. C83, Sec 1 (1813).

Engler, Russell. "Out of Sight and Out of Line," *California Law Review,* 1997.

Federal Rules of Appellate Procedure, Ninth Circuit. San Francisco, California, 2003.

Federal Rules of Civil Procedure. Westbury, New York: The Foundation Press Inc., 1996.

Lawyers Professional Liability Program, Continental Casualty Company, 1991.

Leubsdorf, John. "Toward a History of the American Rule on Attorney Fee Recovery," *Law & Contemporary Problems,* Vol. 47; 9,10–11 (1984)

Moll, Richard W. *The Lure of The Law.* New York: Penguin Books, 1990.

Munneke, Gary A., and Anthony E. Davis. *The Essential Formbook,* Vol. ll. Chicago, Illinois: Law Practice Management Section, American Bar Association, 2001; p. 351.

Prest, Wilfred. *Lawyers in Early Modern Europe and America.* Holmes & Meier Publishers, Inc., 1981.

Profile of Legal Malpractice Claims. Chicago, Illinois: American Bar Association Standing Committee on Lawyer's Professional Liability, American Bar Association, 2001.

Rose, Joel A. "Simplified Timekeeping and Billing Management." *Journal of Legal Economics* (Spring 1975), page. 23.

Ross, William G. *The Honest Hour.* Durham, NC: Carolina Academic Press, 1996.

Rules Regulating the Florida Bar, The Florida Bar, 1998.

Schachner, Robert W. *How and When to Be Your Own Lawyer.* Garden City, NY: Avery Publishing, 2000.

Sells, Benjamin. *The Soul of the Law.* Boston, MA: Element, 1994.

The Legal Reformer (HALTS Membership Newsletter), Washington, D.C., 2001.

Index

About the Authors

Robert W. Schachner studied at Carnegie-Mellon University and Duquesne University Journalism School. Mr. Schachner is the best-selling author of *The Official Scrabble Word Finder* and *Lost Words in the English Language*, and coauthor of *How and When to Be Your Own Lawyer* and *Barefoot Pirate, The Tall Ships and Tales of Windjammer.*

John F. Phillips, Esq., received his BS from the College of William and Mary in Virginia, his MBA from Florida Atlantic University, and his JD from Seton Hall University School of Law. He is admitted to practice in Florida, New Jersey, New York, and Colorado, and to the US District Courts of the Southern District of Florida, Middle District of New Jersey, and Southern District of New York. Currently, he is a practicing attorney in Fort Lauderdale, Florida.